The Turks and E

Gaston Gaillard

Alpha Editions

This edition published in 2024

ISBN : 9789362513915

Design and Setting By
Alpha Editions
www.alphaedis.com
Email - info@alphaedis.com

As per information held with us this book is in Public Domain.
This book is a reproduction of an important historical work. Alpha Editions uses the best technology to reproduce historical work in the same manner it was first published to preserve its original nature. Any marks or number seen are left intentionally to preserve its true form.

Contents

I THE TURKS ....- 1 -
II THE TURKISH EMPIRE ....- 7 -
III TURKEY AND THE WAR..- 19 -
IV TURKEY AND THE CONFERENCE ....- 29 -
V THE OCCUPATION OF CONSTANTINOPLE ....- 99 -
VI THE TREATY WITH TURKEY ....- 110 -
VII THE DISMEMBERMENT OF THE OTTOMAN
    EMPIRE..- 179 -
VIII THE MOSLEMS OF THE FORMER RUSSIAN EMPIRE
AND TURKEY..- 234 -
IX TURKEY AND THE SLAVS ....- 242 -

I

THE TURKS

THE peoples who speak the various Turkish dialects and who bear the generic name of Turcomans, or Turco-Tatars, are distributed over huge territories occupying nearly half of Asia and an important part of Eastern Europe. But as we are only considering the Turkish question from the European point of view, no lengthy reference is needed to such Eastern groups as those of Turkish or Mongol descent who are connected with the Yenisseians of Northern Asia and the Altaians. The Russians call these peoples Tatars, and they, no doubt, constituted the "Tubbat" nation, referred to by the Chinese historians under the name of "Tou-Kiou" up to the seventh century after Christ. These very brief facts show the importance of the race and are also sufficient to emphasise the point that these people are akin to those Turks of Western Asia who are more closely connected with the Europeans.

The Western Turkish group includes the Turcomans of Persia and Russian or Afghan Turkistan; the Azerbaïjanians, who are probably Turkisised Iranians, living between the Caucasus Mountains and Persia; and, lastly, the Osmanli Turks, who are subjects of the Sultan, speak the Turkish language, and profess Islam.

Close to this group, but farther to the East, the central group also concerns us, for some of its representatives who now inhabit the boundaries of Europe made repeated incursions into Europe in various directions. In the plains lying between the River Irtish and the Caspian Sea live the Kirghiz-Kazaks, and in the Tien-Shien Mountains the Kara-Kirghiz, who have preserved many ancient Old Turkish customs, and seem to have been only slightly Mohammedanised. The Usbegs and the Sartis of Russian Turkistan, on the other hand, have been more or less Iranised. Finally, on the banks of the Volga are to be found the Tatars of European Russia. Among them the Tatars of Kazan, who are descended from the Kiptchaks, came to the banks of the Volga in the thirteenth century and mingled with the Bulgars. These Tatars differ from the Tatars of Astrakhan, who are descendants of the Turco-Mongols of the Golden Horde, and are connected with the Khazars, and from the Nogaïs of the Crimea, who are Tatars of the steppes who more or less inter-married with other races—the Tatars of the Tauris coast being the hybrid descendants of the Adriatic race and the Indo-Afghan race. They are to be found near Astrakhan and in the Caucasus Mountains, and even, perhaps, as far as Lithuania, "where, though still being Mohammedans, they have adopted the language and costume of the Poles."[1]

The invasion of Europe by the Turks appears as the last great ethnic movement that followed the so-called period of migration of peoples (second to sixth centuries A.D.) and the successive movements it entailed.

Let us consider only the migrations of those who concern us most closely, and with whom the Turks were to come into contact later on. First the Slavs spread westward towards the Baltic and beyond the Elbe, and southward to the valley of the Danube and the Balkan Peninsula. This movement brought about the advance of the Germans towards the west, and consequently the advance of the Celts towards Iberia and as far as Spain. Owing to the invasion of the Huns in the fifth century and in the sixth of the Avars, who, after coming as far as Champagne, settled down in the plains of Hungary and the territories lying farther to the south which had already been occupied by the Dacians for several centuries, the Slavs were cut into two groups. About the same time, the Bulgars came from the banks of the Volga and settled on the banks of the Danube.

In the ninth century, owing to a new migration of masses of Slavonic descent, the Hungarians, driven by tribes of Petchenegs and Polovts into Southern Russia, crossed the Carpathian Mountains and took up their abode in the valley of the Tirzah. While the Magyar Turks settled in Hungary, the Kajar Turks occupied the hinterland of Thessalonica in Macedonia. In the twelfth century, the Germans, driving the Western Slavs as far as the banks of the Vistula, brought about a reaction towards the north-east of the Eastern Slavs, whose expansion took place at the expense of the Finnish tribes that lived there.

Only in the thirteenth century did the Turco-Mongols begin to migrate in their turn; they occupied the whole of Russia, as far as Novgorod to the north, and reached Liegnitz in Silesia. But, although they soon drew back from Western Europe, they remained till the fifteenth century in Eastern Russia, and in the eighteenth century they were still in the steppes of Southern Russia, and in the Crimea.

Finally, in the fourteenth and fifteenth centuries, the Osmanli Turks invaded the Balkan Peninsula, where they met such of their kindred as the Kajars, the Tchitaks, and the Pomaks, who were heathens or Christians, and later on embraced Islam. They invaded Hungary and made incursions into Lower Austria.

Then began the migration of the Little Russians into the upper valley of the Dnieper, and in the sixteenth century they set off towards the steppes of

Southern Russia, while the Great Russians began to advance beyond the Volga towards the Ural, a movement which reached Siberia, and still continues.

It follows, necessarily, that in the course of these huge migrations, the so-called Turkish race was greatly modified; the Turks of the Eastern group mixed with the Mongols, the Tunguses, and the Ugrians; and those of the Western group in Asia and Europe with various Indo-Afghan, Assyrian, Arab, and European elements, especially with those living near the Adriatic: the Greeks, the Genoese, the Goths, etc. Thus the Osmanli Turks became a mixture of many races.

Though ethnologists do not agree about the various ethnic elements of the Turco-Tatar group, it is certain, all the same, that those who came to Asia Minor early associated for a long time with the people of Central Asia, and Vambéry considers that a Turkish element penetrated into Europe at a very early date.[2]

Though the Arabs in the seventh century subdued the Turks of Khiva, they did not prevent them from penetrating into Asia Minor, and the Kajars, who were not Mohammedans, founded an empire there in the eighth century. At that period the Turks, among whom Islam was gaining ground, enlisted in the Khalifa's armies, but were not wholly swallowed up by the Arab and Moslem civilisation of the Seljukian dynasty, the first representatives of which had possibly embraced Nestorian Christianity or Islam. Henceforth Asia Minor, whence the previous Turkish elements had almost disappeared, began to turn into a Turkish country.

All the Turks nowadays are Mohammedans, except the Chuvashes (Ugrians) who are Christians, and some Shamanist Yakuts.

As will be shown later on, these ethnographic considerations should not be neglected in settling the future conditions of the Turks and Slavs in Europe, in the interest of European civilisation.

About half a century ago Elisée Reclus wrote as follows:

"For many years has the cry 'Out of Europe' been uttered not only against the Osmanli leaders, but also against the Turks as a whole, and it is well known that this cruel wish has partly been fulfilled; hundreds of thousands of Muslim emigrants from Greek Thessaly, Macedonia, Thrace, and Bulgaria have sought refuge in Asia Minor, and these fugitives are only the remnants of the wretched people who had to leave their ancestral abodes; the exodus is still going on, and, most likely, will not leave off till the whole of Lower Rumelia has become European in language and customs. But now the Turks are being threatened even in Asia. A new cry arises, 'Into the Steppes,' and to our dismay we wonder whether this wish will not be carried out too. Is no conciliation possible between the hostile races, and must the unity of civilisation be obtained by the sacrifice of whole peoples, especially those that are the most conspicuous for the noblest qualities—uprightness, self-respect, courage, and tolerance?"[3]

For a long time this state of affairs did not seem to change much, but after the recent upheaval of Europe it has suddenly become worse.

Very different races, who have more or less intermingled, live on either side of the Bosphorus, for Elisée Reclus says:

"The Peninsula, the western end of the fore part of the continent, was a place where the warlike, wandering, or trading tribes, coming from the south-east and north-east, converged naturally. Semitic peoples inhabited the southern parts of Anatolia, and in the centre of that country their race, dialects, and names seem to have prevailed among numerous populations; in the south-west they seem to have intermingled with coloured men, perhaps the Kushits. In the eastern provinces the chief ethnic elements seem to have been connected with the Persians, and spoke languages akin to Zend; others represented the northern immigrants that bore the generic name of Turanians. In the West migrations took place in a contrary direction to those that came down from the Armenian uplands; Thracians were connected by their trade and civilisation with the coastlands of Europe and Asia sloping towards the Propontis, and between both parts of the world Greeks continually plied across the Ægean Sea."[4]

Thus the common name of "Turks" is wrongly given to some Moslem elements of widely different origin, who are to be found in Rumelia and Turkey-in-Asia, such as the Albanians, who are akin to Greeks through their common ancestors, the Pelasgians, the Bosnians, and the Moslem Bulgars, the offspring of the Georgian and Circassian women who filled the harems, and the descendants of Arabs or even of African negroes.

After the internal conflicts between some of these elements, the quarrels with other foreign elements, and the keen rivalry which existed generally, each section seems to have held the Turk responsible for whatever wrong was done, and the Turk was charged with being the cause of all misfortunes—almost in the same way as the Jews: the Turks have become, as it were, the scapegoats.

Yet, in 1665, in his account of his travels in the East, M. de Thévenot, who died at Mianeh in 1667, praised Turkish morality and tolerance.

Elisée Reclus wrote:

"Turkish domination is merely outward, and does not reach, so to say, the inner soul; so, in many respects, various ethnic groups in Turkey enjoy a fuller autonomy than in the most advanced countries of Western Europe."

Ubicini speaks in the same manner, and Sir H. Bulwer states that:

"As to freedom of faith and conscience, the prevailing religion in Turkey grants the other religions a tolerance that is seldom met with in Christian countries."

Unfortunately the Turk's mentality, in spite of what his enemies say, does not help him. Owing to his nature, he is quite unable to defend himself and to silence his slanderers.

For, as E. Reclus remarked:

"They are not able to cope with the Greeks, who, under pretence of pacific dealings, take vengeance for the war of extermination, the traces of which are still to be seen in Cydonia and Chio. They do not stand an equal chance of winning; most of them only know their own language, while a Greek speaks several languages; they are ignorant and artless by the side of clever, shrewd adversaries. Though he is not lazy, the Turk does not like to hurry; 'Haste is devilish, patience is godly,' he will often say. He cannot do without his 'kief,' an idle dream in which he lives like a mere plant, without any exertion of his mind and will, whereas his rival, always in earnest, can derive profit even from his hours of rest. The very qualities of the Turk do him harm: honest, trustworthy, he will work to the end of his life to pay off a debt, and the business man takes advantage of this to offer him long credits that shall make a slave of him for ever. There is an axiom among business men in Asia Minor: 'If you wish to thrive, do not grant a Christian more credit than one-tenth of his fortune; risk ten times as much with a Mohammedan.' Encumbered with such a credit, the Turk no longer possesses anything of his own; all the produce of his work will go to the usurer. His carpets, his wares, his flocks, even his land, will pass gradually into the hands of the foreigner."[5]

But since the time when this was written the Turkish mind has changed. The Turks have set to work to learn languages, especially French. A large part of the younger generation concern themselves with what takes place in the West, and this transformation, which the Greeks and other Europeans looked upon as endangering their situation in Turkey, may be one of the factors of the present conflict.

Besides, E. Reclus added: "The Greeks already hold, to the great prejudice of the Turks, numerous industries and all the so-called liberal professions, and as dragomans and journalists they are the only informers of the Europeans, and control public opinion in the West."[6]

Footnotes:

[1] J. Deniker, *Les Races et les peuples de la terre* (Paris, 1900), p. 438. Zaborowski, *Tartares de la Lithuanie* (1913).

[2] Deguignes, *Histoire générale des Huns* (1750 and 1756); L. Cahun, *Turcs et Mongols, des origins à 1405* (Paris, 1896); Vambéry, *Das Turkenvolk* (1885).

[3] Elisée Reclus, *Nouvelle géographie universelle* (1884), ix., p. 547.

[4] *Ibid.*, p. 536.

[5] Elisée Reclus, *Nouvelle géographie universelle* (1884), ix., p. 546.

[6] *Ibid.*, p. 550.

II

THE TURKISH EMPIRE

THE Turks who lived in Turkistan and territories lying to the north of China arrived in the tenth century and settled down in Persia and Asia Minor, together with some allied or subject races, such as the Tatars. There they founded several dynasties. Out of the numerous branches of the Turkish race we will only deal with the Ottomans, who were to establish their rule in Asia Minor and Europe.

People too often forget the wonderful rise of the Turkish Empire, which for nearly three centuries increased its power and enlarged its territories; and they lay too much stress on its decline, which began two centuries and a half ago.

The Oghouz tribe of Kaï, following the Seljuks more or less closely in their migrations, reached the uplands of Asia Minor about the end of the tenth century. While part of the latter retraced their steps towards the territories from which they had started, the others settled down and founded the Empire of Rum. The Seljukian chief, Ala Eddin Kaï Kobad I, gave to Erthoghrul, a son of Suleiman Khan, the ancestor of the Seljukian dynasty of Konia, the summer pasturage of Mount Toumanitch, south of Brusa, on the boundaries of the Roman Empire of Byzantium. Erthoghrul and his successors strengthened and enlarged their dominions and laid the foundation of Ottoman power.

Othman, or Osman, settled at Karahissar about the end of the thirteenth century, at the time when the Seljukian Empire of Rum was destroyed by Mongol inroads, and he conquered several of its principalities.

Orkhan conquered the rest of Asia Minor and set foot in Europe in 1355. Amurath I took Adrianople, subjugated Macedonia and Albania, and defeated the Serbs at the battle of Kossowo in 1389. By the victory of Nicopolis in 1396 Bajazet I conquered Bulgaria and threatened Constantinople, but Tamerlain's invasion and Bajazet's defeat in 1402 at Ancyra postponed the downfall of the Byzantine Empire. The Turkish Empire recovered under Mohammed I and Amurath II, who made new conquests and entirely subdued the Serbians in 1459, Mohammed II took Constantinople in 1453, quickly subdued the Greek peninsula, and annihilated the Byzantine Empire. He also took Carmania, the Empire of Trebizond in 1461, Bosnia, Wallachia in 1462, and Lesser Tartary, and even made an incursion into Italy. The Turkish Empire continued to expand for nearly another century. In 1517 Selim I turned Syria, Palestine, and Egypt into Ottoman provinces; he took Mecca and acquired Algiers in 1520.

Soliman II made new conquests. In Asia he added to the Empire Aldjeziresh and parts of Armenia, Kurdistan, and Arabia; in Europe, after capturing part of Hungary, Transylvania, Esclavonia, and Moldavia, and taking Rhodes from the Knights, he came to the gates of Vienna in 1529, and in 1534 added Tunis to his empire, and Tripoli in 1551. At the beginning of his reign Selim II conquered the Yemen, and in 1571 took Cyprus from the Venetians; but next year the Turkish fleet was utterly destroyed at the battle of Lepanto.

Turkish domination then reached its climax, and from this time began its downfall. Internal difficulties soon showed that the Ottoman Empire was beginning to decline. From 1595 to 1608 Turkey lost territory in Hungary, though, on the other hand, by the battle of Choczim, she conquered new districts in Poland. After a few perturbed years, in 1669 Mohammed IV took Candia, which Ibrahim had vainly attempted to conquer.

But henceforth the decline of the Empire was rapid, and its territories were dislocated and dismembered. The regencies of Algiers, Tunis, and Tripoli became practically independent. By the fall of Carlovitz, which put an end to the 1682-1699 war, the Turks lost nearly the whole of Hungary. By the treaty of Passarovitz, they lost Temesvar and a part of Serbia, which was restored to them by the peace of Belgrade in 1740. The Russians, with whom they had been fighting since 1672, and who began to get the upper hand during the 1770-74 war, took from them Bukovina and Lesser Tartary, the independence of which was recognised by the treaty of Kuchuk-Kainarji. After a new war from 1809 to 1812, the treaty of Bukharest gave to Russia the provinces lying between the Dnieper and the Danube. In 1809 Turkey lost the Ionian Islands, which became independent under an English protectorate. The victory of Navarino made Greece free in 1827. The Turks were obliged to cede Turkish Armenia to Russia in 1829, and, after a new war with Russia, Wallachia, Moldavia, and Serbia were put under Russian protection by the treaty of Adrianople. France conquered Algeria in 1831. In 1833 the pasha of Egypt, Mehemet Ali, rebelled, captured Syria, defeated the Turks at Konia, and threatened Constantinople. Turkey, lying at the mercy of Russia, opened the Bosphorus to her ships and closed the Dardanelles to the other Powers by the treaty of Hunkiar-Iskelessi in 1833.

Yet a reaction took place, and it seemed that Mehemet Ali, who helped the Sultan to subdue the insurgent Greeks, was likely to stop the downfall of Turkey. But his fleet was annihilated at Navarino, October 20, 1827, by the combined fleets of England, France, and Russia. He received Candia from the Sultan as a reward for his co-operation, but, not having been able to obtain Syria, he broke off with the Sublime Porte. An intervention of the European Powers put an end to his triumph. Turkey recovered the territories she had lost, and, in return for this restitution and for giving back the Turkish fleet, he obtained the hereditary government of Egypt under the suzerainty of the Porte.

Turkey then attempted to revive and to strengthen her condition by organisation on European lines.

As early as 1830 a liberal movement had made itself felt in Turkey as in many other States. The Ottoman Government realised, too, that it was necessary to get rid of the Russian influence imposed upon her by the treaty of Hunkiar-Iskelessi, and so was compelled to institute reforms.

As early as 1861 Midhat Pasha, first as vali of the Danubian province, then as vali of Baghdad in 1869, and later on in Arabia, showed much enterprise and evinced great qualities of organisation and administration. When recalled to Constantinople, he became the leader of the Young Turk party.

Mahmoud II and Abdul Mejid renewed the attempts already made by Selim III at the end of the eighteenth century, with a view to putting an end to the utter confusion of the Empire, and instituted various reforms borrowed from Europe. In 1853 France and England helped Turkey to repel a new Russian aggression, and the treaty of March 30, 1856, after the Crimean war, guaranteed her independence.

But the reign of Abdul Aziz, which had begun in such a brilliant way, proved unfortunate later on. A rising in Crete was suppressed with great difficulty in 1867; in 1875 Herzegovina and Bosnia, urged on by Russia, rebelled, and Serbia, who backed the rebels, was defeated in 1876. Abdul Aziz, on account of his wasteful financial administration as well as his leaning towards Russia, which he considered the only State to be favoured because it was an autocratic government, unconsciously aided the Tsar's policy against his own country, and uselessly exhausted the resources of Turkey. Yet under his reign the judicial system, the army, and the administration were reorganised, the legislation was secularised, and Mussulmans and non-Mussulmans were set on a footing of equality. These reforms, prepared by his two predecessors, were carried out by him. He was forced to abdicate by an insurrection in 1876, and committed suicide.

His successor, Mourad V, became mad and reigned only a few months. He was dethroned and replaced by his brother Abdul Hamid, who, on December 23, 1876, suspended the liberal constitution that the Grand Vizier Midhat Pasha had promulgated. On February 5, 1877, he disgraced Midhat Pasha, who left the country and lived abroad. Midhat Pasha was allowed to come back to Turkey later, and ordered to reside in the Isle of Crete. He was then appointed governor of the vilayet of Smyrna, but was charged with the murder of Abdul Aziz, imprisoned in the fortress of Taïf in Arabia, and assassinated on February 26, 1883.[7] A rising of Bulgaria, which the Turks put down ruthlessly, caused European intervention and a new war with Russia backed by Rumania and Montenegro. The Turks, beaten in 1877, had to sign the preliminaries of San Stefano, modified by the treaty of Berlin in 1878. Rumania, Serbia, and Montenegro became independent States; Eastern Rumelia an autonomous country; and Bulgaria a tributary principality. Austria occupied Bosnia and Herzegovina, England Cyprus, and in Asia the Russians received Kars, Ardahan, and Batum. The Berlin Conference in 1880 allowed Greece to occupy Larissa, Metzovo, and Janina.[8]

In 1898 Turkey slightly recovered, and in seventeen days her armies routed Greece, and the country would have ceased to exist but for the Tsar's intervention with the Sultan.

However, as the condition of Turkey at the end of Abdul Hamid's reign was growing more and more critical, the old ambitions entertained by several Great Powers revived. At the meeting of Edward VII and Nicholas II at Reval, the question of the extension of the European control which already existed in Macedonia was discussed.

The revolution of July 23, 1908, which put an end to Abdul Hamid's autocratic rule, instituted constitutional government in Turkey. The Great Powers were at first taken aback, but without troubling themselves about Turkey's chance of regeneration, they carried on their rivalries, all trying to derive some profit from Turkey in case she should become prosperous and powerful, and at the same time doing their best to prevent her from reviving in order to be able to domineer over her and exhaust her the more easily.

For a long time previously many Turks of the younger generation, who regretted the condition of the Empire, and were acquainted with European ideas, had realised that, if Turkey was not to die, she must reform herself. They had tried to further this aim by literary methods and had carried on propaganda work abroad, being unable to do so in Turkey. The reign of Abdul Hamid, during which the old régime had become more and more intolerable, was to bring about its overthrow, and in this respect the revolutionary movement was the outcome of Turkey's corruption. Among the numerous instigators of this movement, Enver Bey and Niazi Bey, who were then only captains garrisoned in Macedonia, soon became the most prominent. The revolutionary elements were chiefly recruited from the university students, especially those of the School of Medicine and of the Mulkieh School. Officers of the highest rank, such as Marshal Redjeb Pasha, who, when governor of Tripoli, had plotted against Abdul Hamid, were on the committee; but the masses, among whom the Young Turk propaganda had not penetrated, at first stood aloof, as they did not know the views of the members of the committee, who, before the revolution, had been obliged to carry on their propaganda very cautiously and among few people, for fear of the Sultan's reprisals.

The movement started from Albania. Macedonia, the province which was most likely to be wrested from the Empire, and Syria immediately followed the lead, and the revolutionary movement soon met with unanimous approval.

On April 13, 1909, a reactionary movement set in which failed only because of Abdul Hamid's irresolute, tottering mind. It was supported by the garrison of Constantinople, which comprised Albanian troops, the very men who had lent their aid to the revolution at first, but had been brought back to the Sultan's party by the lower clergy and politicians whose interest it was to restore Abdul Hamid's autocratic rule, or whose personal ambitions had been baulked. Troops, comprising Albanians, Bosnians, and Turkish elements, and reinforced by Greek, Bulgarian, and Serbian volunteers, old komitadjis, were summoned to Salonika.

The reaction of April 13 seems to have been partly due to foreign intrigue, especially on the part of England, who, anxious at seeing Turkey attempt to gain a new life, tried to raise internal difficulties by working up the fanaticism of the hodjas, most of whom were paid and lodged in seminaries, and so were interested in maintaining Abdul Hamid's autocratic government. These manœuvres may even have been the original cause of the reactionary movement.

Mr. Fitzmaurice, dragoman of the English embassy, was one of the instigators of the movement, and the chief distributor of the money raised for that purpose. He seems to have succeeded in fomenting the first internal difficulties of the new Turkish Government. After the failure of the reactionary movement, the Committee of Union and Progress demanded the dismissal of Mr. Fitzmaurice, who later on settled at Sofia, where he continued his intrigues.

Then the government passed into the hands of the Committee of Union and Progress which had brought on the revolution, and which practically governed the country from 1908 till the signing of the armistice between the Allies and Turkey.

The Committee of Union and Progress, which at the outset had shown a liberal and enlightened spirit, soon became very powerful; but, being the only ruling power in the country, they soon left the straight path and began to indulge in corrupt practices. The leaders' heads were turned by their sudden success, and they were not sufficiently strong-minded to resist the temptations of office in a time of crisis. All the power was soon concentrated in the hands of a few: Talaat, Enver, and Jemal, all three men of very humble origin, who, when still young, had risen rapidly to the highest eminence in the State.

Enver, born on December 8, 1883, was the son of a road-surveyor. At twenty he left the cadet school of Pancaldi, and became a prominent figure at the time of the revolution. After Abdul Hamid's downfall, he was sent to Berlin, whence he returned an enthusiastic admirer of Germany. After distinguishing himself in Tripoli, he was made War Minister at the end of the Balkan war. He was naturally very bold; his brilliant political career made him vain, and soon a story arose round him. He became rich by marrying a princess of the Imperial Family, the Sultan's niece, but it was wrongly said that he married a daughter of the Sultan—a mistake which is easily accounted for as in Turkey anybody who marries a princess of the Imperial Family bears the title of imperial son-in-law, Damad-i-Hazret-i-Shehriyari. At any rate, Enver's head was turned by his good fortune.

Talaat is supposed to be the son of a *pomak*—that is to say, his ancestors were of Bulgarian descent and had embraced Islam. He was born at Adrianople in 1870, received an elementary education at the School of the Jewish Alliance, then became a clerk in a post-office and later on in a telegraph-office. Owing to the liberal ideas he propounded and the people he associated with, he was sentenced to imprisonment. Two years after, in 1896, when he came out of prison, he was exiled to Salonika, a centre of propaganda of the Young Turks who were then attempting to overthrow Abdul Hamid. He had learned very little at school, but had a quick wit and great abilities; so he soon obtained a prominent place among the leaders of the revolutionary movement, and in a short time became a moving spirit in the party, together with Enver, Marniassi Zadé Refik Bey, and Javid Bey. Very strongly built, with huge, square fists on which he always leant in a resolute attitude of defiance, Talaat was a man of great will power. When the constitution was granted to the Turkish people, he went to Adrianople, where he was returned Member of Parliament. Soon after he became Vice-President of the Chamber, then Minister of the Interior. But he always remained an unassuming man and led a quiet life in a plain house. He was among those who desired to turn his country into a modern State, in the Anglo-Saxon sense of the word, with the help of Germany and by using German methods, which was perhaps his greatest mistake. When war broke out, Talaat was Minister of the Interior in the Cabinet in which the Egyptian prince Said Halim was Grand Vizier. On February 4, 1917, when this Ministry resigned, he became Grand Vizier, and on February 17, in the course of the sitting of the Constantinople Parliament, he declared that he intended to maintain the alliance with Germany to the end.

Jemal Pasha is of Turkish descent. He left the War Academy as Captain of the Staff, and married the daughter of Bekir Pasha, who commanded a division of the second army garrisoned at Adrianople. This Bekir Pasha had risen from the ranks, and when he was still a non-commissioned officer had throttled Midhat Pasha with his own hands. It has been wrongly stated that his father was the public executioner at Constantinople during the reign of Mahmoud II. Whereas Talaat's and Enver's manners were distant, Jemal professed to be affable and strove to please, though he was very cruel at heart. He was looked upon as a friend of France when he came to Paris in 1914 to raise the Ottoman loan. He was appointed military governor of Constantinople after Nazim Pasha's murder, January 10, 1913, in which he and Talaat and Enver had a share; then he became Minister of Marine.

Talaat fully represented the Committee of Union and Progress, and was supported by it, but Enver and Jemal, though also members, did not make use of their connection with the party. Indeed Enver, who disagreed with Talaat, had nothing to do with the party after he had been appointed War Minister, and when he was called upon to resign during the war, he retained his office with the support of Germany. Only the difficulties which the Empire experienced could have brought together three men who were actuated by such widely different motives; at any rate the omnipotence of the Union and Progress Committee, which even caused some liberals to regret the passing of the old régime, was contrary to the constitutional system which the party had purposed to institute in Turkey.

Though the leaders of the Unionist movement drove Turkey to the verge of ruin, yet the movement itself to a certain extent aroused in the Turkish people a consciousness of their rights, which they had nearly given up under the control of foreign countries; the movements of opinion brought about, and even the reaction that set in finally, roused that national feeling, which found expression soon after the events of the last war.

It must be acknowledged that the Capitulations, the extension of which led to the improper interference of foreign nations in the home affairs of the Ottoman State and gave them a paramount power over it, formed one of the chief causes of the modern ruin of Turkey, by weakening and disintegrating it. The extension of the economic Capitulations was made possible by the carelessness of the Mussulmans in commercial matters, and by their natural indolence, while the extension of the judicial Capitulations, which originated in a Moslem custom dating from the Middle Ages, seems to have been due to the condescension of the Sultans.

It is a well-known fact that Mehmet II, by the treaty he signed in 1434, granted to the Republic of Venice extra-territorial privileges consisting of commercial immunities, the benefit of which was claimed afterwards by the Powers the Porte had then to deal with. Those immunities, renewed with slight alterations, constituted what was later on called the Capitulations.

In 1528 Soliman II officially ratified the privileges which French and Catalonian merchants living in Constantinople had been enjoying for a long time, according to an old custom. The treaty signed by this monarch in 1535 confirmed the old state of affairs. By this treaty the French king, Francis I, both secured the help of Turkey against his enemies, and promised the Ottoman Empire the protection of France; at the same time he obtained for French merchants the privilege of trading in the Eastern seas, preferential customs duties on their goods, the obligation for all foreigners trading in the East to sail under the French flag, and the privilege of appointing consuls in the Levant who had jurisdiction over their fellow-countrymen. Lastly, the treaty not only secured to France the protectorate of the Holy Places, but also entrusted her with the defence of all the Latin religious orders, of whatever nationality, which were beginning at that time to found establishments in the East.

These stipulations, renewed in 1569, 1581, 1604, and 1673, secured to France both commercial supremacy and much prestige throughout the Ottoman Empire, and gave a permanent character to the concessions made by Turkey. The agreement that sealed them and seemed unchangeable soon induced other foreign nations to claim further privileges.

By the end of the sixteenth century Turkey had to grant similar privileges to Great Britain, and the contest between the British representative, Sir Thomas Glover, and Jean de Gontaut-Biron, the French ambassador, has become historical. Nevertheless France for nearly two centuries maintained her position and influence.

So it was with Russia in 1711 and the United States in 1830. The Ottoman Empire had even to concede almost equal advantages to Greece and Rumania, countries which had enlarged their boundaries at her expense.

Such privileges, which were justifiable at the outset, soon brought on unrestricted and unjustifiable interference by foreign Powers in Turkish affairs. The Powers attempted to justify the establishment and maintenance of this régime by alleging they had to protect their subjects against the delays or evil practices of the Turkish courts of justice, though the Powers that had managed to gain great influence in Turkey were already able, through their embassies, to defend fully the rights and interests of their own subjects.

In virtue of the judicial privileges, all differences or misdemeanours concerning foreigners of the same nationality were amenable to the consuls of the country concerned, whose right of jurisdiction included that of arrest and imprisonment; cases between foreigners of different nationalities were heard in the court of the defendant, this applying to both lawsuits and criminal cases; while, in lawsuits between Turkish subjects and foreigners, the jurisdiction belonged to the Ottoman tribunals; but, as the Consul was represented in court by an assessor or a dragoman, the sentence depended chiefly on the latter. As a matter of fact, these privileges only favoured the worst class of foreigners, and merely served to make fraud easier.

Lastly, from an economic point of view, the Capitulations injured the Turkish treasury by binding the Ottoman State and preventing it from establishing differential duties, at a time when a war of tariffs was being carried on between all States.

During the reign of Abdul Hamid, owing to the facilities given by this state of things, the interference of the Powers in Turkish affairs reached such a climax that they succeeded not only in bringing Turkey into a condition of subjection, but in disposing of her territories, after dividing them into regions where their respective influence was paramount. The greediness of the Powers was only restrained by the conflicts their rivalry threatened to raise. If one of them obtained a concession, such as the building of a railway line in the region assigned to it, the others at once demanded compensation, such as the opening of harbours on the sea-fronts assigned to them. Things went so far that Russia, though she could not compete with the Powers whose rivalry gave itself free scope at the expense of the Ottoman Empire, intervened to hinder Turkey from constructing a system of railways in Eastern Asia Minor, alleging that the building of these lines would endanger her zone of influence. The railway concessions had to be given to her, though she never attempted to construct any of the lines.

In addition, by laying stress on the Capitulations, in which nothing could be found that supported their demands, the Great Powers established foreign post-offices in the ports of the Empire. These post-offices, which enjoyed the privilege of extra-territoriality, were only used by foreign merchants and persons of note to smuggle in small parcels, and by native agitators to correspond safely with agitators living abroad.

Of course Turkey, being thus brought into subjection, did not develop so rapidly as the nations which, not being under any foreign tutelage, enjoyed independence; and it is unfair to reproach her with keeping behind them.

After the revolution, and owing to many requests of the Turkish Government, some economic alterations were made in the Capitulations, such as the paying of the tradesman's licence tax by foreigners, and the right of the State to establish monopolies. Austria-Hungary, when the question of Bosnia-Herzegovina was settled, consented to give up her privilege concerning the customs duties, on condition that other Powers did the same.

A short time after Germany promised to do so, but, among the other Powers, some refused, and others laid down conditions that would have brought more servitude to Turkey and would have cost her new sacrifices.

The Unionist Government, as will be shown later, cancelled the Capitulations during the last war.

After recalling the wonderful political fortune of the Turkish Empire, we should remember that, after bringing Eastern influences to Western countries, it had also an influence of its own which was plainly felt in Europe. Western art drew its inspiration from Eastern subjects, and at the end of the eighteenth century everything that was Turkish became the fashion for a time.

This influence was the natural outcome of the close intercourse with the Levant from the Renaissance till the eighteenth century, and of the receptions given in honour of Eastern men of mark during their visits to European courts. It is not intended to discuss the question of the relation between Turkish art and Arabian art, and its repercussion on Western art, or of Eastern influence in literature; but it will be well to show how much attraction all Turkish and Eastern things had for the people of the time, and how happily the imitation of the East influenced decorative art and style, as if the widely different tastes of societies so far apart had reached the same stage of refinement and culture.

Records are still extant of the famous embassy sent by the Grand Turk during the reign of Louis XIV, and the embassy sent by the Sultan of Morocco to ask for the hand of the Princess de Conti, for in Coypel's painting in the Versailles Museum can be seen the ambassadors of the Sultan of Morocco witnessing a performance of Italian comedy in Paris in 1682. Later on the Turkish embassy of Mehemet Effendi in 1721 was painted by Ch. Parrocel.

Lievins' "Soliman" in the Royal Palace of Berlin, a few faces drawn by Rembrandt, his famous portrait known as "The Turk with the Stick" in MacK. Tomby's collection, which is more likely to be the portrait of an aristocratic Slav, the carpet in "Bethsabe's Toilet after a Bath," bear witness to the Eastern influence. So do the Turkish buildings of Peter Koeck d'Aelst, who was the director of a Flemish manufactory of tapestry at Constantinople during Soliman's reign; the scenes of Turkish life and paintings of Melchior Lorch, who also lived at Constantinople about the same time and drew the Sultan's and the Sultana's portraits; and the pictures of J.-B. van Mour, born at Valenciennes, who died in Constantinople, where he had been induced to come by M. de Ferriol, the French King's Ambassador; of A. de Favray; and of Melling, the Sultana Hadidge's architect, who was called the painter of the Bosphorus.⁹

There may also be mentioned Charles Amédée van Loo's pictures: "A Sultana's Toilet," "The Sultana ordering the Odalisks some Fancy Work," "The Favourite Sultana with her Women attended by White and Black Eunuchs," "Odalisks dancing before the Sultan and Sultana," most of which were drawn for the king from 1775 to 1777, and were intended as models for tapestries; and also the portrait of Madame de Pompadour as an odalisk, "The Odalisk before her Embroidery Frame," and "A Negress bringing the Sultana's Coffee," by the same painter. To these may be added Lancret's Turkish sketches, the drawings and pastels of Liotard, who left Geneva for Paris about 1762, then lived in the ports of the Levant and Constantinople, and came back to Vienna, London, and Holland, and whose chief pictures are: "A Frankish Lady of Pera receiving a Visit," "A Frankish Lady of Galata attended by her Slave"; and also Fragonard's "New Odalisks introduced to the Pasha," his sepia drawings, Marie Antoinette's so-called Turkish furniture, etc.

In music any sharp, brisk rhythm was styled *alla turca*—that is, in the Turkish style. We also know a Turkish roundelay by Mozart, and a Turkish march in Beethoven's "Ruins of Athens."

At the end of the eighteenth century, not only did people imitate the gorgeousness and vivid colours of Turkish costumes, but every Turkish whim was the fashion of the day. Ingres, too, took from Turkey the subjects of some of his best and most famous paintings: "The Odalisk lying on her Bed," "The Turkish Bath," etc.

Lastly, the Great War should teach us, in other respects too, not to underrate those who became our adversaries owing to the mistake they made in joining the Central Powers. For the "Sick Man" raised an army of nearly 1,600,000 men, about a million of whom belonged to fighting units, and the alliance of Turkey with Germany was a heavy blow to the Allied Powers: Russia was blockaded, the Tsar Ferdinand was enabled to attack Serbia, the blockade of Rumania brought on the peace of Bukharest, Turkish troops threatened Persia, owing to which German emissaries found their way into Afghanistan, General Kress von Kressenstein and his Ottoman troops attacked the Suez Canal, etc. All this gave the Allies a right to enforce on Turkey heavy terms of peace, but did not justify either the harsh treatment inflicted upon her before the treaty was signed, or some of the provisions of that treaty. It would be a great mistake to look upon Turkey as of no account in the future, and to believe that the nation can no longer play an important part in Europe.

7 *Midhat Pacha, Sa vie et son œuvre*, by his son Ali-Haydar-Midhat Bey (Paris, 1908).

8 Janina was occupied by Greece in 1912-18.

9 Cf. A. Boppe, *Les Peintres du Bosphore au dix-huitième siècle* (Paris, 1919).

III

TURKEY AND THE WAR

IT is a well-known fact that Germany, while carefully organising the conflict that was to lay waste the whole world and give her the hegemony of the globe, had not neglected Turkey. Her manœuvres ended, before the war, in concluding a Turco-German treaty of alliance, signed in Constantinople at four o'clock in the afternoon of August 2, 1914, by Baron von Wangenheim and the Grand Vizier Said Halim, an Egyptian prince, cousin to the former Khedive of Egypt and Mehemet Ali's grandson. It seems that the Turkish negotiators had plainly told the German representatives that they only meant to fight against Russia, and they did not even require any guarantee against the action of France and England.

The spirit in which these negotiations were carried on has been lately corroborated by a statement of M. Bompard, former French Ambassador at Constantinople, who, in answer to a newspaper article concerning the circumstances under which Turkey entered into the war, and the episode of the *Goeben* and the *Breslau*,[10] wrote in the same newspaper:[11]

"Owing to the treaty of August 2, Turkey was ipso facto a belligerent; yet though the military authorities acted in conformity with the treaty, the civil authorities—*i.e.*, the Government, properly speaking—had a somewhat different attitude. In the first place, the Government denied it was at war with France and England. The Grand Vizier had even made a formal declaration of neutrality in Paris and London; it only had to do with Russia; besides, the thing was not urgent, as the Russian decree of mobilisation had just been issued."

In the first article of the treaty it was stated that both Powers should maintain a strict neutrality in the conflict between Austria-Hungary and Serbia. This clause, however, was only intended to give the treaty a pacific appearance, for it was said in Clause 2 that if Russia intervened and thus compelled Germany to support her ally, Austria-Hungary, Turkey should be under the same obligation.

Now, on the previous day, Germany had declared war on Russia, and thus the second article came into effect immediately. So by this treaty Germany really wanted to throw Turkey into the war by the side of the Central Powers.

The other clauses laid down the conditions of a military co-operation. The most important one was that Turkey pledged herself to let the German military mission have the control in the conduct of operations, "according to what was agreed between His Excellency the War Minister and the President of the Military Mission." Theoretically the treaty was to come to an end on December 31, 1918, but, if not denounced six months before that date, it was to be renewed for five years more.

Clause 8 and last expressly said that the agreement was to be kept secret.

On October 29, 1914, two Turkish torpedo-boats entered the port of Odessa, sank a Russian gun-boat, and fired at the French liner *Portugal*, and a Turco-German squadron made a surprise attack upon Theodosia and Novorossisk. Then the Allied Powers declared war on Turkey on November 5.

Yet, after keeping neutral during the first three months of the war, Turkey seems to have had some hesitation in entering the conflict, notwithstanding German pressure. Most of her statesmen, who had weighed the financial and political consequences of her intervention, did not seem to consider they were to the advantage of their country; but the ambitious aims of Enver Pasha, who was devoted to Germany, for his success depended on her triumph, prevailed upon Turkey to yield. On the other hand, the Grand Vizier, Said Halim Pasha, pointed out on October 2, 1914, to the Austrian ambassador, who urged Turkey to utilise her fleet, that if the latter was ever defeated by the Russian fleet, Constantinople would be endangered. But a few days after, on October 15, he declared that the only obstacle to Turkish intervention was the penury of the treasury. Indeed, it is probable that Javid Bey, Minister of Finance, who had just signed an agreement with France concerning Turkish railways and finance, was not very eager to declare war on a country whose financial help was indispensable. He had even made overtures on several occasions to the ambassadors of the Entente, on behalf of the moderate members of the Ministry. In August, 1914, he offered to come to an agreement with the Entente providing that the Capitulations were suppressed, and in September he asked them to recognise the suppression of the Capitulations in order to be able to demobilise the Ottoman army. He resigned after the declaration of war, but consented to be member of a new Cabinet the next year.

It seems probable, too, that Talaat for rather a long time favoured an attitude of neutrality in order to obtain for Turkey, among other political and economic advantages, the suppression of the Capitulations, and that only later on he finally, like Jemal, Minister of Marine, sided with Enver Pasha and the Germans. On September 6 Talaat Bey told Sir L. du Pan Mallet that there was no question of Turkey entering the war,[12] and on September 9 he declared to the same ambassador, with regard to the Capitulations, that the time had come to free Turkey from foreign trammels.[13]

Ghalib Kemaly Bey, Turkish Minister at Athens, in a telegram addressed to Said Halim Pasha on June 15, 1914, had informed him he had just learnt that "Greece, by raising a conflict, expected a general conflagration would ensue which might bring on the opening of the question of Turkey-in-Asia." On August 7, 1914, he stated in another dispatch sent from Athens to the Sublime Porte:

"In the present war England, according to all probabilities, will have the last word. So if we are not absolutely certain to triumph finally, it would be a highly venturesome thing for us to rush into an adventure, the consequences of which might be—which God forbid—fatal to our country."

In a long report dated September 9, 1914, he added:

"The present circumstances are so critical and so fraught with danger that I take the liberty humbly to advise the Imperial Government to keep a strict neutrality in the present conflicts, and to endeavour to soothe Russia....

"The compact lately signed in London by the Allies shows that the war is expected to last long.... A State like the Ottoman Empire, which has enormous unprotected sea-coasts and remote provinces open to foreign intrigues, should certainly beware of the enmity of a malignant and vindictive country like England...."

So it appears that the decision of Turkey was not taken unanimously and only after much hesitation.

Henceforth the operations engaged in by both sides followed their due course.

In Europe the Franco-British squadrons under the command of Admiral Carden began on November 3 to bombard the forts which guarded the entrance of the Dardanelles. On February 25, 1915, a combined attack of the Allied fleets took place, and on March 18 a general attack was made by the Franco-British squadrons, in which three of their ironclads were sunk, four were severely damaged, and other ships were disabled.

On April 25 to 27 the English and French troops landed in Gallipoli, and after driving back the Turks advanced on May 6 to 8. But when the expeditionary corps had failed to reach Krithia and the Kareves-Dere, then, after a violent offensive of the Turks, which was repulsed on June 21, and the failure of a diversion against the Sari-Bair Mountains, it was withdrawn on January 8, 1916.

In Asia, after the Turkish naval action in the Black Sea, and the march of the Turkish troops against Kars and Tiflis, the Russians invaded Armenia, in Asia

Minor, on November 4, 1914, and took Ardost. On November 8 they captured Bayazid and Kuprikeui; Ardahan and Sary-Kamysh, where, as will be seen later on, the Armenians were partly responsible for the Turkish retreat, December 21 and 22; on May 19, 1915, Van fell; then, in the following year, Erzerum (February 16, 1916), Mush (February 18), Bitlis (March 2), Trebizond (April 18), Baiburt (July 16), and Erzinjan (July 25). Thus the Russian troops had conquered the four provinces of Erzerum, Van, Trebizond, and Bitlis, extending over an area of 75,000 square miles.

In Mesopotamia the British brigade of Indian troops came into action on November 8, 1914, and captured the little fort at Fao, which commands the entrance of the Shatt-el-Arab. On November 17 it was victorious at Sihan, took Basra on the 22nd, and Korna on December 9 of the same year. Next year, on July 3, 1915, the British troops captured Amara, Suk-esh-Shuyukh on July 21, Naseriya on the 25th of the same month, and on September 29 they occupied Kut-el-Amara, which the Turks recaptured on April 18, 1916, taking General Townshend prisoner. On February 28, 1917, Kut-el-Amara fell again to British arms, then Baghdad on March 11. On April 2, 1917, the English and Russian forces joined together at Kizilrobat on the main road to Persia, and all the Indian frontier was wholly freed from the Turco-German pressure.

But after the Russian revolution, the Turks successively recaptured all the towns the Russian troops had conquered in Transcaucasia and Asia Minor, and soon threatened Caucasus.

Meanwhile in Arabia the Turks had suddenly invaded the Aden area, where they were beaten on the 21st by the British at Sheikh-Othman and on the 25th at Bir-Ahmed.

On June 10, 1916, the Arab rising broke out. On June 14 they were masters of Mecca. On July 1 they took Jeddah, then Rabagh, then Yambo on the Red Sea. On November 6, 1916, the Sherif of Mecca, the Emir Hussein, was proclaimed King of the Hejaz, under the name of Hussein-Ibn-Ali.

As early as November 3, 1914, Turkey, which occupied all the Sinai Peninsula, threatened Egypt. A first Turkish offensive against the Suez Canal was checked from February 2 to 4 simultaneously before El-Kantara, Al-Ferdan, Toussoun, and Serapeum. A second Turkish offensive, started on July 29, 1916, was also crushed before Romani near the Suez Canal, on the 5th at Katia and on the 11th at Bir-el-Abd.

The British army then launched a great offensive in December, 1916, which resulted, on December 21, in the capture of El-Arish, on the boundary of the Sinaitic desert, and in the occupation of Aleppo on October 26, 1918. On January 9, 1917, they took Rafa, then Beersheba on October 31, 1917,

Gaza on November 7, and Jaffa on November 17; and on December 11, 1917, General Allenby entered Jerusalem.

In September, 1918, a new offensive took place, backed by the French troops that took Nablus, and the French navy that made the British advance possible by bombarding the coast. General Allenby entered Haïfa and Acre on September 23 and Tiberias on the 24th, and on the 28th he effected his junction with the troops of the King of the Hejaz. He entered Damascus on October 1 with the Emir Feisal, who commanded the Arabian army. On October 6 the French squadron sailed into the port of Beyrut, which was occupied on the 7th. Tripoli was captured on the 13th, Homs on the 15th, Aleppo on the 26th of October, 1918. By this time Syria, Lebanon, Mesopotamia, and Arabia had fallen into the hands of the Allies.

Meanwhile the disintegration of the Turkish troop was completed by General Franchet d'Espérey's offensive and the capitulation of Bulgaria. Turkey applied to General Townshend—who had been taken prisoner at Kut-el-Amara—to treat with her victors. The negotiations of the armistice were conducted by Rauf Bey, Minister of the Navy; Reshad Hikmet Bey, Under-Secretary of State for Foreign Affairs; and Sadullah Bey, head of the general staff of the Third Army.

As early as 1916 Turkey of her own authority had suppressed the Capitulations—*i.e.*, the conventions through which the Powers, as has been seen, had a right, amongst other privileges, to have their own tribunals and post-offices; and by so doing she had freed herself from the invidious tutelage of Europe.

The Ottoman Government, in a note sent on November 1, 1916, by the Turkish ambassadors in Berlin and Vienna to the German and Austrian Ministers of Foreign Affairs, notified to their respective Governments and the neutrals that henceforth they looked upon the two international treaties of Paris and Berlin as null and void.

Now the treaties of Paris in 1856 and of Berlin in 1878 were the most important deeds that had hitherto regulated the relations between the Ottoman Empire and the other European Powers. The treaty of Paris confirmed the treaty of 1841, according to which the question of the closing of the Straits to foreign warships was considered as an international question which did not depend only on the Turkish Government.

The Berlin treaty of 1878, too, asserted a right of control and tutelage of the Powers over Turkey, and in it Turkey solemnly promised to maintain the principle of religious liberty, to allow Christians to bear evidence in law-courts, and to institute reforms in Armenia.

As the King of Prussia and the Emperor had signed the treaty of Paris, and the Austrian Emperor and the German Emperor had signed the treaty of Berlin, Turkey could not denounce these treaties without the assent of these two allied countries, which thus gave up the patrimonial rights and privileges wrested from the Sultan by Western Europe in the course of the last three centuries. This consideration accounts for the support Turkey consented to give the Central Powers and the sacrifices she engaged to make.

In order to understand the succession of events and the new policy of Turkey, the reader must be referred to the note of the Ottoman Government abrogating the treaties of Paris and Berlin which was handed on November 1, 1916, by the Turkish ambassadors in Berlin and Vienna to the German and Austrian Ministers of Foreign Affairs. This note, recalling the various events which had taken place, pointed out that they justified Turkey in casting off the tutelage of both the Allied Powers and the Central Powers:

"Owing to the events that took place in the second half of the last century, the Imperial Ottoman Empire was compelled, at several times, to sign two important treaties, the Paris treaty on March 30, 1866, and the Berlin treaty on August 3, 1878. The latter had, in most respects, broken the balance established by the former, and they were both trodden underfoot by the signatories that openly or secretly broke their engagements. These Powers, after enforcing the clauses that were to the disadvantage of the Ottoman Empire, not only did not care for those that were to its advantage, but even continually opposed their carrying out.

"The Paris treaty laid down the principle of the territorial integrity and independence of the Ottoman Empire; it also stipulated that this clause should be fully guaranteed by all the Powers, and forbade any meddling, either with the relations between the Imperial Government and its subjects, or with the interior administration of the Ottoman Empire.

"Nevertheless, the French Government kept on interfering by force of arms in Ottoman territory, and demanded the institution of a new administrative organisation in Lebanon. Then the Powers signatory to the treaty were compelled to participate in this action by diplomatic ways, in order not to let France have a free hand in carrying out her plans, which were contrary to the Paris treaty and paved the way to territorial encroachments.

"On the other hand, the Russian Government, pursuing a similar policy, held in check by an ultimatum the action of the Porte against the principalities of Serbia and Montenegro, where it had raised an insurrection, and which it had fully provided with arms, supplies, officers, and soldiers; and after demanding the institution of a new foreign administration in some Ottoman provinces and of a foreign control over their home affairs, it finally declared war against Turkey.

"In the same manner the clauses of the Paris treaty did not hinder either the French Government from occupying Tunis and turning this province of the Ottoman Empire into a French protectorate—or the English from occupying Egypt to become the ruling power there, and from encroaching upon Ottoman sovereignty in the south of the Yemen, in Nejed, Koweit, Elfytyr, and the Persian Gulf. In spite of the same clauses the four Powers now at war against Turkey have also recently modified the condition of Crete and instituted a new state of things inconsistent with the territorial integrity that they had guaranteed.

"Finally Italy, without any serious reason, merely in order to have territorial compensations after the new political situation created in Northern Africa, did not hesitate to declare war against the Ottoman Empire, and did not even comply with the engagement she had taken, in case of a contention with the Imperial Government, to refer the case to the mediation of the Powers signatory of the treaty before resorting to war.

"It is not necessary to mention all the other cases of interference in the home affairs of the Ottoman Empire.

"The Berlin treaty, concluded after the events of 1877-78, completely remodelled the Paris treaty by creating in European Turkey a new state of things, which was even modified by posterior treaties. But soon after the Berlin treaty the Russian Government showed how little it cared for its engagements. Even before capturing Batum it managed to annex that fortified place by declaring openly and officially its intention to turn it into a free trade port. The British Government consented to renew some of its engagements. Yet the Cabinet of Petrograd, after fulfilling its aspirations, simply declared that the clause relating to this case was no longer valid, and turned the town into a naval station. As for the British Government, it did not carry out any of the protective measures it had hinted at, which shows how little it cared for the régime instituted by the Berlin treaty.

"Though the Imperial Ottoman Government scrupulously submitted to the harsh, heavy clauses of the treaty, a few previsions that were favourable to it were never carried out, in spite of its own insistence and that of its protectors, because one of the Powers thought it its own interest to raise difficulties to the Ottoman Empire.

"It ensues from all this that the fundamental and general clauses of the treaties of Paris and Berlin, concerning the Ottoman Empire, were annulled *ipso facto* by some of the signatories. Now, since the clauses of an international deed that are to the advantage of one of the contracting parties have never been carried out, it is impossible that the obligations contracted by this party should be considered as valid still. Such a state of things makes it necessary, as far as the aforesaid party is concerned, to annul such a treaty. It should also be borne in mind that, since the conclusion of these two treaties, the situation has completely changed.

"Since the Imperial Government is at war with four of the signatory Powers, to whose advantage and at whose eager request the aforesaid treaties were concluded, it follows that these treaties have become null and void, as far as the relations between Turkey and these Powers are concerned.

"Besides, the Imperial Government has concluded an alliance on a footing of complete equality with the other two signatory Powers. Henceforth the Ottoman Empire, being definitely freed from its condition of inferiority and from the international tutelage some of the Great Powers had an interest in maintaining, now sits in the European concert with all the rights and privileges of a completely independent State; and this new situation cancels even the causes of the aforesaid international agreements.

"All these considerations deprive the aforesaid contracts of any binding value.

"Nevertheless, that there may lurk no uncertainty on this head in the mind of the contracting Powers that have turned their friendly relations into an alliance with Turkey, the Imperial Government begs to inform the German and Austro-Hungarian Governments that it has annulled the treaties of 1856 and 1878.

"It also feels bound to declare that, in accordance with the principles of international law, it will certainly avail itself of such rights as are to its advantage, and have not yet been recognised.

"On the other hand, the Imperial Government, under the pressure of France, had been compelled to grant the sanjaks of Lebanon a strictly administrative and restricted autonomy, that might be a pretext to a certain extent to the intervention of the Great Powers. Though this situation was never sanctioned by a regular treaty, but by interior laws in 1861 and 1864, the Imperial Ottoman Government, in order to avoid any misunderstanding, feels bound to declare that it puts an end to that state of things, and, for the reasons mentioned above, it institutes in this sandjak the same administrative organisation as in the other parts of the Empire."

After the military defeat of autumn, 1918, the leaders of the Committee of Union and Progress who had governed the Ottoman Empire since 1905 disappeared, and the statesmen of the former régime came into office again.

In the very first days of October, 1918, the Talaat Pasha Cabinet had offered its resignation, which had not been accepted at first by the Sultan.

The new Ottoman Cabinet made a declaration of policy to Parliament on Wednesday, October 23, 1918. In the opening address, read by the Grand Vizier Izzet Pasha, an amnesty was promised to all political offenders. Turkey stated she was quite ready to accept a peace, based on Mr. Wilson's fourteen points, and to grant at once to all the elements of the population, without any distinction of nationality or religion, full political rights and the right to a share in the administration of the country. She also promised to solve the question of the Arabian vilayets, to take into consideration their national aspirations, and to grant them an autonomous administration, provided the bonds existing between them, the Caliphate, and the Sultan, should be maintained. The whole Chamber, with the exception of ten deputies who refused to vote, passed a vote of confidence in the new Cabinet.

After the French victory in the East and the capitulation of Bulgaria, the political changes, which had already begun in Turkey, soon became quite pronounced. Talaat Pasha, whose ideas differed utterly from those of Enver Pasha, and who had more and more confined his activity to the war department, had gradually lost his influence over the policy of the Empire since the death of Mehmed V. After having taken his share, together with Enver and Jemal, in bringing Turkey into the war by the side of the Central Powers in 1914, he now realised that the game was up. Besides, the Ottoman Press now openly attacked the Cabinets of the two Empires, and reproached them with neglecting the interests of the Porte when the additional treaty of Brest-Litovsk was drafted, during the negotiations of Bukharest, and later on in the course of the negotiations with the Cabinet of Sofia.

Talaat, Javid, and Enver sought shelter in Berlin. Their flight greatly affected the new Constantinople Government on account of some financial malversations which had occurred while the leaders of the Committee of Union and Progress were in office. So the Sublime Porte in December, 1918, demanded their extradition, which Germany refused to grant. In April, 1919, Talaat, who lived in Berlin under the name of Sali Ali Bey, and who later on opened a public-house in that city, was sentenced to death by default in Constantinople, and a year later, in March, 1920, England, according to a clause of the Versailles treaty, put him down on the list of the war-criminals[14] whose extradition might be demanded.

10 *L'Éclair:* "Comment le Goeben et le Breslau échappèrent aux flottes alliées," by Henry Miles, June 16, 1921.

11 M. Bompard's letter to the editor of the *Éclair*, June 23, 1921.

12 Blue Book, No. 64.

13 *Ibid.*, No. 70.

14 Since the publication of the French edition of this book Talaat was murdered on March 15, 1921, at Charlottenburg, by an Armenian student named Solomon Teilirian, aged twenty-four, a native of Salmas in Persia.

IV

TURKEY AND THE CONFERENCE

As early as 1916 the Allies seem to have come to an agreement over the principle of the partition of the Ottoman Empire. In their answer to President Wilson they mentioned among their war aims "to enfranchise the populations enslaved to the sanguinary Turks," and "to drive out of Europe the Ottoman Empire, which is decidedly alien to Western civilisation."

According to the conventions about the impending partition of Turkey concluded between the Allies in April and May, 1916, and August, 1917, Russia was to take possession of the whole of Armenia and Eastern Anatolia, Constantinople, and the Straits. In virtue of the treaty signed in London on May 16, 1916, fixing the boundaries of two zones of British influence and two zones of French influence, France and England were to share Mesopotamia and Syria, France getting the northern part with Alexandretta and Mosul, and England the southern part with Haïfa and Baghdad. According to the treaty of August 21, 1917, Italy was to have Western Asia Minor with Smyrna and Adalia. Palestine was to be internationalised and Arabia raised to the rank of an independent kingdom.

But, following the breakdown of Russia and the entrance of America into the war, the conventions of 1916 and 1917 were no longer held valid. President Wilson declared in the fourteenth of his world-famous points that: "The Turkish parts of the present Ottoman Empire should be assured of secure sovereignty, but the other nations now under Turkish rule should be assured security of life and autonomous development."

It follows that the partition of Turkish territories such as Mesopotamia or Syria between Powers that had no right to them, as was foreshadowed in the conventions of 1916, was no longer admitted; and the Conference in February, 1919, decided, at Mr. Wilson's suggestion, that all territories that belonged to the Ottoman Empire before should be put under the control of the League of Nations, which was to assign mandates to certain Great Powers.

According to the decisions taken at that time, and at the special request of M. Venizelos, the Greeks obtained all the western coast of Asia Minor between Aivali and the Gulf of Kos, with Pergamus, Smyrna, Phocœa, Magnesia, Ephesus, and Halicarnassus, and a hinterland including all the vilayet of Aidin, except the sanjak of Denizli and part of that of Mentesha (Mughla).

The Italian delegation thought fit to make reservations about the assignment of Smyrna to Greece.

It seems that in the course of the conversations at St-Jean-de-Maurienne—Greece being still neutral at the time—M. Ribot asked Baron Sonnino whether Italy, to facilitate the conclusion of a separate peace with Austria-Hungary, would eventually consent to give up Trieste in exchange for Smyrna. The Italian delegation had merely noted down the offer, without giving an answer. The Italian diplomats now recalled that offer as an argument, not so much to lay a claim to Smyrna—as their subsequent attitude showed—as to prevent a change to Italy's disadvantage in the balance of power in the Eastern Mediterranean, and an infringement of the London treaty that guaranteed her definite possession of the Dodecanese.

Moreover, according to Article 9 of the London treaty, in case of a partition of Asia Minor, or merely in case zones of influence should be marked out in it, Italy was to have the same share as the other Powers and receive, together with the province of Adalia, where she had acquired a paramount influence and obtained a recognition of her rights from Turkey in 1912, the neighbouring regions. In accordance with this article, the Conference seemed inclined to give Italy an international mandate for all the part of Asia Minor that was to be left to the Turks—namely, all the Anatolian plateau, including the vilayets of Kastamuni, Brusa, Angora, Konia, and Sivas. It is obvious that the difficulties raised by the assignment of Smyrna to Greece could not but be aggravated by the new political situation in case this mandate should be given to the Italians.

Consequently, when the Italians saw Smyrna assigned to Greece, they were all the more anxious to give to their new zone of influence in Asia Minor an outlet to the sea that should not depend on the great port of Western Asia Minor. After considering Adalia, Makri, and Marmaris, which are good harbours but do not communicate with the interior and are not connected with the chief commercial routes of the continent, their attention was drawn to Kush-Adassi, called by the Greeks New Ephesus and by themselves Scala Nuova, a port that numbered about 6,000 souls before the war, lying opposite to Samos, in the Gulf of Ephesus, about ten miles from the ruin of the old town of the same name and the Smyrna-Aidin railway.

This port, which is situated on the mouth of the Meander, might easily be connected by a few miles of railroad with the main railway line to the south of Ayasaluk which brings towards the Ægean Sea all the produce of Asia Minor; then it would divert from Smyrna much of the trade of Aidin, Denizli, and the lake region. To the merchants of Asia Minor—who deal with Syria, Egypt, Greece, Italy, and all Western Europe, excepting those who trade with the Black Sea—the Kush-Adassi line would be both faster and cheaper, if this port was as well equipped as Smyrna.

But, as Kush-Adassi happened to be in the zone which at first had been assigned to Greece and whose frontier goes down to the south as far as Hieronda Bay, Italy endeavoured in every way to carry farther to the north the boundaries of the Italian zone, in order to include this port in it. For this purpose, Italy took advantage of the troubled condition of the area round Aidin, Sokia, and Cape Mycale to send a police force up the Meander and the railway line along it, in order to carry her control up to the Gulf of Ephesus. Of course the territory lying between Hieronda and Kush-Adassi still remained part of the Greek zone of occupation, but, all the same, Italy set foot in it. Her diplomats soon turned this fact into a right of possession.

M. Tittoni soon after agreed to play the part of arbiter in the question of the southern frontier of Bulgaria; and in July, 1919, it was announced that after some conversations between M. Venizelos and M. Tittoni an understanding had been reached about Thrace and Northern Epirus, whereby Greece agreed to enlarge the northern part of the Italian zone of occupation in Asia Minor, and gave up to Italy the valley of the Meander. So, though on the whole M. Tittoni's arbitration was in favour of Greece, Italy obtained the territorial triangle included between Hieronda, Nazili, and Kush-Adassi, the control over the Meander, and to a certain extent over the railway. In return for this, Italy promised to cede to Greece the Dodecanese except one, captured by Italy in 1912 during her war with Turkey, together with the Isle of Rhodes, though she had a right to keep the latter for at least five years. In case England should grant the inhabitants of Cyprus the right to pass under Greek sovereignty, Italy was to hold a plebiscite in Rhodes and let the native population become Greeks if they wished. By supporting the Greek claims in Thrace, Italy won the sympathies of Greece at a time when the latter both consolidated the rights of Italy on the continent and strengthened her own situation in the Dodecanese.

The control over the eastern part of Asia Minor which was to fall to the lot of the Armenians and included the vilayets of Erzerum, Van, Bitlis, Kharput, Diarbekir, and probably Trebizond—the population of the latter vilayet consisting chiefly of Moslems with a Greek minority—was to be assumed, so the Great Powers thought, by the United States.

It should be remembered that the question of the eastern vilayets was raised for the first time by the Tsars of Russia, and gave them a pretext for intervening in the domestic affairs of Turkey and thus carrying out their plans of expansion in Asia Minor. As a matter of fact, those vilayets were not really Armenian. The Armenians were in a minority there, except in two or three districts where, as throughout the Ottoman Empire, they were mixed up with

Turks. They had lived peaceably together till the Powers thought fit to support the claims of the Armenians and incite them to rebel, in order to further their own aims in Turkey, by a misuse of the privileges granted them by the Capitulations.

Constantinople and the Straits seemed likely to be internationalised.

Lastly, the Arabian part of the Turkish Empire was to be cut off from it, though nobody could tell expressly in what manner, but in a way which it was easy to foresee.

We shall deal later on with the negotiations that took place during the war between the British Government and Hussein, Grand Sherif of Mecca, the Emir Feisal's father, and we have already mentioned the help given to the British army by the Emir Feisal's troops, after the aforesaid negotiations. These facts throw a light on the policy pursued by England later on; and besides, immediately after the hostilities, in a speech made in London on Friday, November 1, 1918, Mr. Barnes, a Labour member of the British Cabinet, while speaking on the armistice with Turkey, acknowledged:

"We could have signed it before, for we held the Turks at our discretion. For the last fortnight the Turks had been suing for peace, but we were on the way to Aleppo, which is to be the capital of the future independent Arab State, established in an Arab country and governed by Arabs. So we did not want to have done with the Turks till we had taken Aleppo."

Such was the condition of the Turkish problem when the Peace Conference took it in hand for the first time.

Rivalries naturally soon arose.

The Emir Feisal, supported by England, laid claim not only to the whole of Arabia, but also to Palestine, Syria, and Mesopotamia to make up a huge Arab Empire, under his father's rule. France, who opposed that plan, convened a Syrian Congress in Marseilles, to raise a protest against the partition of Syria as had been laid down by the Franco-English agreement of 1916.

Soon after the landing of Greek troops in Smyrna on the morning of May 15, 1919, brought about a serious conflict.

It is noteworthy that after General Allenby's victories in Palestine and the resignation and flight of Talaat, Enver, and Jemal, General Izzet Pasha, who had been appointed Grand Vizier, had signed, on October 31, 1918, a convention of armistice, which put Turkish ports and railways under the Allies' provisional control and allowed them "in case things should become alarming for them" to occupy "all strategic points." This armistice had been concluded on the basis of Mr. Wilson's principle that "to the Turkish regions of the Ottoman Empire an unqualified sovereignty should be ensured." In no respect had the Turks broken the agreement when the Allies infringed it by allowing the Greeks to occupy Smyrna. This occupation, carried on in spite of France, who was not energetic enough, and one might almost say in spite of Italy, created a very serious situation.

Indeed, no good reason could be given in support of this decision. By the help of misleading or false information cleverly worded and widely distributed by a propaganda which overwhelmed the Press—and was only equalled by the propaganda carried on by Poland—political manœuvres induced the Allies to allow Greece, who wished to become "Greater Greece" and wanted Epirus, Thrace, Constantinople, Smyrna, Trebizond, and Adana, to occupy a region belonging to Anatolia, where the Turkish element predominates more than in all the rest of the Ottoman Empire, for there are only 300,000 Greeks against about 1,300,000 Turks. This permission granted to Greece was the more surprising as it seems to have been obtained because the Greek Government had informed the Supreme Council that the disorder prevailing in the vilayet of Smyrna was a danger to the non-Turkish populations.

Now the report of the Inter-allied Commission about the Greek occupation of Smyrna and the neighbouring territories which was sent later on and was dated from Constantinople, October 12, 1919, began as follows:

"The inquiry has proved that since the armistice the general condition of the Christians of the vilayet of Aidin has been satisfactory, and their security has not been threatened.

"If the occupation of Smyrna was ordered by the Peace Conference owing to inaccurate information, the primary responsibility lies with the individuals or governments that gave or transmitted inconsiderately such information as is mentioned in No. 1 of the established facts.

"It is obvious, therefore, that this occupation was not at all justifiable, and violated the terms of the armistice concluded between the Powers and Turkey."

Moreover, to quote the very words of that report, the Greek occupation, "far from appearing as carrying out a civilising mission, has immediately put on the aspect of a conquest and a crusade."

This inquiry, on the one hand, acknowledged that the responsibility for the events that took place at Smyrna on May 15 and 16 and in the immediate neighbourhood during the first days following the landing, lay with the Greek headquarters and some officers who did not perform their duty. On the other hand it stated that part of the responsibility rested with the Turkish authorities at Smyrna, who took no step to prevent the escape and arming of common law prisoners before the coming of the Greeks. Then it went on as follows:

"In the person of the high civil authority that represents it at Smyrna, the Greek Government is responsible for the serious disturbances that ended in bloodshed in the interior of the country during the advance of the Greek troops.... The Greeks alone are responsible for the bloodshed at Menemen.... The Greek officers who were at Menemen quite neglected their duty."

And the Commission wound up its report with this:

"In the occupied region, putting aside the towns of Smyrna—where the number of Christians is high, but the number of Greek Christians much inferior to that of the Turks—and Aivali, the predominance of the Turkish element over the Greek element is undeniable."

So we easily understand the violent and justifiable indignation felt by the Turks when the Greek troops landed, for they could not forget that now there were no Turks in Thessaly, where they numbered 150,000 in 1878, or in the Morea, where there had once been 300,000, and that in Greece only about 20,000 were left of the 100,000 that had once lived there.

M. Venizelos, in a letter addressed on May 29 to the President of the Conference, thought it his duty to give particulars about the way the occupation had been effected. After setting right what he styled "the wrong and misleading information given by newspapers," he stated that the Greeks had "arrived at Aidin, on the southern side, east of Nymphaton and north of the River Ermos." The Great Powers having asked the Greek Government, as he said expressly in his letter, "to occupy Smyrna and its environs" without stating exactly how far the environs of Smyrna reached, he thought he had a right to look upon this operation—which had been attended with a few incidents and had not been received everywhere with unmixed joy—as the outcome of a settled policy. After this occupation public meetings of protest took place in Constantinople.

An important Crown Council was held in the afternoon of May 26 at Yildiz-Kiosk, in order to enable the various political groups to express their opinion concerning the recent events.

The Sultan, attended by the princes of the Imperial Family, opened the meeting, and stated it had been thought necessary to call together the most eminent men of Turkey that they might express their opinion about the critical condition of the country.

The Grand Vizier, after recalling the events that had taken place in Turkey since the beginning of the war, asked the audience to let him have their opinions.

The Unionist group said they were dissatisfied with the composition of the Ministry, and demanded a Coalition Government, in which all parties should be represented.

Another political group asked the Crown Council to form itself into a National Assembly.

Somebody else showed the inanity of such suggestions and proposed to entrust the mandate of the administration of Turkey to a Great Power—without mentioning which Power. He added: "Otherwise Turkey will be dismembered, which would be her ruin."

As the assembly had merely consultative powers, no decision was reached.

At the beginning of June, 1919, the Ottoman League sent from Geneva to Mr. Montagu, British Secretary for India, the following note:

"The Ottoman League has examined the statements which your Excellency was so kind as to make at the Peace Conference, regarding the subsequent fate of the Ottoman Empire.

"We have always been convinced that His Britannic Majesty's Government in its relations with our country would resume its traditional policy, which was started and advocated by the most famous English statesmen, and that, after obtaining the guarantees required for the safety of its huge dominions, it would refuse to countenance any measure aiming at the oppression and persecution of Moslems.

"The British Government can realise better than any other Power the disastrous consequences that would necessarily follow throughout Islam on the downfall of the Ottoman Empire and any blow struck at its vital parts, especially at its capital, the universally revered seat of the Khilafat, where the best works of Moslem civilisation have been gathered for centuries.

"We feel certain that your Excellency will also realise better than anybody else of what importance would be to Great Britain the loyalty, not only of the Ottoman Moslems without any distinction of race, but of all the Mohammedans whose destiny is presided over by His Britannic Majesty."

At last, about the end of the month, the treaty with Turkey was drafted by the Conference, and on June 11 the Turkish representatives were brought to France on board the French ironclad *Démocratie*.

The delegation included Tewfik Pasha, Riza Tewfik Bey, with Reshid Bey, former Minister of the Interior, as adviser. At its head was Damad Ferid Pasha, the Sultan's brother-in-law, who, after the resignation of the Tewfik Pasha Cabinet at the beginning of March, 1919, had formed a new Ministry.

As was stated in the Allies' answer to the Porte in the letter addressed to the Turkish Premier, Damad Ferid Pasha, Turkey had not attempted in the memorandum handed to the Conference to excuse the Germano-Turkish intrigues which had paved the way for her to take part in the war on the side of the Germans; neither had she attempted to clear herself of all the crimes she was charged with. Damad Ferid Pasha had simply pleaded that only the "Young Turks" of the Committee of Union and Progress were responsible for the Ottoman policy during the last five years, and that, if they had governed the Empire, as it were, in the name of the Germans, the whole Turkish nation could not be held responsible for this.

The Allies pointed out in their reply that they could not accept the distinction which cast all the blame on the Government and alleged the misdeeds were not imputable to the Turkish people merely because these misdeeds were abhorrent to Turkish ideas, as shown in the course of centuries. So the Allies informed the delegation they could not grant their request to restore Ottoman sovereignty over territories that had been taken away from them before.

Yet the Council, though they declared they could not accept such views or enter upon such a controversy, launched into considerations on Turkish ideas and Turkish influence in the world which, to say the least, were most questionable, as will be seen later on.

They stated, for instance, that no section of the Turkish people had ever been able to build up a lasting political organisation, the huge Empires of the Hioung-nous, the Ouigours, and the Kiptchaks having been of short duration. The Supreme Council also asserted that the lack of stability of the Ottoman Empire—which was represented as unable to develop—was due to the various origins of its elements. But other influences were laid aside, which have been at work, especially during the modern period, since the beginning of the decline. It should be borne in mind that three centuries ago the civilisation and prosperity of the Ottoman Empire were not inferior to those of the Western nations, and its inferiority appeared only nowadays, when Germany and Italy founded their unity, while the European States did not do anything in Turkey to improve—or even did much to aggravate—a condition of things that left to Turkey no possibility of recovery. If Moslem civilisation is quite different from Western civilisation, it does not follow necessarily that it is inferior to it. For several centuries its religious and social ideals safeguarded and ruled, to their satisfaction, the lives of numerous populations in the Levant, whereas more modern ideals in the West have not yet succeeded in bringing about conditions of life that can meet the requirements of man's mind and physical nature. As to the so-called combativeness of the Turks and their supposed fanaticism—which may be only due, considering they were nomads at first, to their quick and headstrong nature—they both were certainly lessened by their intercourse and especially intermarriages with the Mongols, a quiet and peaceful people largely influenced by Buddhism and Lamaism, which they all profess, except a few Bouriate tribes that are still Shamanist. Moreover, even if such suppositions were true, their mixing with Western people could only have a good influence in soothing their original nature, whereas their eviction to Asia, by depriving them of any direct and close contact with Europe, would have the effect of reviving their former propensities.

Finally, the aforesaid document, though it was really superficial and rather vague on this point, purposed to give a crushing answer to the arguments of the Ottoman memorandum about the religious rivalries; yet these arguments were well grounded and most important, as appeared when the Protestant campaign broke out and Anglo-American opinion demanded the ejection of the Turks.

On June 27, 1919, the President of the Peace Conference in Paris addressed a second letter to Damad Ferid Pasha to inform him that the solution of the Turkish problem was postponed.

After stating that the declarations made before the Peace Conference by the Ottoman delegation "have been, and will continue to be, examined most attentively, as they deserve to be," the letter went on to say that "they involve other interests than those of Turkey, and raise international questions, the immediate solution of which is unfortunately impossible; and it ended thus:

"Therefore, though the members of the Supreme Council are eager to restore peace definitely and fully realise it is a dangerous thing to protract the present period of uncertainty, yet a sound study of the situation has convinced them that some delay is unavoidable.

"They are of opinion, therefore, that a longer stay in Paris of the Ottoman delegation, which the Ottoman Government had asked to be allowed to send to France, would not be conducive to any good.

"Yet a time will come when an exchange of views will be profitable again; then the Allied and Associated Powers will not fail to communicate with the Ottoman Government as to the best means to settle the question easily and rapidly."

One of the reasons given for this adjournment was the protest handed to Mr. Montagu, Secretary of State for India, by the Maharaja of Bikanir in the name of the Moslems of India, a protest which is supposed to have shaken the decisions already taken by the British Government.

At any rate, instead of maintaining the negotiations on a sound basis, and dealing squarely with the difficulties of the Turkish question, which would have made it possible to reach a better and more permanent solution, the Allies seemed to wish to break off the debates, or at least to postpone the discussion, in order to manœuvre and gain time. Perhaps they did it on purpose, or the negotiations came to an untimely end because, among the men who had assumed the charge of European affairs, some meant to intervene in them all the more eagerly because they did not know anything about them. They were not aware or had forgotten that in dealing with Eastern affairs or in pursuing negotiations with people of ancient civilisation, a great deal of delicacy, discretion, and shrewdness is required at the same time, and that generally diplomatists must expect plenty of haggling and procrastination, must avoid clashing with the adversary, and be able repeatedly to drop and resume a discussion smoothly, sometimes after long delays.

Somebody then quoted the words of the well-known French traveller Chardin in regard to Chevalier Quirini who, about 1671, carried on negotiations in Constantinople with the Vizier Ahmed Küprüli on behalf of the Republic of Venice:

"I heard M. Quirini say, when I had the honour of calling upon him, that the policy of the Turks far excelled that of the Europeans; that it was not restrained by maxims and regulations, but was wholly founded on, and regulated by, discernment. This policy, depending on no art or principles, was almost beyond anybody's reach. So he candidly confessed that the vizier's conduct was an utter mystery to him, and he was unable to fathom its discrimination, depth, secrecy, shrewdness, and artfulness."

It is noteworthy that the same vizier was also able to cope successively with three ambassadors of Louis XIV.

The direction taken from the outset by the deliberations of the Conference, and the standpoint it took to settle the Turkish question, showed it was about to give up the traditional policy of the French kings in the East, which had been started by Francis I, and the last representatives of which had been the Marquis de Villeneuve, Louis XV's ambassador, and the Comte de Bonneval.

As early as the end of the eighteenth century Voltaire, though he extolled Turkish tolerance throughout his "Essai sur la tolérance," and wrote that "two hundred thousand Greeks lived in security in Constantinople," advocated quite a different policy in his "Correspondance," and took sides with the Russians against the Turks. After confessing that "he had no turn for politics," and stating in "Candide" that he only cared for the happiness of peoples, he wrote to Frederick II:

"I devoutly hope the barbarous Turks will be driven out of the land of Xenophon, Socrates, Plato, Sophocles, and Euripides. If Europe really cared, that would soon be done. But seven crusades of superstition were once undertaken, and no crusade of honour will ever be undertaken; all the burden will be left to Catherine."

He did not conceal how highly pleased he was with the events of 1769-71, and he wrote to the "Northern Semiramis," as he styled her:

"It is not sufficient to carry on a fortunate war against such barbarians; it is not enough to humble their pride; they ought to be driven away to Asia for ever. Your Imperial Majesty restores me to life by killing the Turks. It has always been my opinion that if their empire is ever destroyed, it will be by yours."

Indeed, some people maliciously hinted at the time that Voltaire's opinion of the Turks was due to his disappointment at the failure of his play "Mahomet, ou le fanatisme," and that it was for the same reason he wrote in his "Essai sur les mœurs et l'esprit des nations" while he was Madame du Chatelet's guest:

"Force and rapine built up the Ottoman Empire, and the quarrels between Christians have kept it up. Hardly any town has ever been built by the Turks. They have allowed the finest works of antiquity to fall to decay; they rule over ruins."

It seems that the members of the Supreme Council, in their answer to the Turkish delegation, only harped upon this old theme, and amplified it, and that in their settlement of the question they were inspired by similar considerations, evincing the same misunderstanding of Turkey and the same political error. The Supreme Council might have remembered J. J. Rousseau's prophecy in his "Contrat Social," which might very well be fulfilled now: "The Russian Empire will endeavour to subjugate Europe, but will be subjugated. The Tatars, its subjects and neighbours, will become its masters and ours too."[15]

The negotiations which had just been broken off could only have been usefully carried on if the Allies had quite altered their policy and had realised the true condition of the Ottoman Empire and the interests of the Western nations, especially those of France.

The condition of the Ottoman Empire, as will be seen later on, when we shall dwell upon the slow and deep disintegration which had taken place among the Turkish and Arabian populations, was on the whole as follows: The Young Turk revolution, on which great hopes were built, had ended lamentably: the Austrians had wrested Bosnia-Herzegovina from Turkey; the Turco-Italian war had taken from her another slice of her territory; then the coalition of the Balkan States had arisen, which seems to have been prepared and supported by England and by the other nations which followed her policy. Finally, the treaty of Bukharest confirmed the failure of the principle—once solemnly proclaimed by France and England—of the territorial integrity of Turkey. So the Turks no longer had any confidence in Europe, and, being sacrificed once more in the Balkan war, and as they could no longer trust England, they were necessarily thrown into the arms of Germany.

After Abdul Hamid, Mehmed V, with his weak, religious mind, allowed himself to be led by Enver, and his reign, disturbed by three wars, cost Turkey huge territorial losses. Mehmed VI, being more energetic and straightforward, tried to restore order in the State, and to put an end to the doings of the Committee of Union and Progress.

Then, too, the Crown Prince, Abdul Mejid, a man about fifty, who speaks French very well, evinces the same turn of mind. After seeing what Germany could do with the Turkish Empire, such men, who had not kept aloof from modern ideas, and to whom European methods were not unfamiliar, had made up their mind that the Turks should not be driven out of Europe. But Mejid Effendi was soon deprived of influence through intrigues, and henceforth engaged in his favourite hobby, painting, in his palace on Skutari Hill, and kept away from politics.

Mustafa Kemal, who had been sent to Amasia as Inspector-General of the Eastern army, had secretly raised an army on his own account, with the help of Reouf Bey, once Minister of Marine in the Izzet Cabinet. When recalled to Constantinople by the Turkish Government in July, 1919, he had refused to obey, and had proclaimed himself his own master. Though he had once gone to Berlin with the Sultan, who was only Crown Prince at the time, the latter degraded him and deprived him of the right of wearing his decorations—which could only have been a political measure intended to show that the throne and the Government could not openly countenance the movement that was taking place in Anatolia.

Mustafa Kemal, brought up at Salonika, had only become well known in Constantinople during the Revolution of 1908. During the war in the Balkan Peninsula he had distinguished himself at Chatalja, and after being promoted colonel he was sent as military attaché to Sofia, and then charged with a mission in Paris. He came back to Constantinople in 1914, a short time before war broke out.

Of course, when he had started his career a long time previously, Mustafa Kemal had been connected indirectly with the Union and Progress party, as he was at the head of the revolutionary group in which this association originated, but he was never a member of the Merkez-i-Oumimi, the central seat of the Committee of Union and Progress. He was a good officer, very fond of his profession, and, as he loathed politics, he had soon kept away from them, and consequently never played any part in them, and was hardly ever influenced by them. Yet the supporters of the Committee of Union and Progress, who have made great mistakes, but have always been patriots, have necessarily been compelled lately to co-operate with him, though they did not like to do so at the outset.

Mustafa Kemal was undoubtedly the real leader of the movement which had already spread over the whole of Anatolian Turkey. As his influence was enormous and he had an undeniable ascendancy over the Turkish troops he had recruited, his power was soon acknowledged from Cartal, close to Constantinople to the Persian frontier. He had compelled Liman von Sanders to give him command of a sector at a moment when the Turks seemed to be in a critical situation during the attack of the Anglo-French fleet in the Dardanelles, and by not complying with his orders he had saved the Turkish army by the victory of Anafarta, and perhaps prevented the capture of Constantinople, for two hours after the Allies, whose casualties had been heavy, retired.

But he had soon come into conflict with Enver Pasha. Their disagreement had begun during the war of Tripoli; it had increased during the Balkan war, and had now reached an acute state. The chief reason seems to be that they held quite different opinions about the organisation of the army and the conduct of the war operations. Mustafa Kemal having always refused to take part in politics after the Young Turk revolution of 1908, it seems difficult to believe this hostility could be accounted for by political reasons, though the situation had now completely changed. As to Mustafa Kemal's bickerings and petty quarrels with several German generals during the war, they seem to have had no other cause than a divergence of views on technical points.

In consequence of this disagreement Mustafa Kemal was sent to Mesopotamia in disgrace. He came back to Constantinople a few weeks before the armistice. After the occupation of Smyrna he was appointed Inspector-General of Anatolia, where he organised the national movement.

By Mustafa Kemal's side there stood Reouf Bey, once Minister of Marine, who, during the Balkan war, as commander of the cruiser *Hamidié*, had made several raids in Greek waters, had then been one of the signatories of the Moudros armistice, and now was able to bring over to the Anatolian movement many naval officers and sailors, and General Ali Fuad Pasha, the defender of Fort Pisani at Janina during the Balkan war, who had a great prestige among the troops.

Bekir Sami Bey, once Governor-General, and Ahmed Rustem Bey, formerly ambassador at Washington, were the first political men of note who joined the nationalist movement. On Mustafa Kemal's arrival at Erzerum, Kiazim Karabekir, together with the other commanders, acknowledged him as their chief, and pledged themselves to support him against Constantinople.

Mustafa Kemal openly charged the Government with betraying Turkey to the Allies, and asked all those who wanted to defend their country and their religion to join him. At that time he only had at his disposal two divisions of regular troops; he sent an appeal to the populations of Sivas and Ushak, and many volunteers joined his colours. Colonel Bekir Sami, who commanded the Panderma-Smyrna line and all the district, also rebelled against the Constantinople Government, and soon his 10,000 soldiers joined the troops of Mustafa Kemal, who assumed the general command of all the insurgent troops. On the other hand, Kiazim Bey threatened to resume hostilities, in case too heavy conditions should be forced on Turkey. Mustafa Kemal, as he refused to make any concessions to the victors of Turkey, and opposed any separatist idea or the cession of any Ottoman territories, of course had with him a large section of public opinion, which was roused by the Allies' threat to take from Turkey half her possessions, Thrace, Smyrna, and Kurdistan, and to drive the Sultan into Asia.

On July 23, a Congress of the committees which had been established in various parts of the Empire for the defence of the national rights was held at Erzerum.

The proceedings were secret, but at the end of the congress an official report was sent to the High Commissioners of the Allies in Constantinople.

An "Anatolian and Rumelian League for the Defence of the National Rights" was formed, which later on was called the "National Organisation." According to what has become known about the sittings of the Congress, the principles that were to control the action of the National Organisation and to constitute its programme were the following: (1) Grouping of the various Moslem nationalities of the Empire into a whole politically and geographically indivisible and administered so as to ensure the respect of their ethnic and social differences. (2) Equality of rights for non-Moslem communities so far as consistent with the principle of the political unity of the State. (3) Integrity of the Empire within the boundaries of Turkish sovereignty as they were in September, 1918, when the armistice was concluded—which are almost the same as the ethnic boundaries of Turkey. (4) No infringement whatever on the sovereignty of the Turkish Empire. A special article expressed the sincere wish on the part of the Turkish nation, with a view to the general restoration of Turkey, to accept the support of any Western country, providing the latter did not aim at an economic or political subjection of any kind.

This programme was sanctioned in the course of a second Congress which was held at Sivas at the beginning of September, 1919, to allow the local committees which had not been able to send delegates to Erzerum to give their approbation to it and to adhere to the national movement.

The executive functions of the Congress were entrusted to a representative committee presided over by Mustafa Kemal, and consisting of members chosen by the Congress, who were: Reouf Bey, Bekir Sami Bey, Hoja Raif Effendi, Mazhar Bey, once vali of Bitlis, and later on Ahmed Rustem Bey, once Turkish ambassador at Washington, Haidar Bey, once vali of Kharput, and Hakki Behij Bey.

The local militias which had been raised took the name of national forces; and when they had been linked with the regular army, they were put by Mustafa Kemal under the command of Kara Bekir Kiazim Pasha, who became commander-in-chief in Eastern Anatolia, and Ali Fuad Pasha, who had the command of the forces of Western Anatolia.

Two delegates of the "Liberal Entente," some leaders of which group seemed open to foreign influence, were sent to Constantinople to ask the Central Committee what attitude was to be taken, and were prudently ordered to enjoin the supporters of the Liberal Entente to be most careful.

But though part of the Constantinople Press seemed to deny any importance to the Anatolian movement, the Stambul Government deemed it proper to send missions to Trebizond, Angora, and Eskishehr, headed by influential men, in order to restore order in those regions. It also directed two of its members to go to the rebellious provinces to see how things stood, and come to terms with Mustafa Kemal. Some of these missions never reached the end of their journey; most of them had to retrace their steps, some did not even set out. In September, 1919, Marshal Abdullah Pasha, who had instructions to reach Mustafa Kemal at Trebizond, and enjoin him to give up his self-assumed command, did not stir from Constantinople. The Government also sent General Kemal Pasha, commander of the gendarmerie, to scatter the nationalist irregular troops, but nothing was heard of him after a while, and he was supposed to have been taken prisoner by, or gone over to, the rebels. The Anatolian valis and commanders who had been summoned to Constantinople did not come, protesting they could not do so or were ill.

On the other hand, Mustafa Kemal sent back to Constantinople Jemal Bey, vali of Konia, and a few functionaries, who had remained loyal to the Stambul Government. Ismaïl Bey, vali of Brusa, one of the most important leaders of the Liberal Entente, was driven out of office by both Governments.

In addition, the cleavages already existing in the Ottoman Empire, which since 1913 only included the prominently Moslem provinces, had widened, and endangered the unity of the Empire. In the provinces where the Arabic-speaking Moslems were in a majority the authority of the Turkish Government dwindled every day; they meant to shake off the Ottoman yoke, and at the same time to keep off any Western influence; they also wished more and more eagerly to part from the provinces where the Turks and Ottoman Kurds—who aim at uniting together—are in a majority.

For the last four centuries France had enjoyed an exceptional situation in Turkey. Her intellectual influence was paramount; French was not only known among the upper classes, but it was also in current use in politics and business, and even a good many clerks in post-offices and booking-offices at Constantinople understood it.

French schools, owing to their very tolerant spirit, were very popular among nearly all classes of the Turkish population, and the sympathies we had thus acquired and the intellectual prestige we enjoyed were still more important than our material interests. Nearly 25,000 children attended the French elementary schools, most of them religious schools, which bears witness both to the confidence the Mahommedans had in us, and the tolerance they showed. The Grammar School of Galata-Serai, established in 1868 by Sultan Abdul Aziz with the co-operation of Duruy, French Minister of Public Education, and several other secondary schools which are now closed, diffused French culture and maintained sympathy between the two peoples. The Jesuits' school of medicine at Beyrut also spread our influence.

The material interests of France in Turkey were also of great importance; and it was, therefore, a great mistake for France to follow a policy that was bound to ruin the paramount influence she had acquired. The other Western States had as important interests as France; and it was necessary to take all these facts into account if an equitable settlement of the Turkish question was to be reached.

France, England, and Germany were, before the war, the three Powers that owned the most important financial concerns in Turkey, France easily holding the premier position, owing to the amount of French capital invested in Turkish securities, Government stocks, and private companies.

From 1854 to 1875 thirteen loans—almost one every year—were issued by the Ottoman Government, ten being entrusted to the care of French banks or financial establishments controlled by French capital.

These thirteen loans have only an historical interest now, except the three loans issued in 1854, 1855, and 1871, secured on the Egyptian tribute, which still exist with some modifications, but may be looked upon as Egyptian or rather English securities, and were not included in the settlement effected in 1881 which converted them into new bonds, and the 1870-71 loan, styled "Lots Turcs," the whole of which at the time was subscribed by Baron Hirsch in return for the concession of railways in Europe. To them let us add another financial operation effected about 1865, consisting in the unification of the various bonds of the interior debt and their conversion into bonds representing a foreign debt.

Most of these operations were controlled by the Imperial Ottoman Bank, founded by the most influential English and French financial groups, to which the Ottoman Government by its firmans of 1863 and 1875 granted the privilege of being the State bank. It thus has the exclusive right of issuing banknotes, and has the privilege of being the general paymaster of the Empire and the financial agent of the Government, both at home and abroad.

The financial activity of the French companies was only interrupted by the 1870 war. The only competition met with was that of a few English banks, which no doubt intended to second the views of the British Government in Egypt, and of an Austrian syndicate for the building of the Balkan railways which, later on, furthered the penetration of Austria-Hungary in Eastern Europe.

In 1875 the nominal capital of the Ottoman debt rose to 5,297,676,500 francs. The Ottoman Government, finding it impossible to pay the interest on the Government stocks, announced its decision on October 6, 1875, to give only one-half in cash in the future. The Imperial Ottoman Bank, which was practically under French control owing to the importance of the French capital invested in it, raised a protest on behalf of the bondholders.

The Porte then agreed to make arrangements with the French, the Italians, the Austrians, the Germans, and the Belgians. The claims of the bondholders were laid before the plenipotentiaries who had met at Berlin to revise the preliminaries of San Stefano, and were sanctioned by the Berlin treaty signed on July 13, 1878. They had three chief objects: First, to secure the right of first mortgage which the creditors of the Empire held from the loans secured on the Russian war indemnity; secondly, to appoint the contributive share of the Ottoman debt incumbent on the provinces detached from the Empire; thirdly, to decide what was to be done to restore Turkish finance.

After the conversations with the plenipotentiaries assembled at Berlin, and chiefly owing to the intervention of the French representative, M. Waddington, the Congress embodied the following clauses in the treaty in order to protect the interests of the bond-holders: Bulgaria was to pay the Sultan a tribute; part of the revenue of Eastern Rumelia was to be assigned to the payment of the Ottoman Public Debt; Bulgaria, Serbia, and Montenegro were to assume a part of the Ottoman debt proportionately to the Turkish territories annexed by each of them; all the rights and duties of the Porte relating to the railways of Eastern Rumelia were to be wholly maintained; finally, the Powers advised the Sublime Porte to establish an international financial commission in Constantinople.

In this way the Berlin treaty laid down the principles on which every financial reorganisation was to be based whenever a province should be detached from the Ottoman Empire.

Then the mandatories of the bondholders began to negotiate directly with the Ottoman Empire, but as the various schemes that were proferred failed, the Imperial Ottoman Bank, supported by the Galata bankers, proposed an arrangement that was sanctioned by the Convention of November 10 to 22, 1879. In this way the administration of the Six Contributions was created, to which were farmed out for a period of ten years the revenues derived from stamp duties, spirits in some provinces, the fisheries of Constantinople and the suburbs, and the silk tax within the same area and in the suburbs of Adrianople, Brusa, and Samsun; it was also entrusted with the collection and administration of the revenues proceeding from the monopolies in salt and tobacco.

At the request of the Imperial Ottoman Bank the revenues of this administration, first allocated to the Priority Bonds, of which she owned the greater part, were divided later on between all the bondholders.

In this way the important agreement known as the decree of Muharrem, in which the French played a paramount part, was made possible (December 8 to 20, 1881), according to which the original capital of the foreign Turkish loans was brought down to the average price of issue, plus 10 per cent. of this new capital as a compensation for the interest that had not been paid since 1876. The old bonds were stamped, converted, and exchanged for new bonds called Bonds of the Unified Converted Debt, except the "Lots Turcs," which, being premium bonds, were treated separately.

The interest of the Converted Debt was fixed at from 1 to 4 per cent. of the new capital.

As to the amortisation, the decree divided the various foreign loans into several series according to the value of the mortgage; this classification stated in what order they would be subject to amortisation.

The outcome of these negotiations, the decree of Muharrem, also established a set of concessions which could not be revoked before the extinction of the debt, and organised the administration of the Ottoman Public Debt, which was to collect and administer, on behalf of the Ottoman bondholders, the revenues conceded as guarantee of the debt.

The Ottoman Government pledged itself to allocate to the payment of the interest and to the amortisation of the reduced debt till its extinction the following revenues: the monopolies in salt and tobacco; the Six Contributions (tobacco, salt, spirits, stamps, fisheries, silk); any increase in the customs duties resulting from the modification of the commercial treaties; any increase of the revenues resulting from new regulations affecting patents and licences (*temettu*); the tribute of the principality of Bulgaria; any surplus of the Cyprus revenues; the tribute of Eastern Rumelia; the produce of the tax on pipe tobacco (*tumbeki*); any sums which might be fixed as contributions due from Greece, Serbia, Bulgaria, and Montenegro for the service of the debt.

The administration of the Ottoman Public Debt was entrusted to "the Council for the Administration of the Ottoman Public Debt," commonly known as "the Public Debt," consisting of delegates of Ottoman bondholders of all nations. The French owned by far the greater part of the debt. The English represented the Belgians in the Council, the shares of these two countries in the debt being about equal.

This international council, who attended to the strict execution of the provisions of the decree, deducted all the sums required for the interest and the sinking fund, and made over the balance to the Imperial treasury.

The decree of Muharrem also entrusted to the Public Debt the control of the cultivation and the monopoly of the sale of tobacco throughout the Turkish Empire. Later on, in 1883, the Public Debt farmed out its rights to an Ottoman limited company, the "Régie Co-intéressée des Tabacs de l'Empire," formed by a financial consortium including three groups: the Imperial Ottoman Bank, which was a Franco-English concern; the German group of the B. Bleichröder Bank; and the Austrian group of the Kredit Anstalt with a capital of 100 million francs. Only one-half of this capital was paid up—*i.e.*, 50 million francs—which was cut down to 40 million francs on November 28, 1899, to make up for the losses of the first three years. It is thought in French financial circles that half this capital—viz., 20 million francs—is French, and the rest chiefly Austrian.

The "Régie," whose activities extend throughout the Empire, may be looked upon as one of the most important financial concerns of the Ottoman Empire. It has branches in all the chief centres, controls the cultivation of tobacco, records the production, buys native and foreign tobaccos, issues licences for the sale of tobacco, and advances money to the growers; its chief factories are at Samsun, Aleppo, Adana, Smyrna, etc. In return for the monopoly it enjoys, it owes the Public Debt a fixed yearly payment, and has to divide a fixed proportion of its net profits between the Public Debt and the Ottoman Government.

The share of France in the Council of the Public Debt, in which French was the official language, gave her a paramount influence and prestige in the Ottoman Empire. Owing to the importance and extent of the part played by the Council of the Debt, in which the influence of France was paramount, the latter country indirectly acquired an influence in the administration of the *Malié*—*i.e.*, in the administration of the Turkish treasury—and in this way Turkey was obliged on several occasions to call for the advice of French specialists for her financial reorganisation.

But the Ottoman Government, in order to consolidate its floating debt, which had not been included in the previous liquidation, was soon compelled to borrow money abroad. Besides, it wanted to construct a system of railways at that time.

The loan guaranteed by the customs duties in 1886, the Osmanie loan in 1890, the 4 per cent. Tombac preferential loan in 1893, the Eastern Railway loan in 1894, the 5 per cent. 1896 loan, and the 4 per cent. 1901 loan, were all floated in France, and the English had no share in the financial operations between 1881 and 1904.

During the same period Germany, through the Deutsche Bank, took up the Fishery loan in 1888 and the 4 per cent. Baghdad Railway loan in 1903. Later on the German financial companies, together with the Deutsche Bank, gave Turkey as much support as the French banks, in order to promote Pan-Germanism in the East and oust French influence. The chief financial operations carried on by these companies were the Baghdad Railway loan, the Tejhizat loan for the payment of military supplies, and the 1911 loan, which were both a guarantee and an encouragement for the German policy of penetration in Turkey, and paved the way to a Germano-Ottoman understanding.

France continued to subscribe all the same, from 1903 to 1914, to six of the twelve Turkish loans raised by the Ottoman Government; four others were taken up by Germany, another by England, and the sixth—the 4 per cent. 1908 loan—was issued one-half in France, one-fourth in Germany, and one-fourth in England. In 1914, as a reward for issuing a loan of 800 million francs in Paris—the first slice being 500 million—France obtained the settlement of several litigious cases and new concessions of railways and ports.

At the outbreak of the war, the external debt of Turkey, including the Unified Debt and other loans, amounted to 3½ milliards of francs, whereas the Turkish revenue hardly exceeded 500 million francs. One-third of this sum went to the sinking fund of the external debt, of which, roughly speaking, France alone owned nearly 60 per cent., Germany nearly 26 per cent., and England a little more than 14 per cent.

In addition to this, in the sums lent to Turkey by private companies, the share of France was about 50 per cent.—*i.e.*, over 830 million francs; that of Germany rose to 35 per cent.; and that of England a little more than 14 per cent.

Foreign participation in the great works and the various economic or financial concerns in Turkey may be summed up as follows:

	France.	*England.*	*Germany.*
Banks	37·7	33·3	28·0
Railways	46·9	10·4	46·6
Ports and wharves	67·9	12·2	19·7
Water	88·6	—	11·3
Mines	100·0	—	—
Various concerns	62·8	24·1	13·0
Total per cent.	50·5	14·3	35·0
Capital (million Francs)	830	235	575

Not only had France an important share in the organisation of Turkish finances, but had opened three banks while the English established but one, the National Bank of Turkey, which holds no privilege from the State, and is merely a local bank for business men. Two German banks—the Deutsche Orient Bank and the Deutsche Palästina Bank, founded almost as soon as Germany began to show her policy regarding Turkish Asia—had turned their activity towards Turkey, as we have just seen.

France incurred an outlay of 550 million francs—not including the sums invested in companies which were not predominantly French, such as the

Baghdad Railway—for the building of 1,500 miles of railway lines, while the Germans built almost as many, and the English only 450 miles; and France spent 58 million francs for the ports, whereas the English only spent 10 million francs.

The railway concessions worked by French capital included the Damascus-Hama line, which afterwards reached Jaffa and Jerusalem; the tramways of Lebanon; the Mudania-Brusa line; the Smyrna-Kassaba railway; the Black Sea railways which, according to the 1914 agreement, were to extend from Kastamuni to Erzerum, and from Trebizond to Kharput, and be connected with the Rayak-Ramleh line—viz., 1,600 miles of railway altogether in Syria; the Salonika-Constantinople line.

Before the London treaty, the Eastern railways in European Turkey, representing 600 miles, were worked by Austro-German capital, and the Salonika-Monastir line, 136 miles in length, had a German capital of 70 million francs.

The concessions with German capital in Asia Minor formed a complete system of railways, including the Anatolian railways, with a length of 360 miles and a capital of 344,500,000 francs; the Mersina-Tarsus-Adana line, 42 miles, capital 9,200,000 francs; the Baghdad Railway, whose concession was first given to the Anatolian railways but was ceded in 1903 to the Baghdad Railway Company, and which before the war was about 190 miles in length.

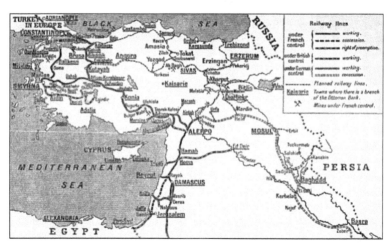

MAP OF THE RAILWAYS OF THE OTTOMAN EMPIRE AND THE CHIEF MINING CONCERNS UNDER FOREIGN CONTROL BEFORE THE WAR.

(191 kB)

As the building of this system of railways closely concerned the French companies of the Smyrna-Kassaba and Beyrut-Damascus railways and the English company of the Smyrna-Aidin railway, the French companies and the Ottoman Imperial Bank concluded arrangements with the holders of the concessions to safeguard French interests as much as possible. Thus a French financial group took up a good many of the Baghdad bonds (22,500 and 21,155 bonds) and numerous shares of the "Société de construction du chemin de fer" established in 1909. On the whole, the share of the French consortium before the war amounted to 4,000,000 francs on the one hand, and 1,950,000 francs on the other; the share of the German consortium was 11,000,000 and 8,050,000 francs.

The concessions controlled by English capital were the Smyrna-Aidin line, 380 miles long, with a capital of 114,693,675 francs, and the Smyrna-Kassaba line, which was ceded later on to the company controlled by French capital which has already been mentioned. They were the first two railway concessions given in Turkey (1856 and 1863).

In Constantinople the port, the lighthouses, the gasworks, the waterworks, and the tramways were planned and built by French capital and labour.

The port of Smyrna, whose concession was given in 1867 to an English company and two years after passed into the hands of some Marseilles contractors, was completed by the "Société des quais de Smyrne," a French limited company. The diversion of the Ghedis into the Gulf of Phocea in order to prevent the port being blocked up with sand was the work of a French engineer, Rivet.

The Bay of Beyrut has also been equipped by a French company founded in 1888 under the patronage of the Ottoman Bank by a group of the chief French shareholders of the Beyrut-Damascus road and other French financial companies.

Moreover, according to the 1914 agreements, the ports of Ineboli and Heraclea on the Black Sea, and the ports of Tripoli, Jaffa, and Haïfa in Syria, were to be built exclusively by French capital. So it was with the intended concessions of the ports of Samsun and Trebizond.

At Beyrut a French group in 1909 bought up the English concession for the building of the waterworks and pipelines, and formed a new company. French capital, together with Belgian capital, also control the Gas Company, Tramway Company, and Electric Company of Beyrut. Only at Smyrna, where the gasworks are in the hands of an English company and the waterworks are owned by a Belgian company has France not taken part in the organisation of the municipal services.

Only the port of Haïdar-Pasha, the terminus of the Anatolian Railway, has been ceded by this company to a financial company whose shares are in German hands.

To these public establishments should be added such purely private industrial or commercial concerns as the Orosdi-Back establishments; the Oriental Tobacco Company; the Tombac Company; the "Société nationale pour le commerce, l'industrie et l'agriculture dans l'Empire ottoman"; the concession of Shukur-ova, the only French concession of landed property situated in the Gulf of Alexandretta on the intended track of the Baghdad Railway, including about 150,000 acres of Imperial land, which represent an entirely French capital of 64 million francs; the Oriental Carpet Company, which is a Franco-British concern; the Joint Stock Imperial Company of the Docks, Dockyards, and Shipbuilding Yard, which is entirely under British control, etc.

During the war, the share of France and that of England were increased, as far as the Public Debt is concerned, by the amount of the coupons which were not cashed by the stockholders of the Allied countries, while the holders of Ottoman securities belonging to the Central Powers cashed theirs.

Beyond this, Turkey borrowed of Germany about 3½ milliards of francs. An internal loan of 400 million francs had also been raised. To these sums should be added 2 milliards of francs for buying war supplies and war material, and the treasury bonds issued by Turkey for her requisitions, which cannot be cashed but may amount to about 700 million francs. As the requisitions already made during the Balkan wars, which amounted to 300 or 400 million francs, have not yet been liquidated, the whole Turkish debt may be valued at over 10 billion francs.

Finally, in the settlement of the Turkish question, the war damages borne by the French in Turkey should also be taken into account, which means an additional sum of about 2 milliards of francs.

The French owned in Turkey great industrial or agricultural establishments, which were wholly or partly destroyed. At Constantinople and on the shores of the Marmora alone they had about fifty religious or undenominational schools, which were half destroyed, together with everything they contained, perhaps in compliance with the wishes of Germany, who wanted to ruin French influence for ever in that country.

In order to keep up French influence in the East, the High Commissioner of the Republic had, in the early days of the armistice, warned his Government it was necessary to provide a fund at once to defray the expenses of the schools and other institutions established by the French in Turkey in pre-war time—which sums of money were to be advanced on the outstanding indemnity. For want of any existing law, this request could not be complied with; but, as will be seen later on, the Peace Treaty, though it says nothing about this urgent question, states that the indemnities due to the subjects of the Allied Powers for damages suffered by them in their persons or in their property shall be allotted by an inter-Allied financial commission, which alone shall have a right to dispose of Turkish revenue and to sanction the payment of war damages. But all this postpones the solution of the question indefinitely.

In the settlement of the Turkish question, the chief point is how Turkey will be able to carry out her engagements, and so, in her present condition, the policy which England and America, followed by Italy and France, seem to advocate, is a most questionable one.

Javid Bey has even published an account of the condition of Turkey, in which he finds arguments to justify the adhesion of his country to the policy of Germany.

Nevertheless it seems that Turkey, where the average taxation is now from 23 to 25 francs per head, can raise fresh taxes. The revenue of the State will also necessarily increase owing to the increase of production, as a tithe of 10 to 12 per cent. is levied on all agricultural produce. Finally, the building of new railway lines and the establishment of new manufactures—to which, it must be said, some competing States have always objected for their own benefit but to the prejudice of Turkey—would enable her to make herself the manufactured goods she bought at a very high price before, instead of sending abroad her raw materials: silk, wool, cotton, hemp, opium, etc.

The soil of Turkey, on the other hand, contains a good deal of mineral and other wealth, most of which has not been exploited yet. There is a good deal of iron in Asia Minor, though there exists but one iron-mine, at Ayasmat, opposite to Mitylene, the yearly output of which is only 30,000 tons. The most important beds now known are those of the Berut Hills, north of the town of Zeitun, about fifty miles from the Gulf of Alexandretta, which may produce 300,000 tons a year. Chrome, manganese, and antimony are also found there.

There is copper everywhere in the north, in thin but rich layers, containing 20 per cent. of metal. The chief mine, which is at Argana, in the centre of Anatolia, is a State property. A French company, the Syndicate of Argana, founded for the prospecting and exploitation of the copper concessions at Argana and Malatia, and the concessions of argentiferous lead at Bulgar-Maden, had begun prospecting before the war.

Lead, zinc, and silver are found, too, in the Karahissar area, where is the argentiferous lead mine of Bukar-Dagh, once a State property. Before the war a French company of the same type as the one above mentioned, the Syndicate of Ak-Dagh, had obtained the right to explore the layers of zinc and argentiferous lead in the vilayet of Angora. The mines of Balia-Karaidin (argentiferous lead and lignite) lying north-east of the Gulf of Adramyti in the sanjak of Karassi, are controlled by French capital. The English syndicate Borax Consolidated has the concession of the boracite mines in the same sandjak.

The range of Gumich-Dagh, or "Silver Mountain," contains much emery. At Eskishehr there are mines of meerschaum, and in the Brusa vilayet quarries of white, pink, and old-blue marble, lapis-lazuli, etc.

A few years ago gold layers were being exploited at Mender-Aidin, near Smyrna, and others have been found at Chanak-Kale, near the Dardanelles. Some gold-mines had been worked in Arabia in remote ages.

There are oil-fields throughout the peninsula, lying in four parallel lines from the north-west to the south-east. The best-known fields are in the provinces of Mosul and Baghdad, where nearly two hundred have been identified; others have also been found near the Lake of Van, and at Pulk, west of Erzerum, which are not inferior to those of Mesopotamia; and others fifty miles to the south of Sinope.

There are almost inexhaustible layers of excellent asphalt at Latakieh, on the slopes of the Libanus, and others, quite as good, at Kerkuk, Hit, and in several parts of Mesopotamia.

Finally, some coal-mines are being worked at Heraclea which are controlled by French capital, and coal outcrops have been found lately in the Mosul area near the Persian frontier, between Bashkala and Rowanduz and Zahku, close to the Baghdad Railway. But the treaty, as will be shown later on, is to deprive Turkey of most of these sources of wealth.

Among the other products of Turkey may be mentioned carpets, furs (fox, weasel, marten, and otter), and, particularly, silks. The silks of Brusa are more valuable than those of Syria—the latter being difficult to wind; their output has decreased because many mulberry-trees were cut down during the war, but the industry will soon resume its importance.

Turkey also produces a great quantity of leather and hides, and various materials used for tanning: valonia, nut-gall, acacia. It is well known that for centuries the leather trade has been most important in the East, numerous little tanyards are scattered about the country, and there are large leather factories in many important towns. The Young Turks, realising the bright prospects of that trade, had attempted to prohibit the exportation of leathers and hides, and to develop the leather manufacture. During the summer of 1917 the National Ottoman Bank of Credit opened a leather factory at

Smyrna, and appointed an Austrian tanner as its director. Owing to recent events, it has been impossible to establish other leather factories, but this scheme is likely to be resumed with the protection of the Government, for the leather industry may become one of the chief national industries.

The Peace Conference, by postponing the solution of the Turkish problem indefinitely, endangered not only French interests in Turkey, but the condition of Eastern Europe.

The consequences of such a policy soon became obvious, and at the beginning of August it was reported that a strong Unionist agitation had started. The Cabinet of Damad Ferid Pasha, after the answer given by the Entente to the delegation he presided over, was discredited, as it could not even give the main features of the forthcoming peace, or state an approximate date for its conclusion. He could have remained in office only if the Allies had supported him by quickly solving the Turkish problem. Besides, he soon lost all control over the events that hurried on.

In the first days of summer, the former groups of Young Turks were reorganised in Asia Minor; some congresses of supporters of the Union and Progress Committee, who made no secret of their determination not to submit to the decisions that the Versailles Congress was likely to take later on, were held at Erzerum, Sivas, and Amasia, and openly supported motions of rebellion against the Government. At the same time the Turkish Army was being quickly reorganised, outside the Government's control, under the leadership of Mustafa Kemal and Reouf Bey. An openly nationalist, or rather national, movement asserted itself, which publicly protested both against the restoration of the old régime and the dismemberment of Turkey.

Even in Constantinople the Unionist Committee carried on an unrestrained propaganda and plotted to overthrow Damad Ferid Pasha and put in his place Izzet Pasha, a shrewd man, who had signed the armistice with the Allies, and favoured a policy of compromise.

This movement had started after the resignation of the Izzet Pasha Cabinet, when the prominent men of the Unionist party had to leave Constantinople. First, it had been chiefly a Unionist party, but had soon become decidedly national in character. Everywhere, but chiefly in Constantinople, it had found many supporters, and the majority of the cultured classes sympathised with the leaders of the Anatolian Government.

Moreover, the Allies, by allowing the Greeks to land in Smyrna without any valid reason, had started a current of opinion which strengthened the nationalist movement, and raised the whole of Turkey against them.

At the beginning of October, 1919, the Sultan replaced Damad Ferid Pasha by Ali Riza Pasha as Prime Minister. Reshid Pasha, formerly Minister of Public Works and ambassador at Vienna, who had been ambassador at Rome till the revolution of 1908, and had been first Turkish delegate in the Balkan Conference in London in 1912-13, became Minister of Foreign Affairs.

The Grand Vizier General Ali Riza had been Minister of War, and Reshid Pasha Foreign Minister in the Tewfik Cabinet, which had come into office in December, 1918, at a time when the Porte was anxious to conciliate the Allies. Ali Riza had led the operations on the Balkan front in 1912 and 1913, but had refused to assume any command during the Great War, as he had always opposed the participation of Turkey in this war. As he was rather a soldier than a diplomat, his policy seemed likely to be led by his Minister of Foreign Affairs, Reshid Pasha, who was said to be a friend of France.

General Jemal Pasha Kushuk, who became War Minister, was quite a Nationalist. He was called Jemal Junior, to distinguish him from the other Jemal who had been Commander-in-Chief of the Fourth Turkish Army during the war. He, too, had commanded in Palestine. He was popular in the army and among the Unionists. Rightly or wrongly, he was supposed to be in correspondence with Kemal, the leader of the Nationalist movement in Asia Minor, and his appointment intimated that Ali Riza did not want to break off with Kemal, whose rebellion had brought about Damad Ferid's resignation.

Said Mollah, Under-Secretary of Justice, a friend of England, edited the newspaper *Turkje Stambul*, in which he carried on a strong pro-English propaganda. It was said he was paid by Abdul Hamid to spy upon a former Sheik-ul-Islam, Jemal ed Din Effendi, his uncle and benefactor. It seems that by appointing him the Sultan wished to create a link within the new Government between the supporters of England and those of France, in order to show that in his opinion Turkey's interest was, not to put these two nations in opposition to each other, but, on the contrary, to collaborate closely with them both for the solution of Eastern affairs.

Sultan Mehemet VI, by doing so, endeavoured to restore calm and order in Turkey, and also to enhance his prestige and authority over the Nationalist rebels in Anatolia who, at the Congress of Sivas, had plainly stated they refused to make any compromise either with the Porte or the Allies. The choice of the new Ministers marked a concession to the Nationalist and revolutionary spirit.

About the end of 1919 there were serious indications that the Nationalist movement was gaining ground in Cilicia, and in January, 1920, disturbances broke out in the Marash area.

In September, 1919, some armed bands, wearing the khaki uniform of the regular Turkish Army, had been recruited at Mustafa Kemal's instigation. A French officer had been sent to Marash for the first time to watch over the Jebel Bereket district, which commands all the tunnels of the Baghdad Railway between Mamurah and Islahie. In December one of those armed bands, numbering about 200 men, occupied the road leading from Islahie to Marash, and intercepted the mail.

As the conditions that were likely to be enforced upon Turkey were becoming known, discontent increased. General Dutieux, commanding the French troops of Cilicia, determined to send a battalion as reinforcement. The battalion set off at the beginning of January and arrived at Marash on the 10th, after some pretty sharp fighting on the way at El Oglo. As the attacks were getting more numerous and the Nationalist forces increased in number, a new French detachment, more important than the first, and provided with artillery, was dispatched to Islahie, which it reached on the 14th. This column met with no serious incident on the way from Islahie to Marash; it reached Marash on the 17th, at which date it was stated that all the district of Urfa, Aintab, Antioch, Marash, and Islahie was pacified.

That was a mistake, for it soon became known that the chiefs of Bazarjik, a place lying halfway between Marash and Aintab, had gone over to the Kemalists, and had just sent an ultimatum to the French commander demanding the evacuation of the country.

On February 3 the French troops at Marash were attacked by Turkish and Arabian troops coming from the East, who intended to drive them away, and join the main body of the Arabian army.

A French column under the command of Colonel Normand reached Marash, and after a good deal of hard fighting with the Nationalists, who were well armed, relieved the French. But Armenian legionaries had most imprudently been sent; and after some squabbles, which might have been foreseen, between Moslems and Armenians, the French commander had bombarded the town, and then had been compelled to evacuate it. These events, later on, led to the recall of Colonel Brémond, whose policy, after the organisation of the Armenian legions, had displeased the Moslem population.

Two months after the Marash affair on February 10 the tribes in the neighbourhood of Urfa, which the French, according to the Anglo-French agreement of 1916, had occupied at the end of 1919 after about a year of British occupation, attacked the stations of the Baghdad Railway lying to the south, and cut off the town from the neighbouring posts. The French detachment was first blocked up in the Armenian quarter, was then attacked, and after two months' fighting, being on the verge of starvation, had to enter into a parley with the Turkish authorities and evacuate the town on April 10. But while the French column retreated southwards, it was assailed by forces far superior in number, and had to surrender; some men were slaughtered, others marched back to Urfa or reached the French posts lying farther south of Arab Punar or Tel-Abiad.

On April 1—that is to say, nearly at the same time—the Turks attacked the American mission at Aintab. French troops were sent to their help as soon as the American consul-general at Beyrut asked for help. They arrived on April 17, and, after resisting for eighteen days, the few members of the American mission were able to withdraw to Aleppo, where they met with American refugees from Urfa, with the French column sent to relieve them.

In a speech made in the Ottoman Chamber of Deputies about the validation of the mandate of the members for Adana, Mersina, and other districts of Asia Minor, Reouf Bey, a deputy and former Minister of Marine, maintained that the occupation of Cilicia had not been allowed in the armistice, and so the occupation of this province by the French was a violation of the treaty.

In the middle of February the Grand Vizier and the Minister of Foreign Affairs handed the Allied representatives a memorandum drawn up by the Government to expound the situation brought about by the postponement of the conclusion of the Peace Treaty, and chiefly requested:

(1) That the Turkish inhabitants, in the districts where they were in a majority, should be left under Turkish sovereignty, and that their rights should be guaranteed.

(2) That the position of the regions occupied by the Allies should be altered.

(3) That the Turkish delegation should be heard before irrevocable decisions were taken.

The Allies, too, felt it was necessary to come to a settlement; and as they had waited too long since they had dismissed the Turkish delegation in July of the previous year, the situation was getting critical now. As the United States, which took less and less interest in European affairs, did not seem anxious to intervene in the solution of the Eastern problem, Mr. Lloyd George, on Thursday, December 18, 1919, in an important speech in which he gave some information about the diplomatic conversations that were taking place in

London, came to the Turkish question and stated that the terms of the treaty would soon be submitted to Turkey.

"My noble friend said: Why could you not make peace with Turkey, cutting out all the non-Turkish territories, and then leaving Constantinople and Anatolia to be dealt with?' I think on consideration he will see that is not possible. What is to be done with Constantinople? What is to be done with the Straits?... If those doors had been open, and if our fleet and our merchant ships had been free to go through ... the war would have been shortened by two or three years. They were shut treacherously in our faces. We cannot trust the same porter. As to what will remain much depended on whether America came in.... Would America take a share, and, if so, what share? France has great burdens, Britain has great burdens, Italy has great burdens. Much depended on whether America, which has no great extraneous burdens, and which has gigantic resources, was prepared to take her share.... But until America declared what she would do, any attempt to precipitate the position might have led to misunderstandings with America and would have caused a good deal of suspicion, and we regard a good understanding with America as something vital. That is the reason why we could not make peace with Turkey....

"We are entitled to say now: 'We have waited up to the very limits we promised, and we have waited beyond that.' The decision of America does not look promising.... Therefore we consider now, without any disrespect to our colleagues at the Peace Conference, and without in the least wishing to deprive the United States of America of sharing the honour of guardianship over these Christian communities, that we are entitled to proceed to make peace with Turkey, and we propose to do so at the earliest possible moment. We have had some preliminary discussions on the subject. As far as they went they were very promising. They will be renewed, partly in this country, partly probably in France, in the course of the next few days, and I hope that it will be possible to submit to Turkey the terms of peace at an early date."

But as the Allies, instead of dictating terms of peace to Turkey at the end of 1918, had postponed the settlement of the Turkish question for fourteen months, as they had dismissed the Ottoman delegation after summoning it themselves, and as the question was now about to be resumed under widely different circumstances and in quite another frame of mind, the Paris Conference found itself in an awkward situation.

―――

About the end of the first half of February, 1920, the Peace Conference at last resumed the discussion of the Turkish question.

The task of working out a first draft of the treaty of peace with Turkey had been entrusted by the Supreme Council to three commissions. The first was to draw up a report on the frontiers of the new Republic of Armenia; the second was to hold an inquiry into the Ottoman debt and the financial situation of Turkey; and the third was to examine the claims of Greece to Smyrna.

It had been definitely settled that the Dardanelles should be placed under international control, and the Conference was to decide what kind of control it would be, what forces would be necessary to enforce it, and what nationalities would provide these forces. There remained for settlement what the boundaries of the Constantinople area would be, and what rights the Turks would have over Adrianople.

The discussion of the Turkish question was resumed in an untoward way, which at first brought about a misunderstanding. The English wanted the debate to be held in London, and the French insisted upon Paris. Finally it was decided that the principles should be discussed in London, and the treaty itself should be drawn up in Paris.

At the first meetings of the Allies concerning Constantinople, the English strongly urged that the Turks should be turned out of Europe, and the French held the contrary opinion. Later on a change seems to have taken place in the respective opinions of the two Allies. The English, who were far from being unanimous in demanding the eviction of the Turks, gradually drew nearer to the opinion of the French, who now, however, did not plead for the Turks quite so earnestly as before.

This change in the English point of view requires an explanation.

The English, who are prone to believe only what affects them, did not seem to dread the Bolshevist peril for Europe, perhaps because they fancied England was quite secure from it; on the contrary, they thought this peril was more to be dreaded for the populations of Asia, no doubt because it could have an easier access to the English possessions. The success of Bolshevism with the Emir of Bokhara, close to the frontiers of India, seemed to justify their fears. Bolshevism, however, is something quite special to the Russian mind; other nations may be led astray or perverted by it for a time, but on the whole they cannot fully adhere to it permanently. Besides, it appears that Bolshevism has been wrongly looked upon as something Asiatic. Of course, it has been welcomed by the Slavs on the confines of Europe, and seems to agree with their mentality; but in fact it does not come from Asia, but from Europe. Lenin and Trotsky, who were sent by Germany from Berlin to St. Petersburg in a sealed railway-carriage and had lived before in Western Europe, imported no Asiatic ideas into Russia. They brought with them a mixture of Marxist socialism and Tolstoist catholicism, dressed up in Russian style to make it palatable to the moujik, and presented to the intellectual class, to flatter Slav conceit, as about to renovate the face of Europe.

The English did not realise that their own policy, as well as that of their Allies, had run counter to their own aims, that they had actually succeeded in strengthening the position of the Soviets, and that if they kept on encroaching upon the independence and territorial integrity of the heterogeneous Eastern populations of Russia and the peoples of Asia Minor, they would definitely bring them over to Bolshevism. Of course, these peoples were playing a dangerous game, and ran the risk of losing their liberty in another way, but they clung to any force that might uphold them. Mustafa Kemal was thus induced not to reject the offers the Moscow Government soon made him, but it did not seem likely he would be so foolish as to keep in the wake of the Soviets, for the latter are doomed to disappear sooner or later, unless they consent to evolution, supposing they have time to change. The Allies, on the other hand, especially the English, forgot that their policy risked giving Constantinople indirectly to Russia, where Tsarist imperialism had been replaced by Bolshevist imperialism, both of which are actuated by the same covetous spirit.

The fear of Bolshevism, however, had a fortunate consequence later on, as it brought about in 1920 a complete change in British ideas concerning Turkey and Constantinople. The London Cabinet realised that the Turks were the first nation that the Bolshevist propaganda could reach, and to which the Moscow Government could most easily and effectually give its support against British policy in Asia Minor, which would make the situation in the East still more complicated. So, in order not to drive the Ottoman Government into open resistance, England first showed an inclination to share the view, held by France from the outset, that the Turks should be allowed to remain in Constantinople.

So the British Government instructed Admiral de Robeck, British High Commissioner in Constantinople, to bring to the knowledge of the Turks that the Allies had decided not to take Constantinople from them, but also warn them that, should the Armenian persecutions continue, the treaty of peace with Turkey might be remodelled.

The Turkish Press did not conceal its satisfaction at seeing that Constantinople was likely to remain the capital of the Empire, and was thankful to France for proposing and supporting this solution. Meanwhile a new party, "the Party of Defence and Deliverance of the Country," to which a certain number of deputies adhered, and which was supposed to be accepted and supported by the whole nation, had solemnly declared that no sacrifice could be made concerning the independence of the Ottoman Empire, and the integrity of Constantinople and the coast of the Marmora, merely recognising the freedom of passage of the Straits for all nations. This party now held great demonstrations.

At the end of February the Minister of the Interior at Constantinople addressed to all the public authorities in the provinces the following circular:

"I have great pleasure in informing you that Constantinople, the capital of the Khilafat and Sultanate, will remain ours, by decision of the Peace Conference.

"God be praised for this! This decision implies that, as we earnestly hope, our rights will be safeguarded and maintained.

"You should do the utmost in your power and take all proper measures to prevent at all times and especially at the present delicate juncture untoward incidents against the non-Moslem population. Such incidents might lead to complaints, and affect the good dispositions of the Allies towards us."

In the comments of the Ottoman Press on the deliberations of the Peace Conference regarding the peace with Turkey, the more moderate newspapers held the Nationalists responsible for the stern decisions contemplated by the Powers, and asked the Government to resist them earnestly.

Great was the surprise, therefore, and deep the emotion among the Turks, when, after the aforesaid declarations, on February 29, the English fleet arrived and a large number of sailors and soldiers marched along the main streets of Pera, with fixed bayonets, bands playing, and colours flying.

A similar demonstration took place at Stambul on the same day, and another on the following Wednesday at Skutari.

A sudden wave of discussion spread over Great Britain at the news that the Turks were going to keep Constantinople, and made an impression on the Conference, in which there were still some advocates of the eviction of the Turks.

A memorandum signed by Lord Robert Cecil and Mr. J. H. Thomas, requiring that the Turks should be driven out of Europe, raised some discussion in the House of Commons. In answer to this memorandum some members sent a circular to their colleagues, to ask them to avoid, during the sittings of the Peace Conference, all manifestations that might influence its decisions concerning foreign affairs. Another group, in an appeal to Mr. Lloyd George, reminded him that in his declaration of January 5, 1918, he had stated that the English did not fight to wrest her capital from Turkey, and that any departure from this policy would be deeply resented in India.

Lord Robert Cecil and Lord Bryce proved the most determined adversaries of the retention of the Turks in Europe.

According to the *Daily Mail*, even within the British Cabinet widely different views were held about Constantinople. One section of the Cabinet, led by Lord Curzon, asked that the Turks should be evicted from Europe; and another, led by Mr. Montagu, Indian Secretary, favoured the retention of the Turks in Constantinople, provided they should give up their internal struggles and submit to the decisions of the Allies.

The Times severely blamed the Government for leaving the Turks in Constantinople; it maintained it was not too late to reconsider their decision; and it asked that Constantinople should in some way be placed under international control.

The *Daily Chronicle* also stated that it would have been better if the Turks had been evicted from Constantinople, and expressed the hope that at any rate public opinion would not forget the Armenian question. At the same time—*i.e.*, at the end of February, 1920—American leaders also asked that the Turks should be compelled to leave Constantinople, and a strong Protestant campaign started a powerful current of opinion.

On Sunday evening, February 29, a meeting of so-called "non-sectarians" was held in New York, with the support of the dignitaries of St. John's Cathedral.

The Bishop of Western Pennsylvania, after holding France responsible for the present situation because it owned millions of dollars of Turkish securities, declared: "Though I love England and France, we must let these two countries know that we will not shake hands with them so long as they hold out their hands to the sanguinary Turk."

Messages from Senator Lodge, the presidents of Harvard and Princeton Universities, M. Myron, T. Herrick, and other Americans of mark were read; asking President Wilson and the Supreme Council that the Ottoman rule in Constantinople should come to an end. Motions were also carried requesting that the Turks should be expelled from Europe, that the Christians should no longer be kept under Moslem sway, and that the Allies should carry out their engagements with regard to Armenia.

Another movement, similar in character to the American one, was started in England at the same time.

The Archbishop of Canterbury, with the other Anglican bishops and some influential men, addressed a similar appeal to the British Government.

Twelve bishops belonging to the Holy Synod of Constantinople sent a telegram to the Archbishop of Canterbury, entreating his support that no Turk might be left in Constantinople. In his answer, the Archbishop assured the Holy Synod that the Anglican Church would continue to do everything conducive to that end.

The Bishop of New York also telegraphed to the Archbishop of Canterbury on behalf of about a hundred American bishops, to thank him for taking the lead in the crusade against the retention of the Turks in Constantinople. The Archbishop replied that he hoped America would assume a share in the protection of the oppressed nationalities in the East.

The personality of the promoters plainly showed that religious interests were the leading factors in this opposition, and played a paramount part in it, for the instigators of the movement availed themselves of the wrongs Turkey had committed in order to fight against Islam and further their own interests under pretence of upholding the cause of Christendom.

So, in February, after the formidable campaign started in Great Britain and the United States, at the very time when the treaty of peace with Turkey was going to be discussed again, and definitely settled, the retention of the Turkish Government in Constantinople was still an open question.

On February 12 the Anglo-Ottoman Society addressed to Mr. Lloyd George an appeal signed by Lord Mowbray, Lord Lamington, General Sir Bryan Mahon, Professor Browne, Mr. Marmaduke Pickthall, and several other well-known men, referring to the pledge he had made on January 5, 1918, to leave Constantinople to the Turks. The appeal ran as follows:

"We, the undersigned, being in touch with Oriental opinion, view with shame the occupation of the vilayet of Aidin, a province 'of which the population is predominantly Turkish,' by Hellenic troops; and have noticed with alarm the further rumours in the Press to the effect that part of Thrace—and even Constantinople itself—may be severed from the Turkish Empire at the peace settlement, in spite of the solemn pledge or declaration aforesaid, on the one hand, and, on the other, the undeniable growth of anti-British feeling throughout the length and breadth of Asia, and in Egypt, owing to such facts and rumours.

"We beg you, in the interests not only of England or of India but of the peace of the world, to make good that solemn declaration not to deprive Turkey of Thrace and Asia Minor, with Constantinople as her capital."

The next week a memorandum was handed to Mr. Lloyd George and printed in the issue of *The Times* of February 23. It was signed by, among others, the Archbishops of Canterbury and York, the Bishop of London, Lord Robert

Cecil, Mr. A. G. Gardiner (late editor of the *Daily News*), the socialist leader Hyndman, Lord Bryce (formerly ambassador to the United States), the well-known writer Seton-Watson, Dr. Burrows, Principal of King's College, Professor Oman, and many professors of universities. In it the same desires lurked behind the same religious arguments, under cover of the same social and humanitarian considerations—viz., that the Turks should no longer be allowed to slaughter the Armenians, and that they should be expelled from Constantinople.

"As to Constantinople itself, it will be a misfortune and indeed a scandal if this city is left in Turkish hands. It has been for centuries a focus of intrigue and corruption; and it will so continue as long as the Turkish Government has power there. If Constantinople were transferred to the control of the League of Nations, there would be no offence to genuine Moslem sentiment. For the Khilafat is not, and never has been, attached to Constantinople. The Sultan, if he retains the Khilafat, will be just as much a Khalifa, in the eyes of Moslems all over the world, at Brusa or Konia, as at Stambul."

Now the absurdity of such arguments is patent to all those who know that "the focus of intrigue and corruption" denounced in this document is the outcome of the political intrigues carried on by foreigners in Constantinople, and kept up by international rivalries. As to the exile of the Sultan to Brusa or Konia, it could only have raised a feeling of discontent and resentment among Moslems and roused their religious zeal.

Such a movement was resented by the Turks all the more deeply as, it must be remembered, they have great reverence for any religious feeling. For instance, they still look upon the Crusades with respect, because they had a noble aim, a legitimate one for Catholics—viz., the conquest of the Holy Places; though later on behind the Crusaders, as behind all armies, there came all sorts of people eager to derive personal profit from those migrations of men. But they cannot entertain the least consideration or regard for a spurious religious movement, essentially Protestant, behind which Anglo-Saxon covetousness is lurking, and the real aim of which is to start huge commercial undertakings.

Moreover, the Greek claims which asserted themselves during the settlement of the Turkish question partly originated in the connection between the Orthodox Church, not with Hellenism in the old and classical sense of the word, as has been wrongly asserted, but with Greek aspirations. For the Œcumenical Patriarch, whose see is Constantinople, is the head of the Eastern Church, and he still enjoys temporal privileges owing to which he is, in the Sultan's territory, the real leader of the Greek subjects of the Sultan. Though the countries of Orthodox faith in Turkey have long enjoyed religious autonomy, their leaders keep their eyes bent on Constantinople, for in their mind the religious cause is linked with that of the Empire, and the eventual restoration of the Greek Empire in Constantinople would both consolidate their religious faith and sanction their claims.

In spite of what has often been said, it seems that the Christian Church did not so much protect Hellenism against the Turks as the Orthodox Church enhanced the prosperity of the Greeks within the Turkish Empire. The Greek Church, thanks to the independence it enjoyed in the Ottoman Empire, was a sort of State within the State, and had a right to open and maintain schools which kept up moral unity among the Greek elements. So it paved the way to the revolutionary movement of 1821, which was to bring about the restoration of the Greek kingdom with Athens as its capital; and now it serves the plans of the advocates of Greater Greece. Let us add that nowadays the Greek Church, like the Churches of all the States that have arisen on the ruins of Turkey, has its own head, and has freed itself from the tutelage of the Patriarch for the administration of its property.

Lord Robert Cecil, who had taken the lead in that politico-religious movement, wrote on February 23 in the *Evening Standard* a strong article in which he said something to this purpose: "Constantinople is a trophy of victories, not the capital of a nation. From Constantinople the Turks issue cruel orders against the Christian population. From the point of view both of morality and of prudence, the Stambul Government must not be strengthened by such an exorbitant concession on the part of the Allies."

In the debate which took place on Wednesday, February 25, 1920, in the House of Commons regarding the retention of the Turks in Constantinople, after a question of Lord Edmund Talbot, Sir Donald Maclean, who spoke first, urged that if the Turks were not expelled from Constantinople all the worst difficulties of the past would occur again, and would endanger the peace of the world.

"The decision of the Peace Conference was a great surprise to most people. We owed nothing to the Turks. They came into the war gladly and without any provocation on our part. They became the willing and most useful ally of Germany. If the Turks were left in the gateway of the world, they would be at their old game again."[16]

Sir Edward Carson said just the reverse:

"It was suggested that we should drive the Turks out of Constantinople.... If the Allies wanted to drive the Turks out of Constantinople, ... they would have to commence another war, and it would not be a small war. You must not talk of cutting down the Army and the Navy, and at the same moment censure the Government because they had not settled the question of driving the Turks out."[17]

Mr. Lloyd George, speaking after them both, began thus:

"This is not a decision, whichever way you go, which is free from difficulty and objection. I do not know whether my right hon. friend is under the impression that if we decided to expel the Turk from Constantinople the course would be absolutely clear. As a matter of fact, it is a balancing of the advantages and the disadvantages, and it is upon that balance and after weighing very carefully and for some time all the arguments in favour and all the arguments against, all the difficulties along the one path and all the difficulties you may encounter on the other, and all the obstacles and all the perils on both sides, that the Allied Conference came to the conclusion that on the whole the better course was to retain the Turk in Constantinople for achieving a common end."

Then he explained that the agreement concerning the substitution of the Russians for the Turks in Constantinople had become null and void after the Russian revolution and the Brest-Litovsk peace, and that at the present date the Bolshevists were not ready to assume such a responsibility, should it be offered to them.

"I will deal with two other pledges which are important. My right hon. friend referred to a pledge I gave to the House in December last, that there would not be the same gate-keeper, but there would be a different porter at the gates.... It would have been the height of folly to trust the guardianship of these gates to the people who betrayed their trust. That will never be done. They will never be closed by the Turk in the face of a British ship again....

"The second pledge, given in January, 1918, was given after full consultation with all parties, and the right hon. member for Paisley and Lord Grey acquiesced. There was a real desire to make a national statement of war aims, a statement that would carry all parties along with it, and they all agreed. It was a carefully prepared declaration, which I read out, as follows: 'Nor are we fighting to destroy Austria-Hungary, or to deprive Turkey of its capital, or of the rich and renowned lands of Asia Minor and Thrace, which are predominantly Turkish in race. Outside Europe we believe that the same principle should be applied.... While we do not challenge the maintenance of the Turkish Empire in the homeland of the Turkish race, with its capital in Constantinople, the passage between the Mediterranean and the Black Sea being internationalised and neutralised' (as they will be), 'Arabia, Armenia, Mesopotamia, Syria, and Palestine are in our judgment entitled to recognition of their separate national conditions.' That declaration was specific, unqualified, and deliberate. It was made with the consent of all parties in the community....

"The effect of the statement in India was that recruiting went up appreciably from that very moment....

"Now we are told: 'That was an offer you made to Turkey, and they rejected it, and therefore you were absolutely free.' It was more than that. It was a statement of our war aims for the workers of this country, a statement of our war aims for India. It is too often forgotten that we are the greatest Mohammedan Power in the world. One-fourth of the population of the British Empire is Mohammedan.... We gave a solemn pledge and they accepted it, and they are disturbed at the prospect of our not abiding by it.... There is nothing which would damage British power in Asia more than the feeling that you could not trust the British word. That is the danger. Of course it would be a fatal reputation for us....

"When the peace terms are published there is no friend of the Turk, should there be any left, who will not realise that he has been terribly punished for his follies, his blunders, his crimes, and his iniquities. Stripped of more than half his Empire, his country under the Allied guns, deprived of his army, his navy, his prestige—the punishment will be terrible enough to satisfy the bitterest foe of the Turkish Empire, drastic enough for the sternest judge. My right hon. friend suggested that there was a religious issue involved. That would be the most dangerous of all, and the most fatal. I am afraid that underneath the agitation there is not only the movement for the expulsion of the Turk, but there is something of the old feeling of Christendom against the Crescent. If it is believed in the Mohammedan world that our terms are dictated by the purpose of lowering the flag of the Prophet before that of Christendom, it will be fatal to our government in India. It is an unworthy purpose to achieve by force. It is unworthy of Britain, and it is unworthy of our faith.

"Let us examine our legitimate peace aims in Turkey. The first is the freedom of the Straits. I put that first for two reasons, which I shall refer to later on. It was put first by my right hon. friend, and I accept it. The second is the freeing of the non-Turkish communities from the Ottoman sway; the preservation for the Turk of self-government in communities which are mainly Turkish, subject to two most important reservations. The first is that there must be adequate safeguards within our power for protecting the minorities that have been oppressed by the Turk in the past. The second is that the Turk must be deprived of his power of vetoing the development of the rich lands under his rule which were once the granary of the Mediterranean....

"You can get the great power of Constantinople from its geographical situation. That is the main point. It is the main point for two reasons. The first is, when you consider the future possibilities of the Black Sea. You have there six or seven independent communities or nations to whom we want access. It is essential that we should have a free road, a right-of-way to these countries, whatever the opinion of the Turk may be. His keeping of the gates prolonged the war, and we cannot have that again. Therefore, for that reason, it is coming to an end. The second reason why the guardianship of the gates is important is because of its effect upon the protection of minorities. How do we propose that that should be achieved? Turkey is to be deprived entirely of the guardianship of the gates. Her forts are to be dismantled. She is to have no troops anywhere within reach of these waters. More than that, the Allies mean to garrison those gates themselves.... I was going to say that we have been advised that, with the assistance of the Navy, we shall be able to garrison the Dardanelles and, if necessary, the Bosphorus, with a much smaller force because of the assistance to be given by the Navy for that purpose. Turkey will not be allowed a navy. What does she want with a navy? It was never of the slightest use to her when she had it. She never could handle it. That is the position in regard to the Straits.

"What is the alternative to that proposal? The alternative to that proposal is international government of Constantinople and the whole of the lands surrounding the Straits. It would mean a population of 1,500,000 governed by the Allies—a committee representing France, Italy, Great Britain, and, I suppose, some day Russia might come in, and, it might be, other countries. America, if she cared to come in. Can anyone imagine anything more calculated to lead to that kind of mischievous intriguing, rivalry, and trouble in Constantinople that my right hon. friend deprecated and, rightly, feared? How would you govern it? Self-government could not be conferred under those conditions. It would have to be a military government.... It would require, according to every advice we have had, a very considerable force, and it would add very considerably to the burdensome expenditure of these countries, and it would be the most unsatisfactory government that anyone could possibly imagine.

"We had hoped that two of the great countries of the world would have been able to help us in sharing the responsibility for the government of this troubled country; but for one reason or another they have fallen out. There was first of all Russia. She is out of the competition for a very unpleasant task. Then there was America. We had hopes, and we had good reason for hoping, that America would have shared these responsibilities. She might probably have taken the guardianship of the Armenians, or she might have taken the guardianship of Constantinople. But America is no claimant now, and I am not going to express an opinion as to whether she ever will be, because it would be dangerous to do so; but for the moment we must reckon America as being entirely out of any arrangement which we contemplate for the government of Turkey and for the protection of the Christian minorities in that land.... I ask my noble friend, if he were an Armenian would he feel more secure if he knew that the Sultan and his Ministers were overlooked by a British garrison on the Bosphorus, and that British ships were there within reach, than if the Sultan were at Konia, with hundreds of miles across the Taurus Mountains to the nearest Allied garrison, and the sea with its great British ships and their guns out of sight and out of mind? I know which I would prefer if I were an Armenian with a home to protect."[18]

The Prime Minister concluded his speech by saying that the Allies chiefly desired to take from the Turks the government of communities of alien race and religion, which would feel adequately protected when they knew that their former persecutors must sign the decree for their liberation under the threat of English, French, and Italian guns. Yet he could not dissemble his own misgivings.

In the discussion that followed Lord Robert Cecil said that, in any settlement with regard to Armenia, he trusted there would not only be a considerable increase in the present area of the Armenian Republic, but that Armenia would be given some access to the Black Sea in the north. Without that he was satisfied that the Armenian Republic would have the greatest difficulty in living. He earnestly hoped that every influence of the British Government would be used to secure that Cilicia should be definitely removed from Turkish sovereignty. He repeated once more that he was sorry the Turks were going to be retained in Constantinople, but that—

"No one wished to turn the Sultan out; the central thing was to get rid of the Sublime Porte as the governor of Constantinople. That did not mean turning anybody out; it merely meant that we were not to hand back Constantinople to the Turkish Government."

He had the greatest regard for the feelings of the Indians in that matter, but was surprised they insisted upon the retention of the Sultan in Constantinople. He thought that there was not the slightest ground for maintaining the Sultan as Caliph of Mohammedanism, and, even if there were, there was nothing at all vital about his remaining in Constantinople. So far as the Turks were concerned, what was Constantinople? It was not a national capital; it had been occupied by the Turks as their great trophy of victory. He entirely approved of the statement of 1918, and, in the same circumstances, he would make it again. It seemed to him perfectly fantastic to say that ever since 1918 we had held out to our Indian fellow-subjects an absolute undertaking that Constantinople should remain in the hands of the Turks.

Then Mr. Bonar Law rose, and declared that it would be easier to have control over the Turkish Government if it was left in Constantinople, instead of transferring it to Konia,

"Our fleet at Constantinople would be a visible emblem of power. The Allies believed that the pressure they would be able to exercise would have an effect throughout the Turkish Empire, but it would not be so if we sent the Turks to Konia. An hon. member had said that some Armenians had told him that they desired the Turks to be sent out of Constantinople. Let the Armenians consider the facts as they now were.

"If there was one thing which more than another was likely to make the League of Nations a failure it was to hand over this question to them. In 1917 it was arranged that if we were victorious in the war, Russia would become the possessor of Constantinople. But all that fell to the ground, and in 1918 a new situation arose, and a solemn document was put before the British people in which it was stated that one of our war aims was not to turn the Turks out of Constantinople. Overwhelming reasons were required to justify departure from that declaration, and those overwhelming reasons had not been forthcoming. When it was hoped and expected that America would accept a mandate in regard to Turkey there was no question of turning the Turks out of Constantinople."[19]

The debate, which came to an end after this statement by Mr. Bonar Law, was not followed by a vote.

Mr. Montagu, Secretary for India, stated in an interview printed in the *Evening Standard*, February 25:

"If one of the results of the war must needs be to take away Constantinople from the Turks, I should take the liberty of respectfully telling Lord Robert Cecil, as president, of the Indian delegation in the Peace Conference, that we ought not to have asked Indians to take part in the war against Turkey. Throughout India, all those who had to express their opinion on this subject, whatever race or religion they may belong to, are of opinion that Constantinople must remain the seat of the Khilafat if the internal and external peace of India is to be preserved.

"The Turks, who are the chief part of the population in Constantinople, have certainly as much right as any other community to the possession of that city. So we have to choose between the Turks and an international régime. Now in the history of Constantinople examples have occurred of the latter régime, and the results were not so good that it cannot be said a Turkish government would not have done better."

This opinion was upheld by a good many British newspapers, notwithstanding Lord Robert Cecil's campaign.

Yet under the pressure of a section of public opinion and the agitation let loose against Turkey, England seemed more and more resolved to occupy Constantinople, and *The Times*, though it had never been averse to the eviction of the Turks from Constantinople, now showed some anxiety:

"We cannot imagine how the greatest lovers of political difficulties in Europe should have ever dreamt that Constantinople should be occupied exclusively by British troops, or that such a decision may have been taken without previously taking the Allies' advice.

"As things now stand, we are not at all surprised that such stories may have given birth to a feeling of distrust towards us. These are the fruits of a policy tainted with contradiction and weakness. The Allied countries refuse to sacrifice any more gold or human lives, unless their honour is concerned. They will not consent to go to war in order to safeguard the interests of a few international financiers, who want to dismember Turkey-in-Asia."

This movement was brought about by the explosion of very old feelings which had been smouldering for nearly forty years, had been kept alive by the Balkan war, and had been roused by the last conflict. Even at the time of Catherine II the merchants of the City of London merely looked upon Russia as a first-rate customer to whom they sold European and Indian goods, and of whom in return they bought raw materials which their ships brought to England. So they felt inclined to support the policy of Russia, and, to quote the words of a French writer in the eighteenth century, the English ambassador at Constantinople was "le chargé d'affaires de la Russie." So a party which took into account only the material advantages to be drawn from a closer commercial connection with Russia arose and soon became influential. William Pitt inveighed against this party when, in one of his speeches, he refused to argue with those who wanted to put an end to the Ottoman Empire. But the opinion that England can only derive economic advantages from the dismemberment of Turkey in favour of Russia soon found a new advocate in Richard Cobden, the leader of the Manchester school, who expounded it in a little book, *Russia, by a Manchester Manufacturer*, printed at Edinburgh in 1835. This dangerous policy was maintained, in spite of David Urquhart's campaign against the Tsarist policy in the East in a periodical, *The Portfolio*, which he had founded in 1833, and, notwithstanding the strenuous efforts made by Blacque, a Frenchman, editor of *The Ottoman Monitor*, to show that Europe was being cheated by Russia, and was going the wrong way in her attitude towards Turkey. And the same foolish policy consistently pursued by Fox, Gladstone, and Grey towards Tsardom is still carried on by Britain towards Bolshevism. The same narrowly utilitarian views, the typical economic principles of the Manchester School, linked with Protestant ideas, and thus strengthened and aggravated by religious feeling, seem still to inspire the Russian policy of Britain as they once inspired the old "bag and baggage" policy of Mr. Gladstone, the "Grand Old Man," that the Turks should be expelled from Constantinople with bag and baggage. Indeed, this policy may be looked upon as an article of faith of the English Liberal party. Mr. Gladstone's religious mind, which was alien to the Islamic spirit, together with the endeavours of the economists who wanted to monopolise the Russian market, brought about an alliance with Holy Orthodox Russia, and within the Anglican Church a movement for union with the Holy Synod had even been started.

That campaign was all the more out of place as the Turks have repeatedly proclaimed their sympathy for England and turned towards her. Just as after the first Balkan war the Kiamil Cabinet had made overtures to Sir Edward Grey, after the armistice of November 11 Tewfik Pasha, now Grand Vizier, had also made open proposals. England had already laid hands on Arabia and Mesopotamia, but could not openly lay claim to Constantinople without upsetting some nations with whom she meant to keep on good terms, though some of her agents and part of public opinion worked to that end. Generally she showed more diplomacy in conforming her conduct with her interests, which she did not defend so harshly and openly.

But religious antagonism and religious intolerance were at the bottom of that policy, and had always instigated and supported it. The Anglicans, and more markedly the Nonconformists, had taken up the cry, "The Turk out of Europe," and it seems certain that the religious influence was paramount and brought on the political action. Mr. Lloyd George, who is a strong and earnest Nonconformist, must have felt it slightly awkward to find himself in direct opposition to his co-religionists on political grounds. Besides, the British Government, which in varied circumstances had supported contradictory policies, was in a difficult situation when brought face to face with such contradictions.

It also seems strange at first that the majority of American public opinion should have suffered itself to be led by the campaign of Protestant propaganda, however important the religious question may be in the United States. Though since 1831 American Protestant missionaries have defrayed the expenses of several centres of propaganda among the Nestorians (who have preserved the Nazarene creed), paid the native priests and supported the schools, America has no interests in those countries, unless she thus means to support her Russian policy. But her economic imperialism, which also aims at a spiritual preponderance, would easily go hand in hand with a cold religious imperialism which would spread its utilitarian formalism over the life and manners of all nations.

At any rate, the plain result of the two countries' policy was necessarily to reinforce the Pan-Turkish and Pan-Arabian movements.

Of course, Mr. Wilson's puritanism and his ignorance of the complex elements and real conditions of European civilisation could not but favour such a movement, and on March 5 the *New York World*, a semi-official organ, plainly said that Mr. Wilson would threaten again, as he had already done about Italy, to withdraw from European affairs, if the treaty of peace with Turkey left Constantinople to the Turks, and gave up all protection of the Christian populations in Turkey.

The traditional hostility of America towards Turkey—one of the essential reasons of which has just been given—demanded that Turkey should be expelled from Europe, and the Empire should be dismembered. President Wilson, in Article 12 of his programme, had mentioned the recognition of the sovereignty of the Ottoman Empire; yet the American leaders, though they pointed out that a state of war had never existed between the United States and Turkey, were the first to demand the eviction of the Turks; and the *Chicago Tribune* of March 8 hinted that an American cruiser might be sent to the Bosphorus. On March 6 Senator Kling criticised in the Senate the Allies' proposals aiming at tolerating Turkish sway in Asia Minor. The United States even backed the Greek claims, and on the same day Mr. Lodge moved that the Peace Conference should give to Greece Northern Epirus, the Dodecanese, and the western coast of Asia Minor.

Mr. Morgenthau, too, criticised the terms of the settlement which allowed Constantinople to remain a Turkish city; he maintained that such a solution could only be another inducement for America to keep away from European affairs, and declared that Europe would fail to do her duty if she did not punish Turkey. Yet at the same time America, and shortly after England, were endeavouring to mitigate the responsibility of Germany, objecting, not to her punishment, which had never been demanded by France, but to the complete execution of the most legitimate measures of reparation, and made concessions on all points that did not affect their own interests. In fact, they merely wanted to resume business with Germany at any cost and as soon as possible.

English newspapers printed an appeal to French and British public opinion drawn up by some eminent American citizens, asking for the eviction of the Turks from Constantinople and the autonomy of Armenia.

The British Press, however, remarked that it was not sufficient to express wishes, and it would have been better if the Americans had assumed a share of responsibility in the reorganisation of Asia Minor.

Now, why did a section of British and American public opinion want to punish Turkey, whereas it refused to support the French and Belgian claims to reparation? In order to form an impartial judgment on Turkey, one should look for the motives and weigh the reasons that induced her to take part in the war, and then ascertain why some members of her political parties most preposterously stood by the side of Germany. If the latter pursued such a policy, perhaps it was because Germany, who aimed at extending her influence over the whole of Eastern Asia, displayed more ability and skill than the Allies did in Turkey, and because the policy of the Powers and their attitude towards the Christians raised much enmity against them.

On such a delicate point, one cannot do better than quote the words of Suleyman Nazif Bey in a lecture delivered in honour of Pierre Loti at the University of Stambul on January 23, 1920:

"When we linked our fate with that of Germany and Austria, the Kaiser's army had already lost the first battle of the Marne. It is under such untoward and dangerous circumstances that we joined the fray. No judicious motive can be brought forward to excuse and absolve the few men who drove us lightheartedly into the conflagration of the world war.

"If Kaiser Wilhelm found it possible to fool some men among us, and if these men were able to draw the nation behind them, the reason is to be found in the events of the time and in the teachings of history. Russia, who, for the last two and a half centuries has not given us a moment of respite, did not enter into the world war in order to take Alsace-Lorraine from Prussia and give it back to France. The Muscovites thought the time had come at last to carry out the dream that had perpetually haunted the Tsars ever since Peter the Great—that is to say, the conquest of Anatolia and the Straits.

"It is not to Europe but to our own country that we must be held responsible for having entered into the war so foolishly, and still more for having conducted it so badly, with so much ignorance and deceit. The Ottoman nation alone has a right to call us to account—the Great Powers had paid us so little regard, nay, they had brought on us such calamities, that the shrewd Kaiser finally managed to stir up our discontent and make us lay aside all discretion and thoughtfulness by rousing the ancient legitimate hatred of the Turks.

"Read the book that the former Bulgarian Premier, Guéchoff, wrote just after the Balkan war. You will see in it that the Tsar Nicholas compelled, as it were by force, the Serbs and Bulgars, who had been enemies for centuries, to conclude an alliance in order to evict us from Europe. Of course, Montenegro followed suit. France approved, then even urged them to do so; and then one of the leading figures of the times intervened to make Greece join that coalition intended to drive the Turks out of Europe. The rest is but too well known. The Bulgarian statesman who owns all this is noted for his hatred of Turkey.

"Let us not forget this: so long as our victory was considered as possible, the Powers declared that the principle of the *status quo ante bellum* should be religiously observed. As soon as we suffered a defeat, a Power declared this principle no longer held good; it was the ally of the nation that has been our enemy for two and a half centuries, and yet it was also most adverse to the crafty policy that meant to cheat us....

"Every time Europe has conferred some benefit upon us we have been thankful for it. I know the history of my country full well; in her annals, many mistakes and evil doings have occurred, but not one line relates one act of ingratitude. After allowing the Moslems of Smyrna to be slaughtered by Hellenic soldiers and after having hushed up this crime, Europe now wants—so it seems at least—to drive us out of Constantinople and transfer the Moslem Khilafat to an Anatolian town, as if it were a common parcel, or shelve it inside the palace of Top-Kapu (the old Seraglio) like the antique curios of the Museum. When the Turks shall have been expelled from Constantinople, the country will be so convulsed that the whole world will be shaken. Let nobody entertain any doubt about this: if we go out of Constantinople a general conflagration will break out, that will last for years or centuries, nobody knows, and will set on fire the whole of the globe.

"At the time when Sultan Mohammed entered the town of Constantinople, which had been praised and promised by Mohammed to his people, the Moslem Empire of Andalusia was falling to decay—that is to say, in the south-east of Europe a Moslem State arose on the ruins of a Christian State, while in the south-west of Europe a Christian State was putting an end to the life of a Moslem State. The victor of Constantinople granted the Christian population he found there larger religious privileges than those granted to it by the Greek Empire. The ulcer of Phanar is still the outcome of Sultan Mohammed's generosity. What did Spain do when she suppressed the Moslem State in the south-west of Europe? She expelled the other religions, burning in ovens or sending to the stake the Moslems and even the Jews who refused to embrace Christianity. I mention this historical fact here, not to criticise or blame the Spaniards, but to give an instance of the way in which the Spaniards availed themselves of the conqueror's right Heaven had awarded them. And I contrast the Christians' cruelty with the Turks' gentleness and magnanimity when they entered Constantinople!"

To adopt the policy advocated by Anglo-American Protestants was tantamount to throwing Islam again towards Germany, who had already managed to derive profit from its defence. Yet Islamism has no natural propensity towards Germanism; on the contrary, Islam in the sixteenth century, at the time of its modern development, intervened in our culture as the vehicle of Eastern influences. That policy also hurt the religious feelings of the Mussulmans and roused their fanaticism not only in Turkey, but even in a country of highly developed intellectual life like Egypt, and in this respect it promoted the cause of the most spirited and most legitimate Nationalism.

Besides, in the note which the Ottoman Minister of Foreign Affairs handed in January, 1920, to the High Commissioners of the Allies, together with a scheme of judicial reforms, it was said notably:

"The Ottoman Government fully realises the cruel situation of Turkey after the war, but an unfortunate war cannot deprive a nation of her right to political existence, this right being based on the principles of justice and humanity confirmed by President Wilson's solemn declaration and recognised by all the belligerents as the basis of the peace of the world. It is in accordance with these principles that an armistice was concluded between the Allied Powers and Turkey. It ensues from this that the treaty to intervene shall restore order and peace to the East.

"Any solution infringing upon Ottoman unity, far from ensuring quietude and prosperity, would turn the East into a hotbed of endless perturbation. Therefore the only way to institute stability in the new state of things is to maintain Ottoman sovereignty.

"Let us add that, if the reforms Turkey tried to institute at various times were not attended with the results she expected, this is due to an unfavourable state of things both abroad and at home.

"Feeling it is absolutely necessary to put an end to an unbearable situation and wishing sincerely and eagerly to modernise its administration so as to open up an era of prosperity and progress in the East, the Sublime Porte has firmly resolved, in a broadminded spirit, to institute a new organisation, including reforms in the judicial system, the finance, and the police, and the protection of the minorities.

"As a token that these reforms will be fully and completely carried out, the Ottoman Government pledges itself to accept the co-operation of one of the Great Powers on condition its independence shall not be infringed upon and its national pride shall not be wounded."

As soon as it was known in what spirit the treaty of peace with Turkey was going to be discussed between the Powers, and what clauses were likely to be inserted in it, a clamour of protest arose throughout the Moslem world.

That treaty could not but affect the most important group of Mohammedans, the Indian group, which numbers over 70 million men and forms nearly one-fourth of the population of India. As soon as the conditions that were to be forced on Turkey were known in India, they roused deep resentment, which reached its climax after the Amritsar massacre. Some of the clauses which the Allies meant to insert in the treaty plainly ran counter to the principles of Mohammedanism; and as they hurt the religious feelings of the Moslems and disregarded the religious guarantees given to the Hindus and all the Moslem world by the present British Cabinet and its predecessors, they could not but bring on new conflicts in the future. Besides, the blunders of the last five years had united Hindus and Mohammedans in India, as they united Copts and Mohammedans in Egypt later on, and it was also feared that the Arabs, whose hopes had been frustrated, would side with the Turkish Nationalists.

At the end of 1918, Dr. Ansari, M.D., M.S., chairman of the Committee of the All-India Muslim League, in the course of the session held at Delhi at that time, set forth the Muslim grievances. But the address he read could not receive any publicity owing to the special repressive measures taken by the Government of India.

In September, 1919, a Congress of Mohammedans, who had come from all parts of India and thus represented Muslim opinion as a whole, was held at Lucknow, one of the chief Muslim centres. In November another congress for the defence of the Caliphate met at Delhi; it included some Hindu leaders, and thus assumed a national character. Next month a third congress, held at Amritsar, in the Punjab, was presided over by Shaukat Ali, founder and secretary of the Society of the Servants of the Ka'ba, who had been imprisoned like his brother Mohammed Ali and released three days before the congress; it was attended by over 20,000 Hindus and Mussulmans.

This meeting confirmed the resolution taken by the previous congress to send to Europe and America a delegation from India for the defence of the Caliphate. On January 19, 1920, a deputation of Indian Mussulmans waited upon the Viceroy of India at Delhi, to request that a delegation might repair to Europe and America, according to the decision of the congress, in order to expound before the allied and associated nations and their governments the Moslems' religious obligations and Muslim and Indian sentiment on the subject of the Caliphate and cognate questions, and to be their representatives at the Peace Conference.

The non-Mussulman Indians supported the claims which the 70 millions of Indian Mussulmans, their fellow-countrymen, considered as a religious obligation. In an address drawn up by the great Hindu leader, the Mahatma Gandhi, and handed on January 19, 1920, by the deputation of the General Congress of India for the Defence of the Caliphate to His Excellency Baron Chelmsford, Viceroy and Governor of India, in order to lay their aims before him, they declared they raised a formal protest lest the Caliphate should be deprived of the privilege of the custody and wardenship of the Holy Places, and lest a non-Muslim control, in any shape or form whatever, should be established over the Island of Arabia, whose boundaries, as defined by Muslim religious authorities, are: the Mediterranean Sea, the Red Sea, the Indian Ocean, the Persian Gulf, the Euphrates, and the Tigris, thus including Syria, Palestine, and Mesopotamia, beside the Peninsula of Arabia.

This General Congress of India, according to the manifesto it adopted during its sittings at Bombay on February 15, 16, and 17, 1920, gave to the delegation sent to Europe the following mandate, with respect to the Muslim claims regarding the Caliphate and the "Jazirat-ul-Arab":

"With respect to the Khilafat it is claimed that the Turkish Empire should be left as it was when the war broke out; however, though the alleged maladministration of Turks has not been proved, the non-Turkish nationalities might, if they wished, have within the Ottoman Empire all guarantees of autonomy compatible with the dignity of a sovereign State."

And the manifesto continued thus:

"The slightest reduction of the Muslim claims would not only hurt the deepest religions feelings of the Moslems, but would plainly violate the solemn declarations and pledges made or taken by responsible statesmen representing the Allied and Associated Powers at a time when they were most anxious to secure the support of the Moslem peoples and soldiers."

The anti-Turkish agitation which had been let loose at the end of December, 1919, and had reached its climax about March, 1920, had an immediate repercussion not only in India, where the Caliphate Conference, held at Calcutta, decided to begin a strike on March 19 and boycott British goods, if the agitation for the expulsion of the Turks from Constantinople did not come to an end in England.

At Tunis, on March 11, after a summons had been posted in one of the mosques calling upon the Muslim population to protest against the occupation of Constantinople, a demonstration took place before the Residency. M. Etienne Flandin received a delegation of native students asking him that France should oppose the measures England was about to take. The minister, after stating what reasons might justify the intervention, evaded the question that was put him by declaring that such measures were mere guarantees, and stated that even if France were to take a share in them, the Mussulmans should feel all the more certain that their religious creed would be respected.

The measures that were being contemplated could not but raise much anxiety and indignation among the Moslem populations and might have had disastrous consequences for France in Northern Africa. This was clearly pointed out by M. Bourgeois, President of the Committee of Foreign Affairs, in his report read to the Senate when the conditions of the peace that was going to be enforced on Turkey came under discussion.

"We cannot ignore the deep repercussions which the intended measures in regard to Turkey may have among the 25 million Moslems who live under our rule in Northern Africa. Their reverence and devotion have displayed themselves most strikingly in the course of the war. Nothing must be done to alter these feelings."

Indeed, as M. Mouktar-el-Farzuk wrote in an article entitled "France, Turkey, and Islam," printed in the *Ikdam*, a newspaper of Algiers, on May 7, 1920—

"If the French Moslems fought heroically for France and turned a deaf ear to the seditious proposals of Germany, they still preserve the deepest sympathy for Turkey, and they would be greatly distressed if the outcome of the victory in which they have had a share was the annihilation of the Ottoman Empire.

"That sympathy is generally looked upon in Europe as a manifestation of the so-called Moslem fanaticism or Pan-Islamism. Yet it is nothing of the kind. The so-called Moslem fanaticism is a mere legend whose insanity has been proved by history. Pan-Islamism, too, only exists in the mind of those who imagined its existence. The independent Moslem populations, such as the Persians and the Afghans, are most jealous of their independence, and do not think in the least of becoming the Sultan's subjects. As to those who live under the dominion of a European Power, they have no wish to rebel against it, and only aim at improving their material and moral condition, and of preserving their personality as a race.

"The true reasons of the Moslems' sympathy for the Ottoman Empire are historical, religious, and sentimental reasons."

The delegation of the Moslems of India for the defence of the Caliphate sent to the Peace Conference was headed by Mohammed Ali, who, in 1914, on behalf of the Government of India, had written to Talaat, Minister of the Interior, to ask him not to side with the Central Empires, and to show him how difficult the situation of the Indian Mussulmans would be if Turkey entered into the war against England. On landing in Venice, he told the correspondent of the *Giornale d'Italia* that the object of his journey was to convince the Allies that the dismemberment of the Ottoman Empire would be a danger to the peace of the world.

"The country we represent numbers 70 million Mohammedans and 230 million men belonging to other religions but agreeing with us on this point. So we hope that if the Allies really want to establish the peace of the world, they will take our reasons into account. Italy has hitherto supported us, and we hope the other nations will follow her example."

This delegation was first received by Mr. Fisher, representing Mr. Montagu, Indian Secretary, to whom they explained the serious consequences which the carrying out of the conditions of peace contemplated for Turkey might have in their country.

Mr. Lloyd George, in his turn, received the delegation on March 19, before it was heard by the Supreme Council. Mohammed Ali, after pointing to the bonds that link together the Mohammedans of India and the Caliphate, because Islam is not only a set of doctrines and dogmas but forms both a moral code and a social polity, recalled that, according to the Muslim doctrine, the Commander of the Faithful must always own a territory, an army, and resources to prevent the aggression of adversaries who have not ceased to arm themselves; he maintained, therefore, that the seat of the Sultan's temporal power must be maintained in Constantinople; that Turkey must not be dismembered; and that Arabia must be left under Turkish sovereignty.

"Islam has always had two centres, the first a personal one and the other a local one. The personal centre is the Caliph, or the Khalifa, as we call him— the successor of the Prophet. Because the Prophet was the personal centre of Islam, his successors, or Khalifas, continue his tradition to this day. The local centre is the region known as the Jazirat-ul-Arab, or the 'Island of Arabia,' the 'Land of the Prophets.' To Islam, Arabia has been not a peninsula but an island, the fourth boundary being the waters of the Euphrates and the Tigris....

"Islam required temporal power for the defence of the Faith, and for that purpose, if the ideal combination of piety and power could not be achieved, the Muslims said, 'Let us get hold of the most powerful person, even if he is not the most pious, so long as he places his power at the disposal of our piety.' That is why we agreed to accept Muslim kings, the Omayyids and the Abbasids, as Khalifas, now the Sultans of Turkey. They have a peculiar succession of their own. We have accepted it for the time being because we must have the strongest Mussulman Power at our disposal to assist us in the defence of the Faith. That is why we have accepted it. If the Turks agreed with other Muslims, and all agreed that the Khalifa may be chosen out of any Muslim community, no matter who he was, the humblest of us might be chosen, as they used to be chosen in the days of the first four Khalifas, the Khulafa-i-Rashideen, or truly guided Khalifas.

"But of course we have to make allowances for human nature. The Turkish Sultan in 1517 did not like to part with his power any more than the Mamluke rulers of Egypt liked to part with their power when they gave asylum to a scion of the Abbasids after the sack of Baghdad in 1258."

It follows that "the standard of temporal power necessary for the preservation of the Caliphate must obviously, therefore, be a relative one," and—

"Not going into the matter more fully, we would say that after the various wars in which Turkey has been engaged recently, and after the Balkan war particularly, the Empire of the Khalifa was reduced to such narrow limits that Muslims considered the irreducible minimum of temporal power adequate for the defence of the Faith to be the restoration of the territorial *status quo ante bellum*....

"When asking for the restoration of the territorial *status quo ante bellum*, Muslims do not rule out changes which would guarantee to the Christians, Jews, and Mussulmans, within the scheme of the Ottoman sovereignty, security of life and property and opportunities of autonomous development, so long as it is consistent with the dignity and independence of the sovereign State. It will not be a difficult matter. We have here an Empire in which the various communities live together. Some already are sufficiently independent and others hope—and here I refer to India—to get a larger degree of autonomy than they possess at the present moment; and consistently with our desire to have autonomous development ourselves, we could not think of denying it to Arabs or Jews or Christians within the Turkish Empire."

He went on as follows:

"The third claim that the Mussulmans have charged us with putting before you is based on a series of injunctions which require the Khalifa to be the warden of the three sacred Harams of Mecca, Medina, and Jerusalem; and overwhelming Muslim sentiment requires that he should be the warden of the holy shrines of Nejef, Kerbela, Kazimain, Samarra, and Baghdad, all of which are situated within the confines of the 'Island of Arabia.'

"Although Muslims rely on their religious obligations for the satisfaction of the claims which I have specified above, they naturally find additional support in your own pledge, Sir, with regard to Constantinople, Thrace, and Asia Minor, the populations of which are overwhelmingly Muslim. They trust that a pledge so solemnly given and recently renewed will be redeemed in its entirety. Although the same degree of sanctity cannot be claimed for Constantinople as for the three sacred Harams—Mecca, Medina, and Jerusalem—Constantinople is nevertheless held very sacred by all the Muslims of the world, and the uninterrupted historic tradition of nearly five centuries has created such an overwhelming sentiment with regard to Islambol, or the 'City of Islam'—a title which no city has up to this time enjoyed—that an effort to drive the Turks out 'bag and baggage' from the seat of the Khilafat is bound to be regarded by the Muslims of the world as a challenge of the modern Crusaders to Islam and of European rule to the entire East, which cannot be taken up by the Muslim world or the East without great peril to our own Empire, and, in fact, to the Allied dominions in Asia and Africa. In this connection, Sir, I might mention one point, that the Muslims cannot tolerate any affront to Islam in keeping the Khalifa as a sort of hostage in Constantinople. He is not the Pope at the Vatican, much less can he be the Pope at Avignon, and I am bound to say that the recent action of the Allied Powers is likely to give rise in the Muslim world to feelings which it will be very difficult to restrain, and which would be very dangerous to the peace of the world."

With regard to the question of the Caliphate and temporal power, on which the Indian delegation had been instructed to insist particularly, M. Mohammed Ali, in order to make the Moslem point of view quite clear, wrote as follows:[20]

"The moment this claim is put forward we are told that the West has outgrown this stage of human development, and that people who relieved the Head of a Christian Church of all temporal power are not prepared to maintain the temporal power of the Head of the Muslim Church. This idea is urged by the supporters of the Laic Law of France with all the fanaticism of the days of the Spanish Inquisition, and in England, too. Some of the most unprejudiced people wonder at the folly and temerity of those who come to press such an anachronistic claim. Others suggest that the Khalifa should be 'vaticanised' even if he is to retain Constantinople, while the Government of India, who should certainly have known better, say that they cannot acquiesce in Muslim statements which imply temporal allegiance to the Khilafat on the part of Indian Muslims, or suggest that temporal power is of the essence of the Khilafat. Where such criticisms and suggestions go astray is in misunderstanding the very nature and ideal of Islam and the Khilafat, and in relying on analogies from faiths which, whatever their original ideals, have, for all practical purposes, ceased to interpret life as Islam seeks to do."

As he had said in the course of his official interview with the British Premier, as Islam is not "a set of doctrines and dogmas, but a way of life, a moral code, and a social polity,"—

"Muslims regard themselves as created to serve the one Divine purpose that runs through the ages, owing allegiance to God in the first place and acknowledging His authority alone in the last resort. Their religion is not for Sabbaths and Sundays only, or a matter for churches and temples. It is a workaday faith, and meant even more for the market-place than the mosque. Theirs is a federation of faith, a cosmopolitan brotherhood, of which the personal centre is the Khalifa. He is not a Pope and is not even a priest, and he certainly has no pretensions to infallibility. He is the head of Islam's Republic, and it is a mere accident, and an unfortunate accident at that, that he happens to be a king. He is the Commander of the Faithful, the President of their Theocratic Commonwealth, and the Leader of all Mussulmans in all matters for which the Koran and the Traditions of the Prophet, whose successor he is, provide guidance."

Therefore, according to the Moslem doctrine—

"There is no such theory of 'divided allegiance' here, as the Government of India consider to be 'subversive of the constitutional basis on which all Governments are established.' 'There is no government but God's,' says the Koran, 'and Him alone is a Mussulman to serve,' and since He is the Sole Sovereign of all mankind, there can be no divided allegiance. All Governments can command the obedience of the Muslims in the same way as they can command the obedience of other people, but they can do so only so far as they command it, as Mr. H. G. Wells would say, in the name of God and for God, and certainly no Christian Sovereign could expect to exercise unquestioned authority over a Muslim against the clear commandments of his Faith when no Muslim Sovereign could dream of doing it. Mussulmans are required to obey God and His Prophet and 'the men in authority from amongst themselves,' which include the Khalifa; but they are also required, in case of every dispute, to refer back to the Holy Koran and to the Traditions of the Prophet, which are to act as arbitrator. Thus the Khalifa himself will be disobeyed if he orders that which the Faith forbids, and if he persists in such unauthorised conduct, he may not only be disobeyed, but also be deposed.

"But whatever he could or could not do, the Khalifa was certainly not a pious old gentleman whose only function in life was to mumble his prayers and repeat his beads.

"The best way to understand what he is and what he is not is to go back to the Prophet whose Khalifa or Successor he is. The Koran regards man as the vicegerent of God on earth, and Adam was the first Khalifa of God, and free-willed instrument of divine will. This succession continued from prophet to prophet, and they were the guides of the people in all the affairs of life. The fuller and final revelation came with Mohammed, and since then the Commanders of the Faithful have been his Khalifas or Successors. But as religion is not a part of life but the whole of it, and since it is not an affair of the next world but of this, which it teaches us to make better, cleaner, and happier, so every Muslim religious authority has laid it down unequivocally and emphatically that the allegiance which Muslims owe to the Khalifa is both temporal and spiritual. The only limits recognised to his authority are the Commandments of God, which he is not allowed to disobey or defy....

"The Mussulmans, therefore, do not believe that Christ, for instance, could have said that His was the kingdom not of this earth but of Heaven alone; or that men were to render to Cæsar what was due to Cæsar, and to God what was due to God. Cæsar could not share the world with God or demand from mankind any allegiance, even if only temporal, if he did not demand it for God and on behalf of God. But the ordinary Christian conception has been that the kingdom of Christ was not of this world, and no Pope or priest could, consistently with this conception, demand temporal power. It is doubtful if the Papacy is based on any saying of Christ Himself. At any rate, the Pope has always claimed to be the successor of St. Peter and the inheritor of *his* prerogatives. As such he has been looked upon as the doorkeeper of the kingdom of heaven, his office being strictly and avowedly limited to the spiritual domain. A study of history makes it only too apparent that the doctrine of the Papacy grew in Christianity by the application to the Popes of the epithets which are applied to St. Peter in the Gospels. Just as St. Peter never had any temporal authority, so the Papacy also remained, in the first stages of its growth, devoid of temporal power for long centuries. It was only by a very slow development that the Popes aspired to temporal power. Thus, without meaning any offence, it may be said that the acquisition of temporal power by the Popes was a mere accident, and they have certainly been divested of it without doing the least violence to the religious feelings of one half of the Christian world.

"On the contrary, the temporal power of the Khilafat in Islam is of the very essence of it, and is traceable not only to the earliest Khalifas, but to the Prophet himself. This is obviously not the religious belief of Christian Europe or America; but equally obviously this is the religious Muslim belief, and after all it is with the Muslim belief that we are concerned...."

So, considering the ever-increasing armaments of European and American nations, "even after the creation of a nebulous League of Nations," he asked himself:

"How then can Islam dispense with temporal power? Others maintain armies and navies and air forces for the defence of their territories or their commerce, because they love these more than they hate armaments. To Islam, its culture and ethics are dearer than territory, and it regards faith as greater than finance. It needs no army or navy to advance its boundaries or extend its influence; but it certainly needs them to prevent the aggression of others."

Then M. Mohammed Ali dealt separately with the chief clauses of the Turkish treaty in the course of his interview with Mr. Lloyd George, and made the following remarks:

"As regards Thrace, it is not necessary to support the Turkish claim for the retention of Thrace by any further argument than that of the principle of self-determination. Its fair and honest application will ensure the satisfaction of that claim.

"As regards Smyrna, the occupation of Smyrna by the Greeks, who were not even at war with Turkey, under the auspices of the Allies, has shaken to a great extent the confidence which Muslims reposed in the pledges given to them, and the atrocities perpetrated in that region have driven them almost to desperation. Muslims can discover no justification for this action except the desire of Greek capitalists to exploit the rich and renowned lands of Asia Minor, which are admittedly the homelands of the Turks. If this state of affairs is allowed to continue, not only will the Turk be driven out, 'bag and baggage,' from Europe, but he will have no 'bag and baggage' left to him, even in Asia. He would be paralysed, commercially and industrially, in a landlocked small Emirate in Asia Minor, the speedy bankruptcy of which is certain. The application of the principle of self-determination would entirely rule out the Greek claim in this fertile region, which obviously tempts the greed of the capitalist and the exploiter.

"As regards Cilicia, reasons similar to those that have promoted the action of Greeks in Smyrna seem clearly to prompt the outcry of the Christian population in Cilicia, and obviously it is the Gulf of Alexandretta which is attracting some people as the Gulf of Smyrna is attracting others."

Afterwards, coming to the question of the massacres, M. Mohammed Ali declared:

"The Indian Khilafat delegation must put on record their utter detestation of such conduct and their full sympathy for the sufferers, whether they be Christian or Muslim. But, if the Turk is to be punished as a criminal, and populations of other races and creeds are to be released from their allegiance to the Ottoman Sovereign on the assumption that the Turks have been tyrants in the past and their rule is intolerable, then the delegation claim that the whole question of these massacres must be impartially investigated by an International Commission on which the All-India Khilafat Conference should be adequately represented."

Moreover, the delegation had already said something similar in a telegram sent to Mr. Lloyd George:

"Where casualties have in fact taken place, not only should their true extent be ascertained, but the Commission should go fully into the so-called massacres and the intrigues of Tsarist Russia in Asia Minor after the success of similar intrigues in the Balkans; it should go into the question of the organisation of revolutionary societies by the Christian subjects of the Sultan, the rebellious character of which was subversive of his rule; it should go into the provocation offered to the Muslim majority in this region, and the nature of the struggle between the contending parties and the character of the forces engaged on either side...."

He went on:

"I have no brief for them; I have no brief for the Turks; I have only a brief for Islam and the India Muslims. What we say is this, as I said to Mr. Fisher: let there be a thorough inquiry, and if this thorough inquiry is carried out, and if it establishes to the satisfaction of the world that the Turks really have been guilty of unprovoked murders, and have been guilty of these atrocities and horrible crimes, then we will wash our hands of the Turks.

"To us it is much more important that not a single stain should remain on the fair name of Islam. We want to convert the whole world to our way of thinking, but with what face could we go before the whole world and say we are the brethren of murderers and massacrers?

"But we know the whole history of these massacres to some extent. It is only in Armenia that the Turk is said to be so intolerant; there are other parts of the world where he deals with Christian people, and where he deals with the Jewish community. No complaints of massacres come from those communities. Then the Armenians themselves lived under Turkish rule for centuries and never complained. The farthest back that we can go to discover any trace of this is the beginning of the last century. But in reality the 'massacres' begin only in the last quarter of the last century.

"It is pretty clear that they begin after the success of efforts like those made in the Balkans by Russia, which has never disguised its desire to take Constantinople since the time of Peter the Great. It has always wanted to go to Tsargrad, as it called it—that is, the city of the Tsars. They wanted to go there. They tried these things in the Balkans, and they succeeded beyond their expectation, only probably Bulgaria became too independent when it became Greater Bulgaria. But in the case of the Armenians, they had people who were not very warlike, who had no sovereign ambitions themselves, and who were also to a great extent afraid of conversion to another branch of the Orthodox Church, the Russian branch, so that they were not very willing tools. Still, they were egged on, and plots and intrigues went on all the time. These people were incited, and they understood that if they made a compromise with Tsarist Russia they would get something better. It was then that these massacres came on the scene. No doubt there have been several outcries about them; some evidence has been produced; but there has been no thorough international inquiry which would satisfy the entire world, Muslim as well as Christian. It is in that connection that we earnestly appeal to you, to the whole of Christendom, to the whole of Europe and America, that if the Turk is to be punished on the assumption that he is a tyrant, that his rule is a blasting tyranny, and that he ought to be punished, in that case the evidence should be of such a character that it should be absolutely above suspicion."

Mr. Lloyd George in his reply upbraided Turkey with fighting by the side of the Central Powers though Great Britain had never fought against her, and protracting the hostilities by closing the Black Sea to the British fleet; but he did not seem to realise that the Russian policy of the Allies partly accounted for Turkey's decision. Only at the end of the interview, in answer to a remark of the leader of the Indian delegation, he pleaded in defence of England "that she had made no arrangement of any sort with Russia at the expense of Turkey at the beginning of the war." Then, before coming to the various points M. Mohammed Ali had dealt with, Mr. Lloyd George, who had kept aloof for a long time from the policy of understanding with France, said:

"I do not understand M. Mohammed Ali to claim indulgence for Turkey. He claims justice, and justice she will get. Austria has had justice. Germany has had justice—pretty terrible justice. Why should Turkey escape? Turkey thought she had a feud with us. What feud had Turkey with us? Why did she come in to try and stab us and destroy liberty throughout the world when we were engaged in this life-and-death struggle? Is there any reason why we should apply a different measure to Turkey from that which we have meted out to the Christian communities of Germany and Austria? I want the Mohammedans in India to get it well into their minds that we are not treating Turkey severely because she is Mohammedan: we are applying exactly the same principle to her as we have applied to Austria, which is a great Christian community."

As to Arabia—which will be dealt with later on together with the Pan-Arabian movement—though M. Mohammed Ali had declared that "the delegation felt no anxiety about the possibility of an understanding between the Arabs and the Khalifa," and that the Moslems "did not want British bayonets to subject the Arabs to Turkey," Mr. Lloyd George answered:

"The Arabs have claimed independence. They have proclaimed Feisal King of Syria. They have claimed that they should be severed from Turkish dominion. Is it suggested that the Arabs should remain under Turkish dominion merely because they are Mohammedans? Is not the same measure of independence and freedom to be given to Mohammedans as is given to Christians? Croatia has demanded freedom, and we have given it to her. It is a Christian community. Syria has demanded it, and it is given to her. We are applying exactly the same principles in Christian places, and to impose the dominion of the Sultan upon Arabia, which has no desire for it, is to impose upon Arabs something which we certainly would not dream of imposing upon these Christian communities."

With regard to Thrace, after owning it was difficult to give reliable figures and saying that according to the Greek census and the Turkish census, which differ but little, the Moslem population was in "a considerable minority," Mr. Lloyd George stated that "it would certainly be taken away from Turkish sovereignty." As to Smyrna, he asserted that according to his information "a great majority of the population undoubtedly prefers the Greek rule to the Turkish rule."

Concerning the temporal power of the Khalifa, he seemed to have forgotten the difference which had just been pointed out to him between the Christian religion and Islam on this point, for he declared:

"I am not going to interfere in a religious discussion where men of the same faith take a different view. I know of Mohammedans—sincere, earnest, zealous Mussulmans—who take a very different view of the temporal power from the one which is taken by M. Mohammed Ali to-day, just as I know of Catholics who take one view and other Catholics who take a very different view of the temporal power of the Pope. That is a controversy into which I do not propose to enter."

And as if M. Mohammed Ali's remarks had quite escaped him, he added:

"All I know is this. The Turk will exercise temporal power in Turkish lands. We do not propose to deprive him of Turkish lands. Neither do we propose that he should retain power over lands which are not Turkish. Why? Because that is the principle we are applying to the Christian communities of Europe. The same principles must be applied to the Turk."

Finally, without thoroughly investigating the question of the massacres, he concluded that the responsibility lay with the Ottoman Government, which "cannot, as it is now constituted, protect its own subjects"; that Turkey is a "misgoverned country"—a reproach that might be applied to many other countries, though nobody would think of declaring they must be suppressed on that account; and that as the Turks "have been intolerant and have proved bad and unworthy rulers," the solutions proposed by the Allies are the only remedy and therefore are justified.

And so the old argument that Turkey must be chastised was recapitulated once more, and, through the mouth of her Prime Minister, England resorted to threats again, whereas she did not mean to compel Germany to carry out her engagements fully. This attitude seems to be accounted for by the fact that Turkey was weak, and was not such a good customer as Germany. England, while pretending to do justice and to settle accounts, merely meant to take hold of the Straits.

Islam has instituted a social polity and culture which, though widely different from British and American civilisations, and leading to different methods of life, is not necessarily inferior to them; and all religious sects, whether Protestant or Catholic, are wrong when they look upon their own moral conception as superior, and endeavour to substitute it for that of Islam.

If we refer to the letter which was written to Damad Ferid Pasha, president of the Ottoman delegation, in answer to the memorandum handed on June 17, 1919, to the Peace Conference, and which lacks M. Clémenceau's wit and style though his signature is appended to it, we plainly feel a Puritan inspiration in it, together with the above-mentioned state of mind.

One cannot help being sorry to find in so important a document such a complete ignorance or total lack of comprehension of the Muslim mind, and of the difference existing between our modern civilisation and what constitutes a culture. For instance, we read in it the following:

"History records many Turkish victories and also many Turkish defeats, many nations conquered and many set free. The memorandum itself hints at a loss of territories which not long ago were still under Ottoman sovereignty.

"Yet, in all these changes not one instance occurs in Europe, Asia, or Africa when the establishment of Turkish sovereignty was not attended with a decrease of material prosperity or a lower standard of culture; neither does an instance occur when the withdrawal of Turkish domination was not attended with an increase of material prosperity and a higher standard of culture. Whether among European Christians or among Syrian, Arabian, or African Mussulmans, the Turk has always brought destruction with him wherever he has conquered; he has never proved able to develop in peace what he had won by war. He is not gifted in this respect."

This stagnation, which to a certain extent has been noticed in modern times, may proceed from the fact that the old Turkish spirit was smothered and Islam was checked by the growth of foreign influence in Turkey. This is probably due, not chiefly to foreign intrusion in the affairs of the Ottoman State—for the latter needed the help of foreign nations—but rather to the selfish rivalries between these nations and to the mongrel solutions inherent in international régimes by which Turkish interests were sacrificed.

It is well known that the decadence of the Arabic-speaking countries had begun long before they were subjected by the Turks. It has even been noticed that Turkish domination in Arabia in 1513 checked the decline of Arabian civilisation, and roused the Syrians, who were in a similar predicament.

Besides, the prevailing and paramount concern for material prosperity which asserts itself in the above-mentioned document, together with the way in which business men, especially Anglo-Saxons, understand material prosperity, would account for the variance between the two civilisations, for it enhances the difference between their standpoints, and proves that the superiority conferred by spiritual eminence does not belong to the nations who consider themselves superior to the Turks.

The Turkish mind, enriched both by Islamic ethics and by Arabian, Persian, and Byzantine influences, has risen to a far more definite and lofty outlook on life than the shallow Anglo-Saxon morality. There is as much difference between the two as between the architecture of the Yeshil-Jami, the green mosque of Brusa, the dome of the Suleymanie, or the kiosk of Baghdad, and the art to which we owe the "sky-scrapers," the "flat-iron" buildings, the "Rhine bridges," and the "Leipzig buildings," or between the taste of the man who can appreciate "loukoums" or rose-jam, and the taste of the man who prefers "chewing-gum" or the acidulated drops flavoured with amyl acetate, or even the sweets flavoured with methyl salicylate provided by the American Government for its army. In the same manner, a similar confusion is often made between comfort—or what vulgar people call comfort—and true ease and real welfare; or again between a set of practical commodities inherent in the utilitarian conception of modern life, and what makes up culture. The quality of culture evidently does not depend on the percentage of water-closets or bath-rooms, or the quantity of calico used per thousand of inhabitants, in a country where the walls of the houses were once decorated with beautiful enamels, where the interior courts were adorned with marble fountains, and where women wore costly garments and silk veils.

Before throwing contempt on Islam, despising the Arabian and Turkish civilisations, and hoping that the Moslem outlook on life will make way for the modern Anglo-Saxon ideal, Mr. Lloyd George and all those who repeat after him that the Turks have no peculiar gift for governing peoples, ought to have pondered over Lady Esther Stanhope's words, which apply so fittingly to recent events. Being tired of Europe, she had travelled in the East, and, enticed by the beauty and grandeur of the Orient, she led a retired life in a convent near Said, dressed as a Moslem man. One day she was asked by the "Vicomte de Marcellus" whether she would ever go back to Europe, and she answered in some such words as these—we quote from memory:

"Why should I go to Europe? To see nations that deserve to be in bondage, and kings that do not deserve to reign? Before long the very foundation of your old continent will be shaken. You have just seen Athens, and will soon see Tyre. That's all that remains of those noble commonwealths so famed for art, of those empires that had the mastery of the world's trade and the seas. So will it be with Europe. Everything in it is worn out. The races of kings are getting extinct; they are swept away by death or their own faults, and are getting more and more degenerate. Aristocracy will soon be wiped out, making room for a petty, effete, ephemeral middle class. Only the lower people, those who plough and delve, still have some self-respect and some virtues. You will have to dread everything if they ever become conscious of their strength. I am sick of your Europe. I won't listen to its distant rumours that die away on this lonely beach. Let us not speak of Europe any more. I have done with it."

Besides, all religions accord with the character of the people that practise them and the climate in which they live. Most likely Islam perfectly fitted the physical and moral nature of the Turkish race, since the latter immediately embraced Mohammed's religion, whereas it had kept aloof from the great Christian movement which, 500 years before, had perturbed a large part of the pagan world, and it has remained faithful to it ever since.

If the Allies tried to minimise the part played by that religion, which perfectly suits the character and conditions of life of the people who practise it, and attempted to injure it, they would really benefit the domineering aims of Rome and the imperialistic spirit of Protestantism. In fact, the Vatican tries to avail itself of the recent Protestant effort, as has already been pointed out, and as various manifestations will show, to bring about a Christian hegemony which would not be beneficial either to the peoples of the East or to the civilisation of the world.

By doing so, the Allies would drive those peoples towards Germanism, though they have no natural propensity for it, for they are averse both to the Lutheran spirit and to the Catholic spirit; yet Germanism has succeeded in finding its way and even gaining sympathy among them, because it pretended to come in a friendly spirit.

It cannot be denied that before the war the Turks endeavoured to find support among other nations to counterbalance German influence. But as, above all things, they dreaded the Russian sway—not without reason, as the latter had already grasped several Turkish provinces in Asia Minor and represented its advance as the revenge of Orthodoxy over Islamism—they had turned towards Germany, who, though it secretly favoured Tsardom, yet pursued an anti-Russian policy.

Of course, they could not have any illusion about what a German Protectorate might be to Turkey, for at a sitting of the Reichstag a German deputy had openly declared: "In spite of our sympathy for Turkey, we must not forget that the time of her partition has come." As early as 1898 the Pan-German League issued a manifesto under the title *Deutschlands Ansprüche an das Türkische Erbe (The Rights of Germany to the Heritage of Turkey)*. "As soon as the present events shall bring about the dissolution of Turkey, no other Power will seriously attempt to raise a protest if the German Empire lays a claim to a share of it, for it has a right to a share as a great Power, and it wants it infinitely more than any other great Power, in order to maintain the national and economic life of hundreds of thousands of its emigrants." In the same manner, at the time of the annexation of Bosnia and Herzegovina, von Aerenberg did not scruple to say: "The opening to economic life of Asia Minor and Mesopotamia will always be looked upon as a high deed of German enterprise." And, alluding to the new field of activity which was thus opened to Austria-Hungary, he added: "The possession of Bosnia has made us a Balkan Power; it is our task and duty to discern when the time shall come, and to turn it to account."

But if the Turks chose to side with Germany, it was because the Emperor "Guilloun" represented himself as the protector of Islam, and promised to leave the Ottoman Empire its religious sovereignty and the full enjoyment of Muslim civilisation. Now, as the Turks acknowledge only Allah's will, it is foolish to ask a Christian sovereign or a Christian community to exercise authority over them in order to ensure peace; and yet the Western Powers, urged on by religious interests, have continued to interfere in Ottoman affairs from the Christian point of view and in order to further Christian interests.

Now we see why Germany, in order not to lose the benefit of her previous endeavours, readily welcomed the Central Committee for the Defence of Islam, whose seat was in Berlin, whence it carried on a vigorous propaganda throughout the Muslim world.

At the beginning of December, 1919, that committee held a meeting in Berlin; among the people present were: Talaat Pasha, representing the Turanian movement; Hussein Bey Reshidof, representing the "Eastern Central Committee" instituted by the Moscovite Foreign Commissariat for the liberation of Islam—which is at the head of all the organisations at work in Persia, the Transcaspian areas, Anatolia, Afghanistan, and India; Kutchuk Talaat, a representative of the Union and Progress Committee; Nuri Bedri Bey, representing the Anatolian Kurds; and delegates from Persia and Afghanistan. There they discussed what measures should be taken and what means of action should be resorted to in Muslim countries, especially in Algeria, Tunis, and Morocco.

It must be owned, on the other hand, that the Catholics in Turkey had refused—as they have always tried to do in all countries—to acknowledge the sovereignty of the Turkish Government, and had looked upon themselves as above the laws of the land, though they laid a claim at the same time to a share in the government of the country; in short, they wanted to be both Roman legates and Turkish governors.

All this does not suffice to justify the measures of oppression the Turks resorted to, but explains how they were driven to take such measures, and accounts for the state of mind now prevailing in Turkey, which has brought about the present troubles. For the foreign Powers, urged by the Eastern

Christians, kept on meddling with Turkish home affairs, which caused much resentment and anger among the Turks, and roused religious fanaticism on both sides.

If the liberal Western Powers carried on that policy—that is to say, if they continued to support the Christians against the Moslems—they would make a dangerous mistake.

At the present time the Holy See, which has never given up its ever-cherished dream of universal dominion, plainly shows by its growing activity that it means to develop its religious influence and avail itself of the war to strengthen and enlarge it.

For some time the Austro-Hungarian monarchy, though always a staunch supporter of the Papacy, restrained that tendency and became a moderating influence in Rome; but now the Holy See aims at playing a more important part than ever in all the affairs of Southern Germany and the countries that have broken loose from the former dual monarchy.

In order to strengthen the Church and to realise Catholic unity, the Vatican at the present juncture is exerting all its power in Central Europe and the Slavonic countries; and is doing its best at the same time to get in touch with the Protestant world in order to reinforce its own action by coupling it with the Protestant propaganda.

Benedict XV has revived the scheme of the longed-for Union of the Churches in order to win over to Catholicism part or the whole of the former Orthodox Empire.

In New Germany the Holy See is endeavouring to bring about an understanding between Catholics and Protestants, with a view to a common Christian—rather than strictly Catholic—action. In Austria, after upholding all the elements of the old régime so long as a monarchist movement seemed likely to triumph, it now gives its support to Christian Democracy. In Hungary, where the Jesuits and the Cistercians first worked hand in hand together with an Allied mission in Budapest to maintain Friedrich, or at least a clerical government, in power, the Primate, Mgr. Csernoch, and the Lutheran bishop, Mgr. Sandar Raffaï, have now agreed to work for the same purpose. The Polish Schlachta, of course, supports these schemes and intrigues, which are being carried on at Fribourg, in Switzerland, where certain princes connected with the Imperial House and Prince Louis of Windisch-Graetz used to meet Waitz, Bishop of Innsbrück.

Uniatism, or the rite of the United Greek Church, which, though retaining the Slavonic liturgy, acknowledges the Pope as the supreme head of the

Church, and is paramount in the Carpathian Mountains, Eastern Galicia, and the Ukraine, favours the extension of the Pope's sovereignty over these territories, and naturally the Holy See takes advantage of this movement to support and reinforce the Church and bring Orthodox countries under the dominion of Rome.

Till these great schemes have been carried out, and in order to further them, the Holy See means to establish between the Orthodox and the Catholic world an intermediary zone which would be a favourable ground for its penetration and conquest. To this intent Father Genocchi has been sent as apostolic visitor to the Ukraine by Cardinal Marini, prefect of the congregation newly established for the propaganda in the East, with full powers over both Latin and Greek Catholics, or Uniates. Father Genocchi is to act in close union with Mgr. Ratti, and both stand out as powerful agents of the great scheme of the Roman Church.

While pursuing this direct conquest, Rome endeavours in all countries to gain the support of all believers in Christ, even the Protestants, in order to be able to exert an influence on the policy of the Governments, and thus serve Christian interests.

At a recent conference of the Czecho-Slovak Catholics, Mgr. Kordatch, Archbishop of Prague, declared the Catholics would go so far as to resort to public political action and hold out the hand to the Protestants, who believe, like them, in the Divinity of Christ and the Decalogue.

So any undertaking against Islam or any other Eastern religion cannot but reinforce the power of Rome, for it aims at destroying the power of the other creeds which, as well as Catholicism, gratify the aspirations of the various peoples, and thus legitimately counterbalance its dream of hegemony.

Finally, though any communist conception is abhorrent to the Moslem spirit, which is essentially individualist and so has an aristocratic trend, and though Bolshevism, as we have already pointed out, is a specific doctrine which suits only the Russian mind, the attitude of the Western nations threatened to drive Islam towards Bolshevism, or at least to create a suitable ground for its expansion. In spite of the enlightened leaders of Islam, the attitude of the Powers risked inducing the Moslem masses to lend a willing ear to Bolshevist promises and to adopt Bolshevism in order to defend the Moslem creed and customs. Besides, Bolshevism, which was undergoing an evolution, and was growing more wily, less brutal, but all the more dangerous, no longer required other nations to adopt its social ideal. In order to serve a political purpose, it now turned its efforts towards the Caspian Sea to communicate with Asia

Minor and create disturbances in Central Asia, while, on the other side, it advanced as far as Mongolia.

After the conclusion of the Anglo-Persian agreement forced by Great Britain upon Persia, which, in spite of what was officially said to the contrary, deprived Persia of her independence, Bolshevism saw what an easy prey was offered to it by the English policy, and concentrated its efforts on Asia Minor, where it could most easily worry England. It carried on a very active propaganda in all Asiatic languages in Turkistan and even in Afghanistan— the result being that the latter country sent a mission of inquiry to Moscow.

According to the statement of a Persian reproduced in the *Journal des Débats* of April 4, 1920, the representatives of the Soviet Government made advances to the Persian patriotic organisations and told them:

"England despises your rights. Your Government is in her hand. To organise your resistance, you need a help. We offer it to you, and ask for nothing in return, not even for your adhesion to our social doctrine. The reason that urges us to offer you our support is a political one. Russia, whether she is Bolshevist or not, cannot live by the side of an England ruling over nearly the whole of the East. The real independence of your country is necessary to us."

Such suggestions could not but attract the attention of the Persians at a time when, without even waiting for the opening of the Chamber that had been elected under the influence of British troops in order to sanction the Anglo-Persian agreement, some English administrators had already settled in Teheran.

The same Persian, in agreement with the main body of Persian opinion, went on:

"Shall we have to submit to that shameful régime? Nobody thinks so in our country. Even those who were not bold enough to protest openly against the deed of spoliation which the Anglo-Persian agreement is, are secretly opposed to that agreement. But in order to avail ourselves of that discontent, to concentrate our forces, and chiefly to act fast and well, we need help from abroad, at least at the outset. The Bolshevists offer it to us. I do not know why we should discard the proposition at once. What makes us hesitate is their communist doctrine; yet they declare they do not want at all to 'bolshevikise' Persia. As soon as their promise seems to be quite genuine, it will be our national duty to accept their help.

"Whether the Red Dictator's action in Russia was good or bad is a question that concerns the Russians alone. The only question for us is how to find an ally. Now we have not to choose between many.

"We should have been only too pleased to come to an understanding with Great Britain, even at the cost of some concessions, provided our independence were respected. But the British leaders have preferred trampling upon our rights. Who is to be blamed for this?"

In the same manner as the Kemalist movement, a Nationalist movement was gaining ground in Persia, like the one which had already brought on the Teheran events from 1906 to 1909.

Now, while the Bolshevists, in order to expand and strengthen their position, did their utmost to convince the Eastern nations that Bolshevism alone could free them, the Germans, on the other hand, seized the new opportunity that was given them to offer the Mohammedans their help, and sent them German officers from Russia. In this way, and through our fault, Bolshevism and Germanism united to foment disturbances in the East, and join with it against us. That is why Mr. Winston Churchill said, at the beginning of January: "New forces are now rising in Asia Minor, and if Bolshevism and Turkish Nationalism should unite, the outlook would be a serious one for Great Britain."

Footnotes:

[15] Chapter "Le Peuple."

[16] *The Times*, February 27, 1920, p. 8, col. 4.

[17] *The Times*, February 27, 1920, p. 8, col. 4.

[18] *The Times*, February 27, 1920, p. 9.

[19] *The Times*, February 27, 1920.

[20] *India and the Empire*, reprinted from *Foreign Affairs*, July 1, 1920 (Orchard House, Great Smith Street, Westminster, London, S.W. 1), pp. 3 f.

V

THE OCCUPATION OF CONSTANTINOPLE

THE Allied intervention in Turkey continued to be the subject of frequent diplomatic conversations between the Powers.

Though Italy and France seemed to favour a strictly limited action, England held quite a different opinion, and energetic measures seemed likely to be resorted to. Lord Derby at the meeting of the Ambassadors' Council on March 10 read a telegram from his Government stating it intended to demand of Germany the extradition of Enver Pasha and Talaat Pasha, who were on the list of war criminals drawn up a few weeks before by the British Government, and who at that time were in Berlin.

As the Allies had not requested that these men should be handed over to them at the time of the armistice, and as the war criminals whose extradition had been previously demanded of the Central Powers did not seem likely to be delivered up to them, this seemed rather an idle request at a time when it was openly said the Allies wanted to expel the Turks from Constantinople, when a deep agitation convulsed the Moslem world and discontent was rife in it. What was the use of this new threat to Germany if, like the previous one, it was not to be carried into effect? What would Great Britain do if the two "undesirables" thought of going to Holland, and why did she prepare to punish Turkey when some of her statesmen seemed inclined to make all sorts of concessions, instead of compelling Germany, the promoter of the conflict, who had not yet delivered up any German subject, to execute the treaty without any restriction whatever?

At the beginning of the armistice England had deported the members and chief supporters of the Committee of Union and Progress, and later on the high functionaries who had been arrested by Damad Ferid Pasha, and were about to be court-martialled. One night fifty-four of the latter out of about 130 were suddenly deported to Malta for fear they should be set free by the population of Constantinople. Among them were: Hairi Effendi, ex-Sheik-ul-Islam; the Egyptian prince, Said Halim Pasha, ex-Grand Vizier; Ahmed Nessiny, ex-Minister of Foreign Affairs; Halil Bey, ex-Minister of Justice; Prince Abbas Halim Pasha, ex-Minister of Public Works; Fethy Bey, ex-Minister at Sofia; Rahmi Bey, Governor-General of vilayet of Smyrna; Jambalat Bey, ex-Minister of Interior; Ibrahim Bey, a former Minister; and four members of the Committee: Midhat Shukri; Zia Geuk Alp; Kemal (Kutchuk Effendi); and Bedreddin Bey, temporary vali of Diarbekir, who was deported as responsible for the massacres that had taken place in that town, though at that time he was out of office and had been discharged by a court-martial. The British even evinced a desperate, undignified animosity and an utter lack of generosity in regard to the Turkish generals who had defeated them. They had, as it were, carried away the spirit of Turkey.

Italy, who had followed a most clever, shrewd, and far-sighted policy, and who had kept some independence within the Supreme Council, had been very reserved in regard to the Turkish question.

In regard to Article 9 of the pact of London, which ascribed to Italy, in case Turkey should be dismembered, a "fair part" of the province of Adana in Asia Minor, the newspaper *Il Secolo*, in the middle of January, 1920, expressed the opinion that Italy should give up that acquisition.

"Notwithstanding all that has been written for the last seven or eight years about the Adalia area, we do not think that its possession would improve our present economic condition. It would only estrange from us a nation from which we might perhaps derive great advantages through an open policy of friendship and liberty.

"The most profitable scheme would have been to maintain the national integrity of Turkey and to give Italy, not a mandate over a reduced State, but a mere administrative control, and to assign her a few zones of exploitation with mere economic privileges, for instance, near Heraclea and Adalia.

"But at the present stage of the Asiatic problem, such a scheme could hardly be carried out. We must then lay aside all selfish purposes, and openly and tenaciously defend the integrity and independence of the Turkish State.

"Let the Turks be driven away from the districts which are predominantly Arabian, Greek, or Armenian. But let the Sultan remain in Constantinople, till the League of Nations has become stronger and able to assume control of the Straits. Let us not forget that the Turks chiefly put their confidence in us now, and that Germany, whose policy had never threatened Turkish territorial integrity, had succeeded in gaining Turkish friendship and blind devotion.

"Italy has not many friends to-day, and so she should not despise a hand which is willingly held out to her."

Italy therefore did not warmly approve an expedition against Turkey. Her semi-official newspapers stated it was owing to Italy that the Allies' policy still showed some moderation, and they hinted that the presence of Italian troops in the contingent landed at Constantinople was to be looked upon as the best means to prevent extreme measures.

On Tuesday, March 16, the Allied troops, consisting mostly of British soldiers, under the command of General Milne, occupied the Ottoman Government offices.

It might seem strange that the Allied troops in Constantinople were commanded by a British general, when the town was the residence of General Franchet d'Espérey, commander-in-chief of the inter-Allied troops on the Macedonian front, who, in the decisive battle in which he broke through the Bulgarian front, had had General Milne under him. But, after all, it was better for France that an English general should stand responsible for carrying out the occupation.

To the student of Eastern events this was but the logical outcome of a patient manœuvre of England. The documents that have now been made public plainly show how far-sighted her policy had been.

General Franchet d'Espérey's dispositions were suddenly reversed, for he had not advocated an important military action against Russia or Turkey when he had taken command of the Eastern army—*i.e.*, before his expedition from Salonika towards the Danube—and at the beginning of October, 1918, he had arranged the French and English divisions so as to march against Budapest and Vienna, foreseeing the ultimate advance of the Italian left wing against Munich.

On October 8, 1918, he was formally enjoined from Paris to send the British divisions which made up his right wing against Constantinople under the command of an English general.

Thus, after the defeat of Bulgaria in October, 1918, the British Government required that the troops sent to the Constantinople area should be led by a British general. In this way General Milne assumed command of the British troops stationed round and in Constantinople when Admiral Calthorpe had concluded the armistice with Turkey, and as a consequence General Franchet d'Espérey, though still commander-in-chief of the Allied forces in European Turkey, was now under the orders of General Milne, commander of the Constantinople garrison and the forces in Asia Minor.

Some time after receiving the aforesaid order, General Franchet d'Espérey, on October 27, 1918, received a letter from the War Minister, M. Clémenceau, No. 13644, B.S. 3,[21] forwarding him "copy of a letter giving the outline of a scheme of action that was recommended not only to carry on the war against the Central Powers in Russia, but also to effect the economic blockade of Bolshevism, and thus bring about its downfall." This scheme, after being assented to by the Allied Powers concerned in it, was to be "the natural outcome of the operations entrusted to the Allied armies in the East."

Finally, in a telegram, No. 14041, B.S. 3, dated November 6, containing some very curious recommendations, it was said:

"The operations in Southern Russia should be carried on by means of Greek elements, for instance, which it might be inexpedient to employ in an offensive against Germany, or by means of the French army in Palestine."[22]

Thus all the plans of the French headquarters were altered by England, and to her advantage; at the same time part of our endeavours was broken up and annihilated under the pressure of the Pan-Russian circles that urged France to intervene in Russia, and the French policy in the East was wholly at the mercy of England. By saying this, we do not mean at all to belittle M. Clémenceau's work during the war, but we only mention one of the mistakes to which he was driven, in spite of his energy and determination, by the English and American policy, which had dazzled some of his collaborators.

On March 16, at 9 a.m., some British *estafettes* handed to the Sultan, in his palace at Yildiz-Kiosk, and to the Sublime Porte a note of General Milne, commanding the Allied troops in Asia Minor and the town of Constantinople. It stated that at 10 a.m., with the agreement of the Italian, French, and British High Commissioners, and according to the orders of the British Imperial Headquarters, the Allied contingents would occupy the offices of the Minister of War and the Minister of Marine, the prefecture, the post and telegraph offices, the town gates, and the new bridge of Galata. In fact, the town had been occupied at daybreak by the Allied troops.

The note added that for a short time the political administration would be left to the Turks, but under the control of Allied officers. Martial law was proclaimed, and, in case of resistance, force would be resorted to.

The Ottoman Government gave no answer, and an hour later all the measures mentioned by General Milne were carried out. As these operations took a whole day, all the means of transport and communication were temporarily stopped.

At the War Office the soldiers on duty attempted to resist the British forces. A skirmish ensued, in which two British soldiers were killed, and an officer and three soldiers wounded; nine Turks, including an officer, were killed, and a few more wounded.

At the same hour a Greek destroyer steamed into the Golden Horn, and cast anchor opposite the Patriarch's palace.

Before this, General Milne had had a few deputies and senators arrested, together with a few men considered as having a share in the Nationalist movement, such as Kutchuk Jemal Pasha, ex-War Minister in the Ali Riza Cabinet; Jevad Pasha, formerly head of the staff; Tchourouk Soulou

Mahmoud Pasha, a senator; Dr. Essad Pasha; Galatali Shefket Pasha, commanding the Straits forces; Reouf Bey, Kara Vassif Bey, Shevket Bey, Hassan Tahsin Bey, Nouman Ousta Effendi, Sheref Bey, deputies.

Reouf Bey and Kara Vassif Bey were considered as representing in the Turkish Parliament Mustafa Kemal Pasha and the people who ensured the transmission of his orders.

All these men were arrested illegally and brutally, with the consent of the French Governor, though they had always evinced much sympathy for France, under the pretext that they corresponded with the national army; and yet their intervention might have had favourable consequences.

Among the men arrested that night, Jemal, Jevad, and Mahmoud Pasha, all three former Ministers, were insulted and sent to prison in their nightclothes, with their arms bound. Their doors and windows were broken open, and their Moslem wives were threatened in the harem. Some children of thirteen or fourteen were also arrested and thrashed. Eight Turkish soldiers on duty at Shahzade-Bashi were killed in the morning while they lay asleep on their camp-beds, and the censorship probably suppressed other deeds of the same kind.

The Ottoman Government could not understand how members of Parliament could be imprisoned, especially by the English, the founders of the parliamentary system. The deputy Jelal Noury Bey, who is neither a Nationalist nor a Unionist, was apprehended, merely because he opposed Ferid Pasha's policy.

England, to enhance her influence over public opinion, got control over the chief newspapers which were not friendly to her. Jelal Noury Bey, the director of the *Ileri*, a radical newspaper, and Ahmed Emin Bey, the director of the *Vakit*, were deported. The *Alemdar*, the *Peyam Sabah*, the *Stambul*, edited by Refi Jevad, Ali Kemal, and Said Mollah, which, since the first days of the armistice, had praised the English policy, fell into English hands; which accounts for the varying attitudes successively assumed by those journals in their comments on current events. Their editors were mostly members of the "Club of the Friends of England," and sought in every possible way to increase the number of the adherents of that committee, which was subsidised by the British High Commissioner, and whose chief aim was that the Turkish mandate should be given to England.

On March 21, 1920, the British at Skutari requisitioned the police courts, the law courts, the police station, the town hall, and the prison, thus almost completely disorganising the administration of the town.

In the note signed by the High Commissioners, this occupation was described as a measure of guarantee, with a view to the execution of the treaty that was going to be forced on Turkey. Yet it seemed rather strange that such measures should be taken before the treaty was concluded—or was it because the English, being aware the treaty was unacceptable, thought it necessary to gag the Turks beforehand, or even sought to exasperate them?—for if the Turks offered resistance, then the English would have a right to intervene very sternly, and thus could justify the most unjustifiable measures of repression. What would England and the United States have answered if France had proposed such coercive measures against Germany in addition to those of the armistice? It was stated in this note that the occupation would not last long, and was no infringement upon the Sultan's sovereignty, that it aimed at rallying the Turks in a common endeavour to restore prosperity to Turkey in accordance with the Sultan's orders; but it also threatened that, should disorder last longer in Asia Minor, the occupation might be extended and the provisions of the treaty might be made harder, in which case Constantinople would be severed from Turkey.

The *Daily Telegraph* said about that time:

"The political situation, which has evolved so rapidly, plainly shows it is not enough for the Americans to keep aloof from the present events. Their national honour is at stake.

"Public opinion in Great Britain would unanimously side with France in her operations in Asia Minor, provided France declares herself willing to accept our co-operation.

"We easily understand that the occupation of Constantinople came rather as a surprise to France and Italy, especially if we take into account that this action closely followed another measure of a similar kind taken by England within the last fortnight.

"It seems that this time our Allies have assumed a slightly different attitude: official France is still hesitating; public opinion has changed completely, and the pro-Turkish feeling is on the wane. If France wants to maintain her prestige in the East unimpaired, she must associate with any political, naval, or military measure taken by England.

"The Italian standpoint and interests do not differ much from ours, or from those of France, but Italian circles plainly advocate a policy of non-intervention, or an intervention restricted to a diplomatic action."

If such proceedings emanating from some American or English circles were hardly a matter of surprise, the attitude of some Frenchmen of note was not so easily accounted for.

M. Hanotaux[23] was led by a strange political aberration and a curious oblivion of all the traditional policy of France—unless he deliberately meant to break off with it, or was blinded by prejudice—when he assigned Constantinople to Greece, because, according to him, to give Constantinople to Greece was "to give it to Europe, and to her worthiest, noblest offspring."

Now Hellenism owes nothing to Byzantium, and Byzantinism, imbued with Christianity, is but remotely and indirectly connected with the magnificent pagan bloom of Hellenism. Byzantium, as has been shown, was not only the continuation of Rome in its decay: it had also a character of its own. Neither was Byzantinism a mere continuation of Hellenism. It was rather the propagator of Orthodoxy, so that when the Greeks claimed Byzantium, they could not do so on behalf of Hellenism, but merely on behalf of Christianity. There is a confusion here that many people have sought to perpetuate because it serves numerous interests, those of the Greeks, and also those of the Slavs, who owe their culture to Byzantium. But whereas Byzantium chiefly taught barbarous Russia a religion together with the rudiments of knowledge, and opened for her a door to the Old World, she imparted to Arabian civilisation knowledge of the works and traditions of antiquity. Russia, who only borrowed the rites of the Byzantine Church and exaggerated them, did not derive much profit from that initiation; the Turks and Arabs, on the contrary, thanks to their own culture, were able to imbibe the old knowledge bequeathed and handed down to them by Byzantium—leaving aside the religious bequest. Thus they were enabled to exercise a wholesome influence, driving out of Constantinople both Orthodoxy and the Slavs who aimed at the possession of that town.

As to the so-called Hellenism of Asia Minor, it is true that the civilisation of ancient Greece spread over several districts on the coast; but it should be borne in mind that, long before the Greeks, the Egyptians and various Semitic peoples had settled on the coast of Lydia—which up to the seventh century B.C. bore the name of Meonia—and fought there for a long time; and that the Lydians, a hybrid race akin to the Thracians and Pelasgi commingled with ethnic elements coming from Syria and Cappadocia, kept up an intercourse between the Greeks of the coast and Asia[24] till the Cimmerian invasion convulsed Asia Minor in the eighth century. Lastly, the Medes, against whom the Greeks waged three wars, are considered by Oppert,[25] owing to the etymology of the name, to be of Turanian descent.

In fact, the relations between the Turks and the Greeks and the Byzantians are really most involved. We know to-day that some Turkish elements, who were converted to the Greek Church long before the Ottoman Turks embraced Islam, and whose origin is anterior by far to the establishment of the Seljukian Empire and the Ottoman Empire, faithfully served the Byzantine Empire from the fifth century onwards, and were utilised by

Justinian for the defence of the Asiatic boundaries of the Empire—which were also the boundaries of Christianity—against the attacks of Eastern nations.

It is difficult to account for the sudden fervid enthusiasm of the Allies for Greece. For two years she adhered to Constantine's policy, perpetrating many an act of treachery against both the Hellenic people and the Allies, repeatedly violating the Constitution guaranteed by the Powers that had protected her, and slaughtering many French sailors; and then, after her unfriendly conduct towards the Allies under cover of a pro-German neutrality, she had very tardily sided with them. It was surprising, therefore, that Greece, who had displayed her pro-German feelings during a great part of the war, would probably receive some of the most thoroughly Turkish territories of the Ottoman Empire, though she never fought against that Empire even after she had deposed King Alexander's father, in spite of the deplorable complaisance of some of the Allies.

Finally, the very day after the occupation of Constantinople, General Milne, who commanded the British troops of occupation, enjoined the Salih Pasha Cabinet to resign under pretence that it no longer enjoyed the Sovereign's confidence. The Grand Vizier refused to comply with the English general's request, as the Government had the confidence of the Chamber and the Sovereign need not apply to the commander of the forces of occupation for permission to communicate with his Ministers. After incarcerating a good many deputies, senators, and political men, as has just been seen, the general gave the Grand Vizier to understand that orders had been given for the arrest of the Ministers in case they should attempt to go to their departments. In order to spare his country another humiliation, Salih Pasha handed in his resignation to the Sultan, who, following the advice of England, charged Damad Ferid to form another Cabinet.

It requires all the reasons that have been previously given to enable us to understand why England threatened and humbled Turkey to such an extent—the only Power left in the East that could be a factor for moderation and peace.

Mustafa Kemal never recognised the Damad Ferid Cabinet, and only after the latter had resigned and Ali Riza Pasha had been appointed Grand Vizier did he consent, in order to avoid another conflict with the Sultan, to enter into negotiations with the Constantinople Government. Salih Pasha was charged by the Minister to carry on the negotiations with the Nationalists, and repaired to Amasia. There it was agreed—first, that the National Organisation should be officially recognised as a lawful power which was necessary to the defence of the rights of the country, and should have full liberty of action side by side with the Government; secondly, that the Cabinet should avoid taking any decision sealing the fate of the country before Parliament met; thirdly, that some appointments should be made in agreement with the National Organisation, after which the latter should not interfere in the administration of the country.

Besides, as Mustafa Kemal said later on in a speech made before the Angora Assembly, though the Sultan had been represented by some as lacking energy, not maintaining the dignity of the Imperial throne, and not being a patriot, yet the reason why he had fallen under English tutelage was that he had seen no other means to save both the existence of Turkey and his throne.

The question whether Parliament should meet at Constantinople or in a province brought on a first disagreement between the Government and Mustafa Kemal, who finally yielded. But, owing to the occupation of Constantinople, Parliament soon found itself in a precarious condition, and the National Organisation decided to hold its sittings at Angora.

After all these events a deputy, Riza Nour, at the sitting of March 18, 1920, raised a protest against the occupation of Constantinople and the incarceration of some members of Parliament by the Allies, which measures were an insult to the dignity of the Turkish Parliament, and a contravention of the constitutional laws and the law of nations. This motion, carried unanimously by the Ottoman Chamber and signed by the Vice-President, M. Hussein Kiazim—the President, for fear of being prosecuted by the British authorities, having left his official residence—was forwarded to the Allied and neutral Parliaments, and the Ottoman Chamber adjourned *sine die* till it was possible for the deputies to carry out their mandate safely.

Ahmed Riza, former President of the Chamber and Senate of the Ottoman Empire—who, after the failure of Damad Ferid's mission to Paris, had addressed an open letter to M. Clémenceau on July 17, 1919, almost the anniversary day of the Constitution—joined in that protest and commented upon the treatment some members of Parliament had undergone, as follows:

"It is contrary to all parliamentary rights and principles throughout the world and to the legal dispositions that guarantee the inviolability and immunity of all members of the Turkish Parliament to arrest representatives of the nation while they are carrying out their mandate. So the armed Interference of the foreigner with our Chamber cannot be in any way excused or accounted for.

"Such an arbitrary intrusion, especially on the part of England, that is looked upon as the founder of the parliamentary system, will bring everlasting shame to British civilisation.

"After the illegal arrest of several of its members, the Turkish Parliament adjourned *sine die*, as a token of protest, till the deputies are able to carry out their mandate freely and safely.

"A note communicated to the Press makes out that some deputies had been returned under the pressure of the Nationalists and that, as the Christian elements had had no share in the elections, the session was illegal.

"Now, it should be noticed that these elements abstained from voting at the last elections of their own free will, and that since the armistice no representative of the Christian communities has taken an official part in the public functions in the Imperial Palace. The Nationalist forces cannot be held responsible for this.

"Neither is it the Nationalists' fault if the French authorities in Cilicia arbitrarily prevented the inhabitants of that district from holding the parliamentary election, thus depriving the people of their most sacred rights, and violating the terms of the armistice.

"The acknowledgment of the validity of the mandates of the new members by the unanimity of their colleagues, the official opening of Parliament by the speech from the throne, the good wishes and greetings of the Sultan to the deputies, bear witness that the assembly legally represented the wishes of the nation and had the Sovereign's approbation.

"Besides, these are strictly internal questions in which the Allies' interests are not at all concerned, and with which foreigners have no right to interfere.

"At such a solemn hour it would be an utter denial of justice if the Ottoman deputies were not able to discuss the fundamental stipulations of the intended Peace Treaty which is to seal the future fate of their country.

"Who is to examine the Peace Treaty to-day, and who is to give its assent to it now the nation has been deprived of its representatives?

"Of what value will be a treaty thus worked out secretly, behind closed doors, and concluded in such conditions? How can the signature of the members of the Government be considered as binding the nation? For the new Ministry does not yet represent the Ottoman nation, since no motion of confidence has hitherto been carried by a chamber which does not sit; and so it cannot be looked upon as being legally constituted.

"Whatever may happen, the nation alone can decide its own fate. If, at such a serious juncture, when its very existence is at stake, it were not able to defend its own cause and its own rights freely through the peaceful vote of its own mandatories, it would be looked upon by the whole of mankind as the victim of most unfair treatment, the responsibility of which will one day be determined by history."

During Abdul Hamid's reign Ahmed Riza had of his own will gone into exile, and from Paris he had wielded great influence over the movement that led to the revolution of 1908. But when the Young Turk Government had practically become dictatorial and had yielded to the pressure that drove it towards Germany, he realised that policy was a failure and was leading the Empire to ruin; then, though he had been one of the promoters of the movement, he protested repeatedly in the Senate, of which he was a member, against the illegal doings of the Government and its foolhardy policy. As President of the "National Block"—which, though not a political party properly speaking, aimed at grouping all the conservative constitutional elements friendly to the Entente—he seemed likely to play an important part in public life again when, about the middle of August, 1919, it was rumoured that the Damad Ferid Government was about to take action against him and his political friends; and soon after it was made known that he intended to go to Italy or France till the reopening of the Ottoman Parliament. After staying in Rome, where he had conversations with some political men of note in order to establish an intellectual entente between Italians and Turks, he settled in Paris.

The English censorship, which gagged the Turkish newspapers, went so far as to prevent them from reprinting extracts from French newspapers that were favourable to the Ottoman cause. It brought ridicule upon itself by censuring the Bible; in an article in the *Univers Israélite*, reprinted by the *Aurore*, which quoted and commented on three verses of chapter xix. of Isaiah, the censor cut off the first of these verses, which may be interpreted as foreshadowing a League of Nations, but in which he was afraid the reader might find a hint at a connection between Egypt and Asia and at the claims of the Turkish and Egyptian Nationalists. This is the verse, which any reader could easily restore: "In that day shall there be a highway out of Egypt to Assyria, and the Assyrian shall come into Egypt and the Egyptian into Assyria, and the Egyptians shall serve with the Assyrians."

[21] Cf. the *Matin*, June 17, 1920, an interview of M. Paul Benazet, ex-chairman of the Committee of War Estimates; and the *Œuvre*, July 8, 1920.

[22] Cf. the *Matin*, June 21, 1920, and M. Fribourg's speech in the second sitting of June 25, 1920.

[23] *Figaro*, March 18, 1920.

[24] Radet, *La Lydie et le monde grec au temps des Mermnades* (Paris, 1893).

[25] Oppert, *Le Peuple des Mèdes*.

VI

THE TREATY WITH TURKEY

IN the course of the debate on the foreign policy of England which opened on Thursday, March 25, on the third reading of the Finance Bill, Mr. Asquith, speaking of the Turkish problem as leader of the Opposition, urged that the Ottoman Government should no longer hold in Europe the political power that belonged to it before the war. He urged, however, that the Sultan should not be relegated to Asia Minor, where he would quite escape European control. He proposed, therefore, that the Sultan should be, as it were, "vaticanised"—that is to say, he should remain in Constantinople, but should only retain his spiritual power as Caliph, as the Pope does in Rome.

The Great Powers or the League of Nations would then be entrusted with the political power in Constantinople, and if the Bosphorus or the Dardanelles were neutralised or internationalised, the presence of the Sultan in Constantinople would not be attended with any serious danger.

As to Mesopotamia, Mr. Asquith objected to the *status quo ante bellum*. As the frontiers of that region were not quite definite, sooner or later, he thought, if England remained there, she would be driven to advance to the shores of the Black Sea, or even the Caspian Sea, and she had not adequate means for the present to do so. So it was better for her to confine her action within the Basra zone.

The Prime Minister, rising in response, first remarked that the cause of the delays in the negotiations with Turkey and the settlement of peace was that the Allies had thought it proper to wait for the decision of America, as to the share she intended to take in the negotiations. He recalled that the Allies had hoped the United States would not only assume the protection of Armenia properly speaking, but of Cilicia too, and also accept a mandate for the Straits of Constantinople, and went on as follows:

"If we had not given time for America to make up her mind it might have suspected the Allies wanted to take advantage of some political difficulty to partition Turkey; and it is only when the United States definitely stated she did not intend to take part in the Conference that the Allies proceeded to take definite decisions with regard to the Turkish peace. I think that it is due to the Allies to make that explanation."

Mr. Lloyd George went on to state that the Allies had contemplated maintaining only the spiritual power of the Sultan, but unfortunately this scheme did not seem likely to solve the difficulties of the situation. For

Constantinople had to be administered at the same time, and it is easier to control the Sultan and his Ministers in Constantinople than if they were relegated to Asia Minor.

Then, resorting to the policy of compromise which bore such bad fruits in the course of the Peace Conference, Mr. Lloyd George, in order not to shut out the possibility of reverting to the opposite opinion, added that if it was proved that the Allies' control weakened the power of the Sultan in Asia Minor, it would always be possible to consider the question afresh—but he hoped that would not be necessary.

As to the question of Asia Minor and the distribution of the mandates, he declared:

"If America had accepted the responsibility for controlling Armenia, the French, who, under what is called the Sykes scheme, had Cilicia assigned to their control, were quite willing to hand it over to American control. The British, French, and Italians are quite agreed on the subject, but we have not yet seen a sign. We have only received telegrams from America, asking us to protect the Armenians; we have had no offers up to the present to undertake the responsibility.... We are hoping that France will undertake that responsibility, but it is a good deal to ask of her. We have also got our responsibility, but we cannot take too much upon our own shoulders....

"With regard to the Republic of Erivan, which is Armenia, it depends entirely on the Armenians themselves whether they protect their independence.... I am told that they could easily organise an army of above 40,000 men. If they ask for equipment, we shall be very happy to assist in equipping their army. If they want the assistance of officers to train that army, I am perfectly certain there is no Allied country in Europe that would not be willing to assist in that respect."[26]

Finally, with, respect to Mesopotamia, Mr. Lloyd George urged "it would be a mistake to give up Baghdad and Mosul."

"I say that, after incurring the enormous expenditure which we have incurred in freeing this country from the withering despotism of the Turk, to hand it back to anarchy and confusion, and to take no responsibility for its development, would be an act of folly quite indefensible.... They have been consulted about their wishes in this respect, and I think, almost without exception, they are anxious that we should stay here, though they are divided about the kind of independent Government they would like....

"We have no right, however, to talk as if we were the mandatory of Mesopotamia when the treaty with Turkey has not yet been signed. It is only on the signing of that treaty that the question of mandatories will be decided, but when that time comes we shall certainly claim the right to be the mandatory power of Mesopotamia, including Mosul."

In its leading article, *The Times*, criticising the attitude Mr. Lloyd George had taken in the debate on the Mesopotamian question, wrote on March 27:

"The Prime Minister made statements, about the future of Mesopotamia which require further elucidation. He said that when the Treaty of Peace with Turkey has been finally decided, the British Government would 'claim the right' to be the 'mandatory Power' for Mesopotamia, including the vilayet of Mosul....

"Judging from some passages in his speech, even Mr. Lloyd George himself has never grasped the full and dangerous significance of the adventure he now advocates....

"The Prime Minister's reply conveyed the impression that he has only the very haziest idea about what he proposes to do in this region, which has been the grave of empires ever since written history began."

After pointing out the dangers of a British mandate over Mesopotamia, including the vilayet of Mosul, *The Times* thought, as had been suggested by Mr. Asquith, that England should confine her direct obligations to the zone of Basra, and pointed out that it was only incidentally and almost in spite of himself that Mr. Asquith had been driven in 1915 to occupy the larger part of Mesopotamia.

"Mr. Asquith says—and he is entirely right—that if we hold a line in the mountains of Northern Kurdistan we shall sooner or later be driven to advance to the shores of the Black Sea, or even to the Caspian. His view is in complete accord with every lesson to be derived from our history as an Empire. We have never drawn one of these vague, unsatisfactory frontiers without being eventually compelled to move beyond it. We cannot incur such a risk in the Middle East, and the cost in money and the strain upon our troops are alike prohibitive factors."[27]

The next day, in a similar debate in the French Chamber, M. Millerand, being asked to give information about the leading principles of the French Government in the negotiations that were being carried on in regard to the Turkish treaty, made the following statement, which did not throw much light on the question:

"First of all the Supreme Council deems it necessary to organise a Turkey that can live, and for this purpose—this is the only resolution that was made public and the only one that the British Government disclosed in the House of Commons—for this purpose it has seemed fit to maintain a Sultan in Constantinople.

"The same principle implies that Turkey will include, together with the countries inhabited mainly by Moslems, the economic outlets without which she could not thrive.

"In such a Turkey France, whose traditional prestige has been enhanced by victory, will be able to exercise the influence she is entitled to by the important moral and economic interests she owns in Turkey.

"This idea is quite consistent with an indispensable clause—the war has proved it—viz., the freedom of the Straits, which must necessarily be safeguarded by an international organisation. It is also consistent with the respect of nationalities, in conformity with which some compact ethnic groups who could not possibly develop under Turkish sovereignty will become independent, and other guarantees will be given for the protection of minorities.

"We have in Turkey commercial and financial interests of the first order. We do not intend that any of them should be belittled; we want them to develop safely and fully in the future. We shall see to it especially that the war expenditures of Turkey shall not curtail the previous rights of French creditors.

"In the districts where France owns special interests, these interests must be acknowledged and guaranteed. It goes without saying that the Government intends to base its claims on the agreements already concluded with the Allies."

At the sitting of March 27, after a speech in which M. Bellet asked that the Eastern question should be definitely settled by putting an end to Turkish sovereignty in Europe and Asia Minor, M. P. Lenail revealed that the Emir Feisal received two million francs a month from the English Government and as much from the French Government; he wondered why he was considered such an important man, and demanded the execution of the 1916 agreements, which gave us a free hand in Cilicia, Syria, and the Lebanon. Then M. Briand, who had concluded these agreements, rose to say:

"It is time we should have a policy in Syria and Cilicia. If we are not there, who will be there? The 1916 agreements were inspired, not only by the wish of safeguarding the great interests of France and maintaining her influence in the Mediterranean, but also because the best qualified representatives of the peoples of those countries, who groaned under the Turkish yoke, entreated us not to forsake them. And it is under these circumstances that in the middle of the war, urging that a long-sighted policy always proves the best, we insisted on the settlement of these questions.

"Thus were Syria and Cilicia, with Mosul and Damascus, of course, included in the French zone.

"Shall we always pursue a merely sentimental policy in those countries?

"If we wanted Mosul, it is on account of its oil-bearing lands; and who shall deny that we need our share of the petroleum of the world?

"As for Cilicia, a wonderfully rich land, if we are not there to-morrow, who will take our place? Cilicia has cotton, and many other kinds of wealth; when we shall see other States in our place, then shall we realise what we have lost, but it will be too late!

"It has been said that it will be difficult for us to settle there. As a matter of fact, the difficulties which are foreseen look greater than they are really; and some of these difficulties may have been put forward to dissuade us from going there.

"It remains that the 1916 agreements are signed; they are based on our time-honoured rights, our efforts, our friendships, and the summons of the peoples that hold out their arms to us. The question is whether they shall be countersigned by facts.

"The name of the Emir Feisal has been put forward. It is in our zone he has set up his dominion; why were we not among the populations of that country at the time? If we had been there, the Emir Feisal would have received his investiture from us by our authority; instead of that, he was chosen by others. Who is to be blamed for it?

"Britain knows the power of parliaments of free peoples; if our Parliament makes it clear that it really wants written treaties to be respected, they will be respected."

Mr. Wilson had been asked by a note addressed to him on March 12, 1920, to state his opinion about the draft of the Turkish settlement worked out in London, and at the same time to appoint a plenipotentiary to play a part in the final settlement. His answer was handed to M. Jusserand, French ambassador, on March 24; he came to the conclusion finally that Turkey should come to an end as a European Power.

In this note President Wilson declared that though he fully valued the arguments set forward for retaining the Turks in Constantinople, yet he thought that the arguments against the Turks, based on unimpeachable considerations, were far superior to the others. Moreover, he recalled that the Allies had many a time declared that Turkish sovereignty in Europe was an anomalous thing that should come to an end.

Concerning the southern frontiers to be assigned to Turkey, he thought they should follow the ethnographic boundaries of the Arabian populations, unless it were necessary to alter them slightly; in which case the American Government would be pleased—though that did not imply any criticism—to be told for what reasons new frontiers had been proposed.

Mr. Wilson was pleased to see that Russia would one day be allowed to be represented in the International Council that was going to be instituted for the government of Constantinople and the Straits, as he felt sure that any arrangement would be stillborn that did not recognise what he thought was a vital interest to Russia. For the same reason he was pleased that the condition of the Straits in wartime had not yet been settled, and was still under discussion; he thought no decision should be taken without Russia giving her consent.

Turning to the territorial question, he said:

"In regard to Thrace, it seems fair that the part of Eastern Thrace that is beyond the Constantinople area should belong to Greece, with the exception of the northern part of this province; for the latter region has undoubtedly a Bulgarian population, and so, for the sake of justice and equity, the towns of Adrianople and Kirk Kilisse, together with their surrounding areas, must be given to Bulgaria. Not only are the arguments set forth by Bulgaria quite sound from an ethnic and historical point of view, but her claims on this territory seem to deserve all the more consideration as she had to cede some wholly Bulgarian territories inhabited by thousands of Bulgarians on her western frontier merely that Serbia might have a good strategic frontier."

He was chiefly anxious about the future of Armenia. He demanded for her an outlet to the sea, and the possession of Trebizond. He went on thus:

"With regard to the question whether Turkey should give up her rights over Mesopotamia, Arabia, Palestine, Syria, and the Islands, the American Government recommends the method resorted to in the case of Austria—namely, that Turkey should place these provinces in the hands of the Great Powers, who would decide on their fate.

"As to Smyrna, this Government does not feel qualified to express an opinion, for the question is too important to be solved with the limited information possessed by the Government."

Finally, the President declared he did not think it necessary for his ambassador to be present at the sittings of the Supreme Council; yet he insisted on being informed of the resolutions that would be taken.

The *Philadelphia Ledger*, when this note was sent, commented on Mr. Wilson's opinion as to the Turkish problem, and especially the fate of Constantinople, and did not disguise the fact that he favoured the handing over of Constantinople to Russia, in accordance with the inter-Allied agreements of 1915, 1916, and 1917.

"Mr. Wilson wants Turkey to be expelled from Europe, and the right for democratic Russia to have an outlet to the Mediterranean to be recognised. Thus, to a certain extent, Mr. Wilson will decide in favour of the fulfilment of the secret promises made by the Allies to Russia in the course of the war.

"Mr. Wilson's opinion is that Bolshevism is about to fall, and next autumn the new Russia that he has constantly longed for and encouraged will come into being. It is calculated that if America gives her support to Russia at this fateful juncture, Russia will throw herself into the arms of America, and this understanding between the two countries will be of immense importance."

After the Allies had occupied Constantinople and addressed to the Porte a new collective note requesting the Ministry officially to disown the Nationalist movement, affairs were very difficult for some time. As the Allies thought the Ottoman Cabinet's answer to their note was unsatisfactory, the first dragomans of the English, French, and Italian commissioners on the afternoon of April 1 again called upon the Ottoman Premier.

Owing to the unconciliatory attitude of the English, who made it impossible for it to govern the country, the Ministry resigned. The English required that the new Cabinet should be constituted by Damad Ferid Pasha, on whom they knew they could rely.

Indeed, a secret agreement had already been concluded, on September 12, 1919, between Mr. Fraster, Mr. Nolan, and Mr. Churchill, on behalf of Great Britain, and Damad Ferid Pasha on behalf of the Imperial Ottoman Government. The existence of this agreement was questioned at the time, and was even officially denied in the *Stambul Journal*, April 8, 1920, but most likely there was an exchange of signatures between them. According to this agreement,[28] the Sultan practically acquiesced in the control of Great Britain over Turkey within the limits fixed by Great Britain herself. Constantinople remained the seat of the Caliphate, but the Straits were to be under British control. The Sultan was to use his spiritual and moral power as Caliph on behalf of Great Britain, to support British rule in Syria, Mesopotamia, and the other zones of British influence, not to object to the creation of an independent Kurdistan, and to renounce his rights over Egypt and Cyprus.

Damad Ferid agreed to do so, with the co-operation of the party of the Liberal Entente. If the information given by the Press is reliable, it seems that the composition of the new Cabinet was endangered at the last moment through the opposition of one of the Allied Powers; yet it was constituted at last.

The members of the new Cabinet, headed by Damad Ferid Pasha, who was both Grand Vizier and Foreign Minister, were: Abdullah Effendi, Sheik-ul-Islam; Reshid Bey, an energetic man, an opponent of the Union and Progress Committee, who was Minister of the Interior; and Mehmed Said Pasha, who became Minister of Marine and provisionally Minister of War. The last-named Ministry had been offered to Mahmoud Mukhtar Pasha, son of the famous Ghazi Mukhtar, who broke off with the Committee of Union and Progress in 1912, was dismissed from the army in 1914 by Enver, and was ambassador at Berlin during the first three years of the war; but he refused this post, and also handed in his resignation as a member of the Paris delegation; so the Grand Vizier became War Minister too. The Minister for Public Education was Fakhr ed Din Bey, one of the plenipotentiaries sent to Ouchy to negotiate the peace with Italy. Dr. Jemil Pasha, who had once been prefect of Constantinople, became Minister of Public Works, and Remze Pasha Minister of Commerce.

The investiture of the new Cabinet took place on Monday, April 5, in the afternoon, with the usual ceremonies. The Imperial rescript ran as follows:

"After the resignation of your predecessor, Salih Pasha, considering your great abilities and worth, we hereby entrust to you the Grand Vizierate, and appoint Duri Zade Abdullah Bey Sheik-ul-Islam.

"The disturbances that have been lately fomented, under the name of nationalism, are endangering our political situation, which ever since the armistice had been gradually improving.

"The peaceful measures hitherto taken against this movement have proved useless. Considering the recent events and the persistence of this state of rebellion, which may give rise to the worst evils, it is now our deliberate wish that all those who have organised and still support these disturbances shall be dealt with according to the rigour of the law; but, on the other hand, we want a free pardon to be granted to all those who, having been led astray, have joined and shared in the rebellion. Let quick and energetic measures be taken in order to restore order and security throughout our Empire, and strengthen the feelings of loyalty undoubtedly prevailing among all our faithful subjects to the Khilafat and the throne.

"It is also our earnest desire that you should endeavour to establish trustful and sincere relations with the Great Allied Powers, and to defend the interests of the State and the nation, founding them on the principles of righteousness and justice. Do your utmost to obtain more lenient conditions of peace, to bring about a speedy conclusion of peace, and to alleviate the public distress by resorting to all adequate financial and economic measures."

The Sheik-ul-Islam in a proclamation to the Turkish people denounced the promoters and instigators of the Nationalist movement, and called upon all Moslems to gather round the Sultan against the "rebels."

The Grand Vizier issued an Imperial decree condemning the Nationalist movement, pointing out to Mustafa Kemal the great dangers the country ran on account of his conduct, wishing for the restoration of friendly relations between Turkey and the Allies, and warning the leaders of the movement that harsh measures would be taken against them. The Ottoman Government, in a proclamation to the population—which had no effect, for most of the Turks thought it was dictated by foreign Powers—denounced all the leaders and supporters of the Nationalist movement as guilty of high treason against the nation. The proclamation stated:

"The Government, though eager to avoid bloodshed, is still more eager to save the nation, which is running into great danger. So it will not hesitate to resort to strict measures against those who might refuse to go back to their duty according to the high prescriptions of the Sherif, as is ordered by the Imperial rescript.

"With this view, the Government proclaims:

"First, anyone who, without realising the gravity of his act, has allowed himself to be driven by the threats or misleading instigations of the ringleaders, and has joined the insurrectionist movement, gives tokens of repentance within a week and declares his loyalty to the Sovereign, shall enjoy the benefit of the Imperial pardon.

"Secondly, all the leaders and instigators of the movements, together with whosoever shall continue to support them, shall be punished according to the law and the Sherif's orders.

"Lastly, the Government cannot in any way allow any act of cruelty or misdemeanour to be committed in any part of the Empire either by the Moslem population against other elements, or by non-Moslem subjects against the Moslem population. So it proclaims that whosoever shall commit such acts, or countenance them, or be party to them, shall be severely punished individually."

A Parliamentary commission set off to Anatolia in order to call upon Mustafa Kemal to give up his hostility to the Entente and lay down arms with the least delay.

Moreover, the Government decided to send some delegates in order to make inquiries and point out to the leaders of the Nationalist movement the dangerous consequences of their stubbornness and open rebellion.

The first delegation was to include an aide-de-camp of the War Minister, and an Allied superior officer. Another delegation was to consist of members of Parliament, among whom were Youssouf Kemal Bey, member for Sivas; Vehbi Bey, member for Karassi; Abdulla Azmi Bey, member for Kutahia; and Riza Nuri, member for Sinope, the very man who had brought in a motion against the occupation of Constantinople and the arrest of some members of the Ottoman Parliament, and who was credited with having said: "Anatolia has a false conception of the occupation of Constantinople. We are going to give clear explanations of the seriousness of the situation in order to avoid disastrous consequences. We are going to tell Anatolia the ideas of the Government about the interests of the nation."

An Imperial decree prescribed the dissolution of the Chamber, and the members before whom it was read left the Chamber quietly.

But it was obvious that the Damad Ferid Pasha Cabinet no longer represented the country, and that in the mind of most Turks it could no longer express or uphold the free will of the Turkish people, whose hidden or open sympathies, in view of the foreigner's threat, were given to the Nationalist movement.

It must be owned that the Turkish Nationalist movement had at the outset co-operated with some questionable elements and had been mixed up with the intrigues of the former members of the Committee of Union and Progress. But it now became impossible, in order to belittle it, to look down upon it as a mere plot or insurrectionary movement. In consequence of the successive events that had taken place since the armistice and of the attitude of the Allies, especially England, after the occupation of Constantinople, carried out under British pressure with the approbation of the French Government notwithstanding the protest of the French Press, and in view of the provisions that were likely to be included in the Peace Treaty, Turkish patriotism, which could not allow Turkey to be destroyed and meant to maintain her traditional rights, had tacitly joined that movement. Besides,

Mustafa Kemal, who, at the very outset, had been a member of the Committee of Union and Progress, had soon disagreed with Enver, and it should be borne in mind that he was his enemy during the greater part of the war, as he was an opponent of the German Marshal Falkenhayn. Some people have tried to make out there was only personal enmity between them, and have denied the possibility of political opposition; but the very fact that their enmity would have ruined any common political designs they might have had proves there were no such designs.

So Mustafa Kemal did not seem greatly moved by the measures mentioned in the manifesto issued by the Government under pressure of the foreign occupation and amidst the perturbation caused by recent events.

At the end of March Mustafa Kemal warned the Sultan that, in consequence of the occupation of Constantinople, he broke off all connection with the central Government, which henceforth was quite under foreign control. In a proclamation issued to the Mussulmans, he declared it was necessary to form a new independent Ottoman State in Anatolia and to appoint an assistant Sheik-ul-Islam. The reason he gave was that the Sultan could no longer be looked upon as Caliph, for it is a fundamental principle of Islam that the Caliph must be an independent Sovereign, and, since the Allied occupation of Constantinople, he no longer enjoyed his freedom of action. In that appeal, which was not intended for the Mussulmans of Algeria, Tunis, Morocco, and Tripoli, for it seemed to be aimed at Great Britain alone, he regarded the occupation of Constantinople as a new crusade against Islam.

According to news from Nationalist sources, Mustafa Kemal formed a Cabinet, in which he was War Minister of the new Anatolian Government.

It was said at the time he had proclaimed Viceroy of Anatolia and nahib—*i.e.*, the Sultan's representative in Anatolia—Prince Jemal ed Din, a member of the Imperial Family, son of the late Prince Shevket Effendi, and general inspector of the recruiting service; but the official circles of Constantinople never believed that the prince had allowed him to use his name.

At the same time he had a Constituent Assembly elected, which he intended to convene at Angora. This assembly consisted of the members of Parliament who had been able to escape from Constantinople and of deputies chosen by delegated electors and met on April 23 at Angora, where all sorts of people had come from quite different regions: Constantinople, Marash, Beyrut, Baghdad, etc. The National Assembly of Angora meant to be looked upon as a Constituent Assembly, and strove to introduce wide reforms into the administrative and financial organisation of the Empire. It elected a rather large committee, which styled itself the Government Council, and it included General Mustafa Kemal, Jemal ed Din Chelebi, from Konia, as first Vice-President, and Jelal ed Din Arif Bey as second Vice-President, etc.

The members of the Government which was instituted at Angora when the Great National Assembly met in this town were: General Mustafa Kemal Pasha, President; Bekir Samy Bey, Foreign Affairs; Jamy Bey, Interior; General Feizi Pasha, National Defence; General Ismail Fazil Pasha, Public Works; Youssouf Kemal Bey, National Economy; Hakki Behij Bey, Finance; Dr. Adnan Bey, Public Education; Colonel Ismet Bey, Chief of Staff.

The Sheik of the Senussi, who had joined the National movement, and owing to his prestige had influenced public opinion in favour of this movement, was not appointed, as has been wrongly said, Sheik-ul-Islam; religious affairs were entrusted to a member of a Muslim brotherhood belonging to the National Assembly.

According to the information it was possible to obtain, the political line of conduct adopted by the Nationalists was not only to organise armed resistance, but also to carry on a strong political and religious propaganda, both in Turkey and in foreign countries.

No official letter from Constantinople was to be opened by the functionaries, who, if they obeyed the Constantinople Government, were liable to capital punishment. The religious authorities in the provinces and the heads of the great Muslim brotherhoods were called upon to protest against the *fetva* by which the Sheik-ul-Islam of Constantinople had anathematised the Nationalists.

But the chief difficulty for the Nationalists was how to raise money.

On behalf of that National Assembly, Mustafa Kemal addressed to M. Millerand the following letter, in which he vehemently protested against the occupation of Constantinople and laid down the claims of the Ottoman people:

"I beg to bring to the knowledge of Your Excellency that, owing to the unjustifiable occupation of Constantinople by the Allied troops, the Ottoman people looks upon its Khalifa, together with his Government, as prisoners. So general elections have been held, and on April 23, 1920, the Grand National Assembly held its first sitting, and solemnly declared it would preside over the present and future destiny of Turkey, so long as her Khalifa Sultan and her Eternal City should remain under the dominion and occupation of foreigners.

"The Grand National Assembly has done me the honour to charge me to bring to the knowledge of Your Excellency the earnest protest of its members against that arbitrary deed, which violates the terms of the armistice, and has once more confirmed the Ottoman people in its pessimism as to the results of the Peace Conference. Not long ago our Parliament—

though a Parliament has always been looked upon as a holy sanctuary by all civilised nations—was violated in the course of a sitting; the representatives of the nation were wrested from the bosom of the assembly by the English police like evildoers, notwithstanding the energetic protest of the Parliament; many a senator, deputy, general, or man of letters, was arrested at his home, taken away handcuffed, and deported; lastly, our public and private buildings were occupied by force of arms, for might had become right.

"Now the Ottoman people, considering all its rights have been violated and its sovereignty encroached upon, has, by order of its representatives, assembled at Angora, and appointed an Executive Council chosen among the members of the National Assembly, which Council has taken in hand the government of the country.

"I have also the honour to let Your Excellency know the desiderata of the nation, as expressed and adopted at the sitting of April 29, 1920.

"First, Constantinople, the seat of the Khilafat and Sultanry, together with the Constantinople Government, are henceforth looked upon by the Ottoman people as prisoners of the Allies; thus all orders and *fetvas* issued from Constantinople, so long as it is occupied, cannot have any legal or religious value, and all engagements entered upon by the would-be Constantinople Government are looked upon by the nation as null and void.

"Secondly, the Ottoman people, though maintaining its calm and composure, is bent upon defending its sacred, centuries-old rights as a free, independent State. It expresses its wish to conclude a fair, honourable peace, but declares only its own mandatories have the right to take engagements in its name and on its account.

"Thirdly, the Christian Ottoman element, together with the foreign elements settled in Turkey, remain under the safeguard of the nation; yet they are forbidden to undertake anything against the general security of the country.

"Hoping the righteous claims of the Ottoman nation will meet with a favourable reception, I beg Your Excellency to accept the assurance of the deep respect with which I have the honour to be Your Excellency's most humble, most obedient servant."

On the eve of the San Remo Conference, which met on April 18, 1920, Ahmed Riza Bey, ex-President of the Chamber and Senator of the Ottoman Empire, who kept a keen lookout on the events that were about to seal the fate of his country, though he had been exiled by the Damad Ferid Ministry, addressed another letter to the President of the Conference, in which he said;

"The Turks cannot in any way, in this age of liberty and democracy, acknowledge a peace that would lower them to the level of an inferior race and would treat them worse than the Hungarians or Bulgarians, who have lost comparatively small territories, whereas Turkey is to be utterly crippled. We want to be treated as a vanquished people, not as an inferior people or a people in tutelage. The victors may have a right to take from us the territories they conquered by force of arms; they have no right to intrude into our home affairs. The Turkish people will willingly grant concessions of mines and public works to the foreigners who offer it the most profitable conditions; but it will never allow the arbitrary partition of the wealth of the nation. To get riches at the expense of an unfortunate nation is immoral; it is all the more unfair as the responsibility of Turkey in the world war is comparatively slight as compared with that of Austria-Germany and Bulgaria. In respect of the crimes and atrocities against Armenia and Greece which the Turks are charged with, we deny them earnestly and indignantly. Let a mixed international commission be formed, and sent to hold an impartial inquiry on the spot, and we pledge ourselves to submit to its decisions. Till such an inquiry has proved anything to the contrary, we have a right to look upon all charges brought against us as slanders or mere lies.

"The Sublime Porte had already, on February 12, 1919, addressed to the High Commissioners an official note requesting that neutral States should appoint delegates charged to inquire into facts and establish responsibilities; but the request of the Ottoman Cabinet has hitherto been in vain, as well as that of the League for National Ottoman Unity made on March 17 of the same year.

"Yet the report of the international Commission of Inquiry assembled at Smyrna, which proved the charges of cruelty brought against the Turks were unfounded, should induce the Allies, in the name of justice, to hold an inquiry into the massacres supposed to have taken place in Cilicia and elsewhere.

"I hope Your Excellency will excuse me if this letter is not couched in the usual diplomatic style, and will consider that when the life and rights of his nation are so grievously endangered it is most difficult for a patriot to keep his thoughts and feelings under control."

As early as April 19, the San Remo Conference, which seemed to have come to an agreement about the main lines of the treaty to be submitted to Turkey, but had not yet settled the terms of this treaty, decided to summon the Ottoman plenipotentiaries to Paris on May 10.

In a note sent on April 20, 1920, to M. Nitti, as president of the San Remo Conference, Ghalib Kemaly Bey, formerly Ottoman minister plenipotentiary to Russia, now living in Rome, wrote:

"In order to justify the dismemberment of the Ottoman Empire it has been asserted that the Turks are not able to administer a large country inhabited by various races, and they have been especially charged with hating and oppressing the Christian element. But a history extending over ten centuries at least plainly shows, by innumerable facts and truths, the absurdity of such assertions.

"If the Ottoman Empire, in spite of its wonderful efforts for the last 130 years, has not been able to reform and renovate itself as the other States have done, that is because, in addition to a thousand other difficulties, it has never had, for the last two centuries, either the power or the peacefulness that would have been necessary to bring such a protracted task to a successful end; for every ten, fifteen, or twenty years, it has been attacked by its neighbours, and the events of the last twelve years testify still more forcibly than any others to the fact that any step taken by the Turks on the way to progress—in the European sense of the word—was not only resented, but even violently opposed by their merciless enemies.

"As to the would-be oppression which the Christians are supposed to have endured in the Empire, let us merely consider that, whereas in Europe the Christians mutually slaughtered each other mercilessly and unceasingly in the name of their sacred Faith, and the unfortunate Jews were cruelly driven away and tortured in the name of the same Faith, the Turks, on the contrary, after ruling for a thousand years over Turkish Asia with many vicissitudes, not only tolerated the presence of millions of Christians in their large, powerful Empire, but even granted them without any restriction, under the benefit of Turkish laws and customs, all possibilities to subsist, develop, and become rich, often at the expense of the ruling race; and they offered a wide paternal hospitality to many wretched people banished from Christian Europe.

"To-day Greece, trampling upon justice and right, lays an iniquitous claim to the noble, sacred land of Turkish Thrace and Asia. Yet can she show the same example of tolerance, and give a strict account of her home policy towards the non-Greek elements, especially concerning the condition and fate of the 300,000 Turks who, before 1883, peopled the wide, fertile plains of Thessaly, of the hundreds of thousands of Moslem Albanians, subjects of the Empire, of the 150,000 Moslems in Crete, and of the 800,000 Moslems in Macedonia, whose unfortunate fate it was to pass under her dominion?

"I need not dwell at length on this painful subject, which will be an eternal shame to modern civilisation, for the victorious Powers know a great deal more—after the inter-Allied inquiry held four months ago in Smyrna—about the 'gentle and fatherly' manner in which thousands of Mussulmans were slaughtered and exterminated by the descendants of the civilisation of ancient

Greece, who invaded that essentially Turkish province during the armistice under pretence of restoring order."

And after recalling the figures of the various elements of the population of the Turkish Empire after the 1914 statistics, he concluded:

"Such figures speak but too eloquently, and the painful events that drenched with blood the unfortunate Ottoman land since the armistice raise only too much horror. So the Turkish people most proudly and serenely awaits the righteous, humane, and equitable sanction of the victorious Powers that have assumed before history the heavy responsibility of placing the whole world on a lasting basis of justice, concord, and peace.

"God grant they may choose the best way, the only way, that will lead them to respect, as they solemnly pledged themselves to do, the ethnic, historical, and religious rights of the Ottoman nation and its Sultan, who is, at the same time, the supreme head of the 350 million Mussulmans throughout the world."

On the same date (April 20, 1920) the Indian Caliphate delegation addressed a note to the president of the Allied Supreme Council at San Remo, to the English, French, Italian Prime Ministers, and to the Japanese ambassador. In this note they summed up their mandate with the Allied and Associated Powers, and insisted again on the claims they had previously laid before Mr. Lloyd George in the course of the interview mentioned previously.

"Firstly, the Mussulmans of India, in common with the vast majority of their co-religionists throughout the world, ask that, inasmuch as independent temporal sovereignty, with its concomitants of adequate military and economic resources, is of the essence of the institution of the Khilafat, the Empire of the Khalifa shall not be dismembered under any pretext. As the Sultan of Turkey is recognised by the vast majority of Mussulmans as Khalifa, what is desired is that the fabric of the Ottoman Empire shall be maintained intact territorially on the basis of the *status quo ante bellum*, but without prejudice to such political changes as give all necessary guarantees consistent with the dignity and independence of the sovereign State for the security of life and property, and opportunities of full autonomous development for all the non-Turkish communities, whether Muslim or non-Muslim, comprised within the Turkish Empire. But on no account is a Muslim majority to be placed under the rule of a non-Muslim minority contrary to the principle of self-determination. In behalf of this claim, the delegation draw the attention of the Supreme Council to the declaration of the British Prime Minister, equally binding on all the Allied and Associated Powers, when on January 5, 1918, he said: 'Nor are we fighting to deprive Turkey of its capital, or of the rich and renowned lands of Asia Minor and Thrace, which are predominantly Turkish in race,' and to President Wilson's twelfth point in his message to Congress, dated January 8, 1918, on the basis of which the armistice with Turkey was concluded, and which required 'that the Turkish portions of the present Ottoman Empire should be assured of secure sovereignty; that the other nationalities now under Turkish rule should be assured security of life and autonomous development.' The delegation submit that any departure from the pledges and principles set forth above would be regarded by the people of India, and the Muslim world generally, as a breach of faith. It was on the strength of these and similar assurances that tens of thousands of India Mussulmans were induced to lay down their lives in the late war in defence of the Allied cause.

"Secondly, we have to submit that the most solemn religious obligations of the Muslim Faith require that the area known as the Jazirat-ul-Arab, or the 'Island of Arabia,' which includes, besides the Peninsula of Arabia, Syria, Palestine, and Mesopotamia, shall continue to be, as heretofore for the last 1,300 years, under exclusively Muslim control, and that the Khalifa shall similarly continue to be the Warden and Custodian of the Holy Places and Holy Shrines of Islam—namely, Mecca, Medina, Jerusalem, Nejef, Kerbela, Samarra, Kazimain, and Baghdad, all situated within the Jazirat-ul-Arab.

Any encroachment upon these sanctuaries of Islam by the inauguration of non-Muslim control in whatever guise or form, whether a protectorate or mandate, would be a direct violation of the most binding religious injunctions of Islam and the deepest sentiment of Muslims all the world over, and would, therefore, be utterly unacceptable to the Mussulmans of India and the rest of the Indian community. In this connection, apart from the religious obligations to which we refer, the delegation would draw the attention of the Supreme Council to the proclamation issued by the Government of India, on behalf of His Britannic Majesty's Government, as also the Governments of France and Russia, on November 2, 1914, in which it was specifically declared that 'no question of a religious character was involved' in this war, and it was further categorically promised that 'the Holy Places of Arabia, including the Holy Shrines of Mesopotamia and the port of Jedda, will be immune from attack or molestation.'"

After pointing out that these were the lowest possible claims the Mussulmans could set forth, the note went on as follows:

"But the Mussulmans of India have already submitted to the British Government that a Turkish settlement made in disregard of their religious obligations, on respect for which their loyalty has always been strictly conditional, would be regarded by Indian Mussulmans as incompatible with their allegiance to the British Crown. This is a contingency which the Mussulmans of India, in common with all their compatriots, constituting a population of over three hundred millions, naturally view with the keenest apprehension and anxiety, and are most earnestly desirous of preventing by every means in their power. We believe that the British Government, at any rate, is fully apprised of the range and intensity of public feeling that has been aroused in India on this question, and we content ourselves, therefore, by simply stating here that the Khilafat movement represents an unprecedented demonstration of national feeling and concern. Only on March 19 last, the day when the delegation was received by the British Prime Minister, all business was suspended throughout the continent of India by Mussulmans and Hindus alike, as a reminder and reaffirmation of the Muslim case in respect of the future of the Khilafat. This unprecedented yet peaceful demonstration involved a loss of millions to the public at large, and was undertaken solely with the object of impressing the authorities and others concerned with the universality of Indian and Muslim sentiment on the question. If, notwithstanding all constitutional and loyal representations which the Mussulmans of India have put forward on behalf of the obligation imposed upon them by their Faith, a settlement is imposed upon Turkey which would be destructive of the very essentials of the Khilafat, a situation would arise in which it would be futile to expect peace and harmony to prevail in India and the Muslim world.

"The delegation, therefore, feel it their duty most solemnly to urge upon the Supreme Council the desirability of endeavouring to achieve a peace settlement with the Ottoman Empire which would be in consonance with the most binding religious obligations and overwhelming sentiments of so large and important a section of the world community."

As a consequence of what has just been said:

"The delegation would beg, even at this late hour, that the Supreme Council will defer taking any final decisions on this question in order to afford to them an opportunity, such as they have repeatedly applied for, of laying their case before the Council. In answer to our request to be allowed to appear before the Supreme Council, the British Secretary to the Council intimated to us that only the accredited Governments of the territories with whose future the Peace Conference is dealing are allowed to appear before it, and that at the request of the British Government the official delegation of India had already been heard. But we have already represented that the Turkish settlement, involving as it does the question on the Khilafat, in the preservation of which the Mussulmans of the world are so vitally interested, does not obviously seem to be a question on which the Peace Conference should hear only the Governments of territories with whose future they are dealing. In fact, the concern of the Muslim world for the future of the Khilafat, which is the most essential institution of Islam, transcends in importance the interests of the various Governments that are being set up in different parts of the Khilafat territories; and the delegation trusts that no technical objection will be allowed to stand in the way of doing justice and securing peace."

And, finally, the note concluded:

"With reference to the official delegation of India, which the Supreme Council has already heard, the Indian Khilafat delegation would invite the attention of the Council to the fact that, so far at least, the State and the nation are not one in India, and the delegation submit that a nation numbering more than 315 millions of people is entitled to a hearing before a final decision is taken on a question that has incontestably acquired a national status. The delegation hope that they may, without may disrespect to the members comprising the official delegation of India, also refer to the fact that no Indian Mussulman was represented on the delegation in spite of Muslim protest."

In a second telegram, dated April 24, 1920, the Indian Caliphate delegation, after the reply made to them by the British secretary of the Supreme Council at San Remo on April 20, expressed their deep regret that—

"the Council, while giving a hearing to a number of delegations representing at best microscopic populations inhabiting meagre areas and permitting the Premier of Greece, which was not at war with Turkey, to take part in the discussions relating to the Turkish settlement, should have ignored the claims of a nation numbering more than 315 millions of people inhabiting the vast sub-continent of India even to a hearing, and should have denied the right of several hundred millions more in the rest of the world professing the Muslim Faith to express their views on the question involving the disintegration of the Khilafat. In the name of our compatriots and co-religionists, we deem it to be our duty once more to point out to the Government of Great Britain and to her Allies, that it would be perfectly futile to expect peace and tranquillity if, to the humiliating disregard of the overwhelming national sentiment of India, which would in any case lessen the value of citizenship of the British Empire to the Indian people, is added, as a result of the secret diplomacy of a few persons, however exalted and eminent, who are now settling the fate of Islam behind closed doors, a contemptuous disregard of the most binding and solemn religious obligations imposed on the Muslims by their Faith."

The delegation did not conceal their disappointment at the way they had been received by the Allied representatives and the little attention paid to the objections they had set forth. Yet they had viewed the Ottoman question from a lofty standpoint, and had brought forward powerful arguments in favour of Turkey. While the Indian delegation were setting forth the Turkish claims before the Peace Conference, the Press, public opinion, and political circles which had been influenced in some degree by the coming of the delegates evinced more sympathy for Turkey, and the deliberations of the Conference seemed likely to assume a more favourable attitude towards Turkey. Yet the Conference, in this case as in many others, and in spite of the warnings it had received, kept to its first resolutions, though everything seemed to invite it to modify them.

On May 6 the Ottoman delegation arrived in Paris. It comprised the former Grand Vizier Tewfik Pasha; Reshid Bey, Minister of the Interior; Fakhr ed Din Bey, Minister of Public Education; and Dr. Jemil Pasha, Minister of Public Works, accompanied by seventeen advisers and five secretaries.

On the previous Thursday, before they left Constantinople, the Sultan had received the delegates, and had a long conversation with each of them.

The draft of the treaty was handed to the delegates on the expected date, May 11.

We refer the reader to this document, which contains thirteen chapters; some of the most important provisions are so laboriously worded that they may give rise to various interpretations, and it is impossible to sum them up accurately.

Several clauses of that draft called forth many objections, and we shall only deal with the most important ones.

The treaty assigned to Greece all the Turkish vilayet of Adrianople or Eastern Thrace—that is to say, the territory which includes Adrianople, the second town and former capital of the Ottoman Empire, and the burial-place of Selim the Conqueror. It only left to European Turkey a mere strip of land near Constantinople up to the Chatalja lines. Besides, this region is entirely included in the "Zone of the Straits" to be controlled by a Commission of the Powers which includes Greece, Rumania, and Bulgaria, but excludes Turkey herself.

Now, according to the official census of March, 1914, the Adrianople vilayet which includes Kirk Kilisse, Rodosto, and Gallipoli, had a population of 360,400 Turks—*i.e.*, 57 per cent. of the inhabitants—as against 224,680 Greeks, or 35·5 per cent., and 19,888 Armenians. In addition, though in Eastern Thrace the Moslem populations are mingled with numerous Greek elements, the majority of the people are Mussulmans. Out of the 673,000 inhabitants of Thrace, 455,000 are Mussulmans.

It is noteworthy that after 1914 a good number of the Greeks in that vilayet emigrated into Macedonia, where they were replaced by the Mussulmans expelled by the Greek administration, and that out of the 162,000 Orthodox Greeks amenable to the Greek Patriarch, 88,000 are Gagavous—that is to say, are of Turkish descent and speak Turkish.

Out of about 4,700,000 acres of land which make up the total area of the Adrianople vilayet, 4,000,000 acres, or 84 per cent., are in Moslem hands, and the Orthodox Greeks hardly possess 600,000 acres.

The Moslem population of Western Thrace, which is no longer under Turkish sovereignty, rises to 362,000 souls, or 69 per cent., against 86,000 Greeks, or 16·5 per cent., and if the figures representing the Moslem population in both parts of Thrace are counted, we get a total number of 700,000 Mussulmans—*i.e.*, 62·6 per cent.—against 310,000 Greeks, or 26 per cent.

Mr. Lloyd George had already guaranteed to Turkey the possession of that region on January 5, 1918, when he had solemnly declared: "Nor are we fighting to deprive Turkey of its capital, or of the rich and renowned lands of Asia Minor and Thrace, which are predominantly Turkish in race," and he had repeated this pledge in his speech of February 25, 1920.

Yet a month after he declared to the Indian Caliphate delegation, as has been seen above, that the Turkish population in Thrace was in a considerable minority, and so Thrace should be taken away from Turkish rule. If such was the case, it would have been logical to take from Turkey the whole of Thrace.

As the Indian delegation inquired at once on what figures the Prime Minister based his Statements he answered:

"It is, of course, impossible to obtain absolutely accurate figures at the present moment, partly because all censuses taken since about the beginning of the century are open to suspicion from racial prejudice, and partly because of the policy of expulsion and deportation pursued by the Turkish Government both during and before the war. For instance, apart from the Greeks who were evicted during the Balkan wars, over 100,000 Greeks were deported into Anatolia from Turkish Thrace in the course of these wars, while about 100,000 were driven across the frontiers of Turkish Thrace. These refugees are now returning in large numbers. But after the study of all the evidence judged impartially, the best estimate which the Foreign Office could make is that the population of Turkish Thrace, in 1919, was 313,000 Greeks and 225,000 Turks.... This is confirmed by the study of the Turkish official statistics in 1894, the last census taken before the Greco-Turkish war, after which ... all censuses as to races in these parts became open to suspicion. According to these statistics, the population of Turkish Thrace and of the part of Bulgarian Thrace ceded to the Allies by the treaty of Neuilly was: Greeks, 304,500: Mussulmans, 265,300; Bulgarians, 72,500."

On receipt of this communication, the delegation naturally asked to what region the Greeks "who were evicted during the Balkan wars" had migrated, and to what extent, according to the Foreign Office estimates, "counter-migration of Turks had taken place into what is the present Turkish Thrace," when Macedonia was made, on the authority of Englishmen themselves, "an empty egg-shell" and when the Greeks and Bulgarians had decided to leave no Turks in the occupied territories, to make a "Turkish question" within the newly extended boundaries of Greece and Bulgaria. It was natural that part of the Turkish population driven away from Macedonia should settle down in the Turkish territory conterminous to Eastern Thrace, as it actually did.

With regard to the "100,000" Greeks "deported into Anatolia from Turkish Thrace during the course of these wars," and the "100,000 driven across the frontiers of Turkish Thrace," the delegation asked to what part of Anatolia the deportees had been taken, and to what extent this deportation had affected the proportion of Turkish and Greek populations in that part of Anatolia. It would certainly be unfair to make Turkish Thrace preponderatingly Greek by including in its Greek population figures of Greek deportees who had already served to swell the figures of the Greek population in Anatolia. Under such circumstances, as the figures which the Prime Minister considered as reliable on January 5, 1918, had been discarded since and as the figures of a quarter of a century ago were evidently open to discussion, the delegation proposed that the Supreme Council should be given a complete set of figures for every vilayet, and if possible for every sanjak or kaza, of the Turkish Empire as it was in 1914. But the Prime Minister's secretary merely answered that it was impossible to enter into a discussion "on the vexed question of the population statistics in these areas."

As to Smyrna, the statistics plainly show that, though there is an important Greek colony at Smyrna, all the region nevertheless is essentially Turkish. The figures provided by the Turkish Government, those of the French Yellow Book, and those given by Vital Cuinet agree on this point.

According to the French Yellow Book, the total population of the vilayet included 78·05 per cent. Turks against 14·9 per cent. Greeks.

M. Vital Cuinet gives a total population of 1,254,417 inhabitants (971,850 Turks and 197,257 Greeks), and for the town of Smyrna 96,250 Turks against 57,000 Greeks.

According to the last Ottoman statistics in 1914 the town of Smyrna, where the Greek population had increased, had 111,486 Turks against 87,497 Greeks; but in the whole vilayet there were 299,097 Greeks—*i.e.*, 18 per cent.—against 1,249,067 Turks, or 77 per cent., and 20,766 Armenians.

From the 299,097 Greeks mentioned in the statistics we should deduct the 60,000 or 80,000 Greeks who were expelled from the vilayet, by way of reprisal after the events of Macedonia in January to June, 1914. The latter, according to the agreement between Ghalib Kemaly Bey, Turkish minister at Athens, and M. Venizelos (July, 1914), come under the same head as the Greeks of Thrace and Smyrna who were to be exchanged for the Mussulmans of Macedonia.

Mr. Lloyd George's secretary, whom the Indian delegation also asked, in reference to Smyrna, on what figures he based his statements, answered on behalf of the Prime Minister:

"The pre-war figures for the sanjak of Smyrna, according to the American estimates, which are the most up-to-date and impartial, give the following result: Greeks, 375,000; Mussulmans, 325,000; Jews, 40,000; and Armenians, 18,000. These figures only relate to the sanjak of Smyrna, and there are other kazas in the neighbourhood which also show a majority of Greeks."

Now, according to the official Turkish figures, the sanjak of Smyrna had, before the war, 377,000 Mussulmans as against 218,000 Greeks, while during the war the Muslim figure rose to 407,000 and the Greek figure was considerably reduced. Only in the kazas of Urla, Shesmeh, Phocœa, and Kara-Burun in the sanjak of Smyrna, are there Greek majorities; but in no other kaza, whether of Magnesia, Aidin, or Denizli, is the Greek element in a majority. Moreover, the Greek minority is important only in the kaza of Seuki in the sanjak of Aidin; everywhere else it is, as a rule, less than 10 per cent., and only in two kazas is it 15 or 16 per cent.

The treaty recognises Armenia as a free and independent State, and the President of the United States is to arbitrate on the question of the frontier to be fixed between Turkey and Armenia in the vilayets of Erzerum, Trebizond, Van, and Bitlis. Now, though everybody—including the Turks—acknowledges that as a principle it is legitimate to form an Armenian State, yet when we consider the nature of the population of these vilayets, we cannot help feeling anxious at the condition of things brought about by this decision.

As a matter of fact, in Erzerum there are 673,000 Mussulmans, constituting 82·5 per cent. of the population, as against 136,000 Armenians, or 16·5 per cent. In Trebizond the Mussulmans number 921,000, or 82 per cent. of the population, as against 40,000 Armenians, or 23·5 per cent. In the vilayet of Van the Muslim population is 179,000, or 69 per cent., and the Armenian population 67,000, or 26 per cent. In Bitlis the Mussulmans number 310,000, or 70·5 per cent., as against 119,000 Armenians, constituting 27 per cent. Thus, in these four vilayets the Mussulmans number 2,083,000, and the Armenians 362,000, the average being 80 per cent. against 13 per cent.

On the other hand, it is difficult to prove that Turkey has persistently colonised these territories. The only fact that might countenance such an assertion is that at various times, especially after the Crimean war, many Tatars sought shelter in that part of the Empire, and that in 1864, and again in 1878, Circassians, escaping from the Russian yoke, took refuge there after defending their country. The number of the families that immigrated is estimated about 70,000. Turkey encouraged them to settle down there all the more willingly as they were a safeguard to her against the constant threat of Russia. But as early as 1514, at the time of the Turkish conquest, the Armenians were inferior in number, owing to the Arabian and Persian pressure that repeatedly brought about an exodus of the native population northwards and westwards, and because some Persian, Arabian, Seljukian, Turkish, and Byzantine elements slowly crept into the country. In 1643 Abas Schah, after his victorious campaign against Turkey, drove away nearly 100,000 Armenians, and later on a huge number of Armenians emigrated into Russia of their own free will after the treaty of Turkmen-Tchai in 1828.

It is noteworthy that an Armenian Power first came into existence in the second century before Christ. It consisted of two independent States, Armenia Major and Armenia Minor. After the downfall of Tigrane, King of Armenia Major, defeated by the Romans, Rome and Persia fought for the possession of those regions, and, finally, divided them. Later on there were various Armenian States, which were more or less independent, but none of them lasted long except the State of Armenia Minor, which lasted from the twelfth century to the fourteenth, till Selim II conquered that territory, where the Arabs, the Persians, the Seljukian Turks, and the Byzantines had already brought the Armenian dominion to an end.

Therefore the numerical majority of Mussulmans in Armenia has not been obtained or maintained, as has been alleged, by the "Turkish massacres"; it is the outcome of more complex causes—which, of course, is no excuse for the tragic events that took place there. As the Conference did not seem to pay any attention either to the figures of M. Vital Cuinet (*Turquie d'Asie*, Paris, 1892), or to the figures published by the French Government in the Yellow Book of 1897, based upon the data furnished by the Christian Patriarchates, or to the figures given by General Zeleny to the Caucasian Geographical Society (*Zapiski*, vol. xviii., Tiflis, 1896), the Indian delegation asked that a report should be drawn up by a mixed Moslem and non-Moslem

Commission, consisting of men whose integrity and ability were recognised by their co-religionists; but this suggestion met with no better success than the international inquiry already suggested by the delegation in regard to the population of every vilayet in Thrace.

The chapter dealing with the protection of minorities plainly shows how much influence the aforesaid Protestant Anglo-American movement had on the wording of the treaty. In none of the four previous treaties are included such stipulations as those contained in the Turkish treaty, and there is a great difference in this respect between the Bulgarian treaty and the Turkish treaty. The latter, under the term "minority," only considers the condition of the Christians, and ensures to them privileges and power in every respect over the Mussulmans.

As the Permanent Committee of the Turkish Congress at Lausanne remarked in its critical examination of the treaty:

"Whereas in the Bulgarian treaty freedom of conscience and religion is guaranteed so far as is consistent with morality and order, this clause does not occur in the Turkish treaty.

The Turkish treaty states that all interference with any religious creed shall be punished in the same way; in the Bulgarian treaty this clause is omitted, for here it would imply the protection of a non-Christian religion."

In regard to Article 139, that "Turkey renounces formally all right of suzerainty or jurisdiction of any kind over Moslems who are subject to the sovereignty or protectorate of any other State," the Indian Caliphate delegation raised an objection in a letter addressed to Mr. Lloyd George, dated July 10, 1920:

"It is obvious that Turkey has, and could have, no 'rights of suzerainty or jurisdiction' over Mussulmans who am not her subjects; but it is equally obvious that the Sultan of Turkey, as Khalifa, has, and must continue to have so long as he holds that office, his very considerable 'jurisdiction' over Muslims who are 'subject to the sovereignty or protectorate of any other State.' The law of Islam clearly prescribes the character and extent of the 'jurisdiction' pertaining to the office of Khalifa, and we cannot but protest most emphatically against this indirect, but none the less palpable, attempt on the part of Great Britain and her allies to force on the Khalifa a surrender of such 'jurisdiction,' which must involve the abdication of the Khalifa."

The delegation also considered that Article 131, which lays down that "Turkey definitely renounces all rights and privileges, which, under the treaty of Lausanne of October 12, 1912, were left to the Sultan in Libya," infringes "rights pertaining to the Sultan as Caliph, which had been specially safeguarded and reserved under the said treaty of Lausanne." It also expressed its surprise that "this categorical and inalienable requirement of the Muslim Faith, supported as it is by the unbroken practice of over thirteen hundred years, was totally disregarded by Articles 94 to 97 of the Peace Treaty, read in conjunction with Articles 22 and 132," which cannot admit of any non-Muslim sovereignty over the Jazirat-ul-Arab, including Syria, Palestine, and Mesopotamia.

Referring again to the objection the British Prime Minister pretended to base on the proclamation of the Emir Feisal, King of Syria, and on the Arabs' request to be freed from Turkish dominion, the Indian Caliphate delegation in the same letter answered Mr. Lloyd George, who had asked them in the course of his reception "whether they were to remain under Turkish domination merely because they were Mohammedans":

"We would take the liberty to remind you that if the Arabs, who are an overwhelmingly large majority in these regions, have claimed independence, they have clearly claimed it free from the incubus of so-called mandates, and their claim to be freed from Turkish dominion is not in any way a claim to be subjected to the 'advice and assistance' of a mandatory of the principal Allied Powers. If the principle of self-determination is to be applied at all, it must be applied regardless of the wishes and interests of foreign Powers covetously seeking to exploit regions and peoples exposed to the danger of foreign domination on account of their unprotected character. The Arab Congresses have unequivocally declared that they want neither protectorates nor mandates nor any other form of political or economic control; and the delegation, while reiterating their view that an amicable adjustment of Arab and Turkish claims by the Muslims themselves in accordance with Islamic law is perfectly feasible, must support the Arab demand for complete freedom from the control of mandatories appointed by the Allies.

"With regard to the Hejaz, Article 98, which requires Turkey not only to recognise it as a free and independent State, but to renounce all rights and titles there, and Article 99, which makes no mention of the rights and prerogatives of the Khalifa as Servant of the Holy Places, are, and must ever be, equally unacceptable to the Muslim world."

On the other hand, as the Jewish question and the Eastern question are closely connected and have assumed still more importance owing to the

Zionist movement, the treaty forced on Turkey concerns the Jews in the highest degree.

It must be borne in mind that if Sephardic Judaism has been gradually smothered by Turkish sovereignty, the Ottoman Empire has proved most hospitable to the Jews driven away by Christian fanaticism, and that for five centuries the Jews have enjoyed both tolerance and security, and have even prospered in it. So the Jews naturally feel anxious, like the Moslems in the provinces wrested from the old Ottoman Empire, when, following the precedent of Salonika, they see Greece annex the region of Adrianople and Smyrna; and they have a right to ask whether Greece, carried away by a wild imperialism, will not yield to her nationalist feeling and revive the fanaticism of religious struggles. So the Allies, foreseeing this eventuality, have asked Greece to take no action to make the Jews regret the past; but as the Greek anti-Semitic feeling is rather economic than religious in character, it is to be feared that the competition of the two races in the commercial struggle will keep up that feeling. The annexation of Thrace would probably concern 20,000 Jews—13,000 at Adrianople, 2,000 at Rodosto, 2,800 at Gallipoli, 1,000 at Kirk Kilisse, 1,000 at Demotica, etc. Great Britain having received a mandate for Palestine—that is to say, virtually a protectorate—on the condition of establishing "a national home for the Jews"—whatever the various opinions of the Jews with regard to Zionism may be—a question is now opened and an experiment is to be tried which concerns them deeply, as it is closely connected with Judaism.

In the course of the reception by Mr. Lloyd George of the Indian Caliphate delegation, M. Mohammed Ali told the British Prime Minister in regard to the Jewish claims in Palestine:

"The delegation have no desire to cause an injustice to the Jewish community, and I think Islam can look back with justifiable pride on its treatment of this community in the past. No aspiration of the Jewish community which is reasonable can be incompatible with Muslim control of the Holy Land, and it is hoped that the Ottoman Government will easily accommodate the Jewish community in such aspirations of theirs as are reasonable.

"Some responsible propagandists of the Zionist movement, with whom I have had conversations, frankly admit: 'We do not want political sovereignty there; we want a home; the details can be arranged and discussed.' I asked them: 'Do you mean that Great Britain herself should be the sovereign Power there, or should be the mandatory?' and they said: 'No, what we want is an ordinary, humanly speaking reasonable guarantee that opportunities of autonomous development would be allowed to us.' We, ourselves, who have been living in India, are great believers in a sort of Federation of Faiths. I think the Indian nationality, which is being built up to-day, will probably be one of the first examples in the world of a Federation of Faiths, and we cannot rule out the possibility of development in Palestine on the lines of 'cultural autonomy.' The Jews are, after all, a very small minority there, and I do not believe for one moment that Jews could be attracted there in such large numbers as the Zionist enthusiasts sometimes think. I would say the same thing of an Armenian State, without desiring to say one word which would be considered offensive to any class of people. Because we, ourselves, have suffered so many humiliations, we do not like ourselves to say anything about other people that they would resent. If the Allied Powers brought all the Armenians together and placed them all in a contiguous position, excluding the present Kurdish community from them, no matter what large slice of land you gave them, I think they would very much like to go back to the old status....

"In the same way I would say of the Jewish community, that they are people who prosper very much in other lands, and although they have a great hankering after their home, and no community is so much bound up with a particular territory as the Jewish community is, still, I must say that we do not fear there will be any great migration of such a character that it will form a majority over the Muslim population. The Jewish community has said: 'We have no objection to Turkish sovereignty remaining in that part of the world so long as we are allowed to remain and prosper there and develop on our own lines, and have cultural autonomy.'"

M. Mohammed Ali, in his letter to Mr. Lloyd George, dated July 10, 1920, also observed that—

"With regard to Palestine in particular, the delegation desire to state that Article 99, embodying the declaration of the British Government of November 2, 1917, is extremely vague, and it is not clear in what relation the so-called national home for the Jewish people, which is proposed to be established in Palestine, would stand to the State proposed to be established there. The Mussulmans of the world are not ashamed of their dealings with their Jewish neighbours, and can challenge a comparison with others in this respect; and the delegation, in the course of the interview with you, endeavoured to make it clear that there was every likelihood of all reasonable claims of Jews in search of a home being accepted by the Muslim Government of Palestine. But if the very small Jewish minority in Palestine is intended to exercise over the Muslim, who constitute four-fifths of the population, a dominance now, or in the future, when its numbers have swelled after immigration, then the delegation must categorically and emphatically oppose any such designs."

The telegram in which Tewfik Pasha informed Damad Ferid of the conditions of the treaty, and which the latter communicated to the Press, was printed by the *Peyam Sabah*, surrounded with black mourning lines. Ali Kemal, though he was a supporter of the Government and could not be accused of anglophobia, concluded his article as follows:

"Better die than live blind, deaf, and lame. We have not given up all hope that the statesmen, who hold the fate of the world in their hands and who have officially proclaimed their determination to act equitably, will not allow this country, which has undergone the direst misfortunes for years and has lost its most sacred rights, to suffer a still more heinous injustice."

All the Constantinople newspapers, dealing at full length with the conditions, unanimously declared that the treaty was unacceptable. The *Alemdar*, another pro-English newspaper, said:

"If the treaty is not altered it will be difficult to find a man willing to sign it."

Another newspaper, the *Ileri*, wrote:

"The anguish which depressed our hearts while we were anxiously waiting seems a very light one compared to the pang we felt when we read the treaty."

The aforesaid *Peyam Sabah*, after a survey of the conditions, came to this conclusion:

"Three lines of conduct are open to the Turkish people:

"To beg for mercy and make the Powers realise that the loss of Smyrna will be a great blow to Turkey and will bring no advantage to Greece, and that the Chatalja frontier will be a cause of endless hostility between the various races.

"To sign the treaty and expect that the future will improve the condition of Turkey; but who in Turkey could sign such a treaty?

"To oppose passive resistance to the execution of the conditions of peace, since all hope of armed resistance must be given up."

Public opinion unanimously protested against the provisions of the treaty, but fluctuated and hesitated as to what concessions could be made.

Damad Ferid, receiving a number of deputies who had stayed at Constantinople and wanted to go back to the provinces, told them that he saw no objection to their going away, and that orders to that effect had been given to the police. Then he is said to have declared that they might tell their mandatories that he would never sign a treaty assigning Smyrna and Thrace to Greece and restricting Turkish sovereignty to Constantinople, and that on this point there was no difference of opinion between him and the Nationalists. He also informed them that in due time he would hold fresh elections, and the treaty would be submitted for approval to the new Chamber.

The Grand Vizier, who had asked Tewfik Pasha to let him see the note which was being prepared by the Turkish delegation at Versailles, was, on his side, elaborating the draft of another answer which was to be compared with that of the delegation, before the wording of the Turkish answer to the Peace Conference was definitely settled.

But the occupation of Lampsaki, opposite to Gallipoli, by the Turkish Nationalists, together with the Bolshevist advance in Northern Persia and Asia Minor, made things worse, and soon became a matter of anxiety to England.

After the text of the Peace Treaty had been presented to the Turks, and when the latter had the certainty that their fears were but too well grounded, it appeared clear that the decisions taken by the Allies would be certain to bring about a coalition of the various parties, and that all Turks, without any distinction of opinion, would combine to organise a resistance against any operation aiming at taking from them Eastern Thrace—where the Bulgarian population was also averse to the expulsion of the Turkish authorities—at assigning Smyrna and the Islands to Greece, and at dismembering the Turkish Empire.

Colonel Jafer Tayar, who commanded the Adrianople army corps and had openly declared against the Sultan's Government since the latter was at war with the Nationalists, had come to Constantinople at the beginning of May, and it was easy to guess for what purpose. Of course, it had been rumoured, after he left Constantinople, that the Government was going to appoint a successor to him, but nothing of the kind had been done, and he still kept his command. When he came back to Adrianople, not only had no conflict broken out between him and the troops under his command, but he had been given an enthusiastic greeting. As soon as it was known that the San Remo Conference had decided to give Thrace to Greece, up to the Chatalja lines, resistance against Greek occupation was quickly organised. Jafer Tayar, an Albanian by birth—he was born at Prishtina—became the leader of the movement. He hurriedly gathered some contingents made up of regular soldiers and volunteers, and put in a state of defence, as best he could, the ports of the western coast of the Marmora. Jafer Tayar wondered why Thrace was not granted the right of self-determination like Upper Silesia or Schleswig, or autonomy under the protection of France, whose administration in Western Thrace had proved equitable and had given satisfaction to that province. In face of this denial of justice, he had resolved to fight for the independence of Thrace.

It was soon known that the Moslem population of Adrianople had held a meeting at the beginning of May, in which, after a speech by Jafer Tayar, all the people present had pledged themselves to fight for the liberty of Thrace. A similar demonstration took place at Gumuljina. A congress including above two hundred representatives of the whole of Western Thrace had been held about the same time at Adrianople.

In Bulgaria a movement of protest was also started, and on Sunday, May 9, numerous patriotic demonstrations were held in all the provincial towns.

On May 16 the inhabitants of Philippopolis and refugees from Thrace, Macedonia, and the Dobruja living at that time in the town, held a meeting of several thousand people, and without any distinction of religion, nationality, or political party carried the following motion against the decision taken by the San Remo Conference to cede Thrace to Greece:

"They enter an energetic protest against the resolution to cede Thrace to Greece, for that would be a flagrant injustice and an act of cruelty both to a people of the same blood as we, and to the Bulgarian State itself; they declare that the Bulgarian people cannot, of their own free will, accept such a decision of the San Remo Conference, which would be a cause of everlasting discord in the Balkans—whereas the victorious Powers of the Entente have always professed to fight in order to restore peace to those regions; and they entreat the Governments, which have come to this decision, to cancel it and to raise Thrace to the rank of an autonomous, independent State under the protection of all the Powers of the Entente, or one of them."

On May 25—that is to say, two days before the Greek occupation—a few "Young Turk" and Bulgarian elements proclaimed the autonomy of Western Thrace, and formed a provisional Government to oppose the occupation. At the head of this Government were Tewfik Bey, a Young Turk, Vachel Georgieff, and Dochkoff, Bulgarian komitadjis. But the latter were expelled by General Charpy before the Greek troops and authorities arrived, and the Greek Press did its best to misrepresent that protest against Greek domination. They set off to Adrianople, taking with them the treasury and seals of the Moslem community, and were greeted by Jafer Tayar.

On the other hand, the resistance of the Turkish Nationalists was becoming organised, and as soon as the conditions of peace were known new recruits joined Mustafa Kemal's forces.

The Nationalist elements, owing to the attitude of the Allies towards Turkey, were now almost thrown into the arms of the Russian Bolshevists, who carried on an energetic propaganda in Asia Minor and offered to help them to save their independence, though they did so to serve their own interests.

Damad Ferid, Mustafa Kemal's personal enemy, who stood halfway between the Allied Powers and the Nationalists, believed that if he did not displease the Allies, he could pull his country out of its difficulties.

Before the draft of the treaty was handed to the Turks, the Ottoman Government had already begun to raise troops to fight the Nationalists. They were to be placed under command of Marshal Zeki, who had formerly served under Abdul Hamid. It was soon known that this military organisation had been entrusted by the Turkish War Minister to the care of British officers at whose instigation the first contingents had been sent to Ismid, which was to be the Turkish base.

It was soon announced that Damad Ferid Pasha's troops, who had remained loyal and were commanded by Ahmed Anzavour Pasha and Suleyman Shefik Pasha, had had some hard fighting with the rebels in the Doghandkeui and Geredi area, east of Adabazar, which they had occupied, and that the Nationalists, whose casualties had been heavy, had evacuated Bolu. The information was soon contradicted, and at the beginning of the last week of April it became known that Anzavour and his troops had just been utterly defeated near Panderma, and that this port on the Marmora had fallen into the Nationalists' hands. Ahmed Anzavour had had to leave Panderma for Constantinople on board a Turkish gunboat, and Mustafa Kemal now ruled over all the region round Brusa, Panderma, and Balikesri. Moreover, in the Constantinople area, a great many officers and soldiers were going over to the Nationalists in Anatolia.

It should be kept in mind that Ahmed Anzavour, though he was of Circassian descent, was unknown in his own country. He had been made pasha to command the Government forces against the Nationalists with the help of the Circassians, who are numerous in the Adabazar region, and to co-operate with the British against his fellow-countrymen, who merely wished to be independent.

Suleyman Shefik Pasha resigned, and some defections took place among the troops under his command.

About the same time, the emergency military court had sentenced to death by default Mustafa Kemal, Colonel Kara Yassif Bey, Ali Fuad Pasha, who commanded the 20th army corps, Ahmed Rustem Bey, ex-ambassador at Washington, Bekir Sami Bey, Dr. Adnan Bey, ex-head of the sanitary service, and his wife, Halidé Edib Hanoum, all impeached for high treason as leaders of the Nationalist movement.

Yet, despite all the measures taken by Damad Ferid and the moral and even material support given to him by the Allies, what could be the outcome of a military action against the Nationalists? How could the Ottoman Government compel the Turks to go and fight against their Anatolian brethren in order to force on them a treaty of peace that it seemed unwilling to accept itself, and that sanctioned the ruin of Turkey?

In some Turkish circles it was wondered whether a slightly Nationalist Cabinet co-operating with the Chamber would not have stood a better chance to come to an understanding with Anatolia and induce her to admit the acceptable parts of the treaty; for should Damad Ferid, who was not in a good position to negotiate with the Nationalists, fail, what would be the situation of the Government which remained in office merely because the Allies occupied Constantinople?

Of course, the Foreign Office proclaimed that foreign troops would be maintained in every zone, and that the treaty would be carried out at any cost. Yet the real Ottoman Government was no longer at Constantinople, where Damad Ferid, whose authority did not extend beyond the Ismid-Black Sea line, was cut off from the rest of the Empire; it was at Sivas. As no Government force or Allied army was strong enough to bring the Nationalist party to terms, it was only in Anatolia that the latter Government could be crushed by those who, with Great Britain, had conspired to suppress 12 million Turks and were ready to sacrifice enough soldiers to reach this end.

On the other hand, it soon became known that at Angora the question of the Caliph-Sultan had been set aside, and even the Sultan's name was now being mentioned again in the *namaz*, or public prayer offered every Friday—that is to say, all the parties had practically arrived at an understanding.

Besides, as most likely Greece would have to face difficulties, if not at once, at least in a comparatively short time, inspired information, probably of Greek origin, already intimated that the Supreme Council would decide whether France, England, and Italy would have to support Greece—though one did not see why France and Italy should defray the expenses of that new adventure by which England first, and Greece afterwards, would benefit exclusively.

On Saturday, May 22, the very day on which a Crown Council met under the Sultan's presidency to examine the terms of the treaty, over 3,000 people held a meeting of protest at Stambul, in Sultan Ahmed Square. Some journalists, who were well known for their pro-English feelings—such as Ali Kemal, an ex-Minister, editor of the *Sabah*; Refi Jevad, editor of the *Alemdar*; Mustafa Sabri, a former Sheik-ul-Islam—and some politicians delivered speeches. The platform was draped with black hangings; the Turkish flags and school banners were adorned with crêpe. After the various speakers had explained the clauses of the treaty and showed they were not acceptable, the following motions were passed:

"First, in contradiction to the principle of nationalities, the treaty cuts off from the Empire Thrace, Adrianople, Smyrna, and its area. In case the Allied Powers should maintain their decisions—which seems most unlikely—we want these regions to be given local autonomy.

"Secondly, now the Arabian territories have been cut off from the Ottoman Empire, the Turks, in accordance with the principle of nationalities, should be freed from all fetters and bonds hindering their economic development on the path to progress and peace. To maintain the Capitulations and extend them to other nations is tantamount to declaring the Turks are doomed to misery and slavery for ever.

"Thirdly, the Turks, relying on the fair and equitable feelings of the Allied Powers, require to be treated on the same footing as the other vanquished nations.

"Fourthly, the Turkish people, feeling sure that the peace conditions are tantamount to suppressing Turkey as a nation, ask that the treaty should be modified so as to be made more consistent with right and justice.

"Fifthly, the aforesaid resolutions shall be submitted to the Allied High Commissioners and forwarded to the Peace Conference."

These resolutions were handed after the meeting to M. Defrance, the senior Allied High Commissioner, who was to forward them to the Peace Conference.

As the difficulties increased, and more important and quicker communications with the Ottoman delegation in Paris were becoming necessary, the Cabinet thought of sending the Grand Vizier to Paris. Upon the latter's advice, and probably at the instigation of the English, several members of the dissolved Chamber set off to Anatolia in order to try and bring about an understanding between Damad Ferid and the Nationalists, for the conditions of the treaty, as was to be expected, had now nearly healed the rupture between the Central Government and the Turkish Nationalists, especially as the Anglo-Turkish Army was unable to carry out the treaty and Damad Ferid and his supporters were neither willing nor able to enforce it. Even the English had sent delegates to Mustafa Kemal, who had refused to receive them.

The Grand Vizier, after reviewing the troops at Ismid, found they were not strong enough, and requested the headquarters merely to stand on the defensive. Indeed, after a slight success in the Gulf of Ismid, the Government forces found themselves in a critical condition, for the Anatolian troops had occupied Kum Kale, close to the Dardanelles, and Mustafa Kemal had concentrated forces in that region.

The Chamber, which had been dissolved at Constantinople, resumed its sittings at Angora. It criticised the Allies' policy with regard to Turkey, especially the policy of England, at whose instigation Constantinople had been occupied and military measures had been taken on the coasts of the Black Sea.

In the speech he delivered at the first sitting of the Chamber, Mustafa Kemal showed that the English occupation of Constantinople had been a severe blow at the prestige of the Caliph and Sultan. "We must do our best," he said, "to free the Sultan and his capital. If we do not obey his orders just now, it is because we look upon them as null and void, as he is not really free."

The same state of mind showed itself in a telegram of congratulation addressed to the Sultan on his birthday by the provisional vali of Angora, who, though he did not acknowledge the power of the Central Government, stated that the population of Angora were deeply concerned at the condition to which the seat of the Caliphate and Sultanry was reduced owing to the occupation of Constantinople. This telegram ran thus:

"The people have made up their minds not to shrink from any sacrifice to make the Empire free and independent. They feel certain that their beloved Sovereign is with them at heart and that their chief strength lies in a close union round the Khilafat."

Similar dispatches were sent from the most active Nationalist centres such as Erzerum and Amasia, and by Kiazim Karabekir Pasha, commanding the 15th army corps at Erzerum.

It was plain that, through these demonstrations, Mustafa Kemal and the Anatolian Nationalists aimed at nullifying the religious pretexts Damad Ferid availed himself of to carry on the struggle against them. Mustafa Kemal had even ordered all the ulemas in Anatolia to preach a series of sermons with a view to strengthening the religious feeling among the masses. He had also the same political purpose in view when he sent a circular to the departments concerned to enjoin them to remind all Mussulmans of the duty of keeping the Ramadhan strictly and of the penalties they incurred if they publicly transgressed the Moslem fast.

Besides, the Nationalists strove to turn to account the movement that had taken place among all classes after the terms of the treaty had been made known, and their activity continued to increase. Sali Pasha, who was Grand Vizier before Damad Ferid, had escaped to Anatolia in order to put himself at the disposal of the Nationalists. So their opposition to the Central Government was asserting itself more and more strenuously, and the struggle that ensued assumed many forms.

An armistice, which came into force on May 30, and was to last twenty days, was concluded at Angora by M. Robert de Caix, secretary of the High Commissionership in Syria, between the French authorities and the Turkish Nationalists. Though the terms of this agreement were not made public, it was known that they dealt chiefly with Cilicia and allowed France to use the railway as far as Aleppo. Meanwhile, conversations were being held on the Cilician front, and finally at Angora, to extend the armistice.

Indeed, it was difficult to understand why, after the Italians had evacuated Konia, the French troops had not been withdrawn before the treaty had been handed to Turkey, for it gave France no right to remain in Cilicia; and now the situation of the French there was rather difficult, and their retreat had, of course, become dangerous. It seemed quite plain that the evacuation of Cilicia had become necessary, and that henceforth only the coastlands of Syria properly so called would be occupied.

So the French policy at this juncture had lacked coherency, for it seemed difficult to go on with the war and carry on peace negotiations at the same time.

This armistice was denounced on June 17 by Mustafa Kemal, who demanded the evacuation of Adana, the withdrawal of the French detachments from Heraclea and Zounguldak, and the surrender of the mines to the Nationalists who lacked coal and wanted Constantinople not to have any. Besides, some incidents had occurred in the course of the armistice: some French soldiers who were being drilled near Adana had been fired at, the railway track had been cut east of Toprak Kale, and telegraphic communications interrupted repeatedly between Adana and Mersina.

An encounter occurred on June 11 between the Nationalists and a company which had been detached at the beginning of the month from a battalion of a rifle corps that guarded the port and mining works of Zounguldak. On June 18, after an inquiry, the French commander withdrew from the spot which had been occupied near Heraclea and the company of riflemen was brought back to Zounguldak.

It was obvious that the staff of Cilicia did not seem to have approved of the armistice which had been concluded by the French authorities in order not to have anything to fear in this region, and to send all their forces against the Arabs; and so the head of the Turkish staff, Ismet Bey, naturally did not wish to renew it.

As we had entered into a parley with Mustafa Kemal openly and officially and signed an armistice with him, it seemed likely we meant to pursue a policy that might bring about a local and provisional agreement with the Nationalists, and perhaps a definite agreement later on. If such an armistice was not concluded, a rupture was to be feared on either side later on, in which case the condition of things would remain as intricate as before, or military operations would be resumed in worse conditions than before for both parties. In short, after treating with Mustafa Kemal it was difficult to ignore him in the general settlement that was to ensue.

But no broad view had ever dominated the Allies' policy since they had signed the armistice with Turkey in October, 1918. Eastern affairs had never been carefully sifted or clearly understood; so the Allies' action had been badly started. Conflicting ambitions had led them in a confused way. The policy of England especially, which had proved harsh and grasping, and also highly dangerous, was at the bottom of the difficulties the Allies had experienced in the East. So France, where public opinion and popular feeling were opposed to any Eastern adventure or any action against Turkey, could not be called upon to maintain troops in the East or to fight there alone for the benefit of others. The operations that were being contemplated in the East would have necessarily required an important army, and if adequate credits had been asked for them, a loud protest would have been raised—though later on the French Chamber granted large sums of money for Syria, after a superficial debate, not fully realising what would be the consequence of the vote.

M. d'Estournelles de Constant, a member of the Senate, wrote to the French Prime Minister on May 25 that, "after asking the Government most guardedly—for months in the Foreign Affairs Committee and the day before in the Senate—to give information about the mysterious military operations that had been carried on for a year and a half in Asia Minor and towards Mesopotamia," he found it necessary to start a debate in the Senate upon the following question: "What are our armies doing in Cilicia?"[29]

Meanwhile the Supreme Council urged the Turkish delegation to sign the treaty that had been submitted for its approval, and the Allies were going to negotiate with the representatives of a Government which, on the whole, was no longer acknowledged by the country. Of what value might be the signature wrested by the Allies from these representatives, and how could the stipulations of that treaty be carried out by the Turks? Most of its clauses raised internal difficulties in Turkey, and such a confusion ensued that the members of the delegation did not seem to agree any longer with the members of the Ottoman Cabinet, and at a certain time even the latter seemed unable to accept the treaty, in spite of the pressure brought to bear on the Ottoman Government by the English troops of occupation.

Mustafa Kemal's Nationalist forces conquered not only the whole of Asia Minor, but also all the Asiatic coast and the islands of the Marmora, except Ismid, which was still held by British posts. The Turkish Nationalists soon after captured Marmora Island, which commanded the sea route between Gallipoli and Constantinople.

On June 16 the British forces engaged the Kemalist troops in the Ismid area. About thirty Indian soldiers were wounded and an officer of the Intelligence Department was taken prisoner by the Turks. The civilians evacuated Ismid, and it was hinted that the garrison would do the same. Mustafa Kemal's aeroplanes dropped bombs on the town, and the railway line between Ismid and Hereke was cut by the Nationalists. The British forces on the southern coast of the Dardanelles withdrew towards Shanak, whose fortifications were being hurriedly repaired.

Mustafa Kemal's plan seemed to be to dispose his forces so as not to be outflanked, and be able to threaten Smyrna later on. To this end, the Nationalist forces advanced along the English sector toward the heights of Shamlija, on the Asiatic coast of the Bosphorus, from which point they could bombard Constantinople.

After a long interview with the Sultan, which lasted two hours, on June 11, the Grand Vizier Damad Ferid Pasha, owing to the difficulty of communicating between Paris and Constantinople, and the necessity of co-ordinating the draft of the answer worked out by the Ottoman Government and the reports drawn up by the various commissions with the answer recommended by the delegation, set off to Paris the next day. So it seemed likely that Turkey would ask for further time before giving her answer.

It could already be foreseen that in her answer Turkey would protest against the clauses of the treaty concerning Thrace and Smyrna, against the blow struck at the sovereignty of the Sultan by the internationalisation of the Bosphorus and the Dardanelles, as thus the Sultan could no longer leave his capital and go freely to Asia Minor, and, lastly, against the clauses restoring the privileges of the Capitulations to the States that enjoyed them before the war.

Turkey also intended to ask that the Sultan should keep his religious rights as Caliph over the Mussulmans detached from the Empire, and that a clause should be embodied in the treaty maintaining the guarantee in regard to the interior loan raised during the war, for otherwise a great many subscribers would be ruined and the organisation of the property of the orphans would be jeopardised.

At the beginning of the second week of June it was rumoured that the treaty might be substantially amended in favour of Turkey.[30] Perhaps Great Britain, seeing how things stood in the East, and that her policy in Asia Minor raised serious difficulties, felt it necessary to alter her attitude with regard to Turkish Nationalism which, supported by the Bolshevists, was getting more and more dangerous in Persia. For Mr. Lloyd George, who has always allowed himself to be led by the trend of events, and whose policy had lately been strongly influenced by the Bolshevists, had now altered his mind, as he often does, and seemed now inclined, owing to the failure of his advances to the Soviet Government, to modify his attitude towards Constantinople—after having exasperated Turkish Nationalism. The debate that was to take place on June 15 in the House of Lords as to what charges and responsibilities England had assumed in Mesopotamia, was postponed—which meant much; and the difficulties just met with by the British in the Upper Valley of the Tigris and the Euphrates in their struggle with the Arabs convinced them of the advisability of a revision of the British policy towards both the Arabs and the Turks.

On the other hand, it did not seem unlikely that M. Venizelos, who was being expected in London, might have seen the mistake the Supreme Council had made when it had granted the Greek claims so fully, and that the apprehension he was entitled to feel about the reality of the huge advantages obtained by Greece might have a salutary influence on him. Yet nothing of the kind happened, and in a long letter to the *Daily Telegraph* (June 18) he asserted not only the rights of Greece to Smyrna, but his determination to have them respected and to prevent the revision of the treaty.

M. Venizelos, "the great victor of the war in the East," as he was called in London, even supported his claims by drawing public attention to the intrigues carried on by Constantine's supporters to restore him to the throne. He maintained that the revision of the treaty would second the efforts which were then being made in Athens by the old party of the Crown, which, he said, was bound to triumph if Greece was deprived of the fruits of her victory and if the Allies did not redeem their pledges towards her. But then it became obvious that the Greeks did not despise Constantine so much after all, and their present attitude could not in any way be looked upon as disinterested.

It might have been expected, on the other hand, that Count Sforza, who had been High Commissioner in Constantinople, where he had won warm sympathies, would maintain the friendly policy pursued by Italy since the armistice towards Turkey—that is to say, he would urge that the time had come to revise the treaty of peace with Turkey which, since it had been drawn up at San Remo, had constantly been opposed by the Italian Press. All the parties shared this view, even the clerical party, and one of its members in the Chamber, M. Vassalo, who had just come back from Turkey, energetically maintained it was impossible to suppress the Ottoman Empire without setting on fire the whole of Asia. The Congress of the Popular Party in Naples held the same opinion. Recent events also induced Italy to preserve the cautious attitude she had assumed in Eastern affairs since the armistice, and she naturally aimed at counterbalancing the supremacy that England, if she once ruled over Constantinople and controlled Greater Greece, would enjoy over not only the western part, but the whole, of the Mediterranean Sea.

Henceforth it was obvious that the chief stipulations of the treaty that was to be enforced on Turkey were doomed to failure, and it was asked with no little anxiety whether the Powers would be wise enough to take facts into account and reconsider their decisions accordingly, or maintain them and thus pave the way to numerous conflicts and fresh difficulties. Indeed, the outcome of the arrangements they had laboriously elaborated was that things in the East had become more intricate and critical than before. No State wished to assume the task of organising the Armenian State: the American Senate flatly refused; Mr. Bonar Law formally declared in the House of Commons that England had already too many responsibilities; France did not see why she should take charge of it; Italy accepted no mandate in Asia Minor. Syria, on the other hand, protested against its dismemberment. Mesopotamia was rising against the English at the very time when the Ottoman Nationalists entered an indignant protest against the cession of Smyrna and Thrace to Greece.

It was to be wished, therefore, from every point of view that not only some articles of the treaty presented to the Turks, but the whole document, should be remodelled, and more regard should be paid to the lawful rights of the Ottoman Empire, a change which could only serve French interests.

But though reason and her interest urged France to maintain the Ottoman Empire—which she attempted to do to some extent—she allowed herself to be driven in a contrary direction by England, who thought she could take advantage of the perturbation caused by the war within the Turkish Empire to dismember it—not realising that this undertaking went against her own Asiatic interests, which were already seriously endangered. Such a submission to the English policy was all the more to be regretted as Mr. Lloyd George had but grudgingly supported the French policy with regard to Germany, and after the San Remo conversations it seemed that France would have to consent to heavy sacrifices in the East in return for the semi-approbation he had finally granted her. This policy of England well might surprise the French—who have always reverenced the British parliamentary system; for the so-styled imperialist policy of Queen Victoria or King Edward, though it has been violently criticised, had really kept up the old traditions of British Liberalism, and had nothing in common with the greed and cool selfishness of such demagogues and would-be advanced minds as Mr. Lloyd George, who stands forth before the masses as the enemy of every imperialism and the champion of the freedom of peoples. But the former leaders of English foreign policy were not constantly influenced by their own political interests; they knew something of men and countries; and they had long been thoroughly acquainted with the ways of diplomacy. Both in England and France, everyone should now acknowledge their fair-mindedness, and pay homage alike to their wisdom and perspicacity.

Many people in France now wondered with some reason what the 80,000 French soldiers round Beyrut were doing—whether it was to carry out the expedition that had long been contemplated against Damascus, or to launch into an adventure in Cilicia.

M. d'Estournelles de Constant, who had first wished to start a debate in the French Chamber on the military operations in Syria and Cilicia, addressed the following letter, after the information given by M. Millerand before the Commission of Foreign Affairs, to M. de Selves, chairman of this Commission:

"I feel bound to let the Commission know for what reasons I have determined not to give up, but merely postpone the debate I wanted to start in the Chamber concerning our military operations in Syria and Cilicia.

"The Premier has given as much consideration as he could to the anxieties we had expressed before him. He has inherited a situation he is not responsible for, and seems to do his best to prevent France from falling into the dreadful chasm we had pointed out to him. We must help him in his most intricate endeavours, for France is not the only nation that has to grapple with the perilous Eastern problem. She must work hand in hand with her allies to avert this peril. The whole world is threatened by it. Our Allies should understand that the interest of France is closely connected with their interests. France guards the Rhine; she is practically responsible for the execution of the treaty with Germany.

"How can she perform such a task, together with the administration of Alsace and Lorraine and the restoration of her provinces laid waste by the Germans, if she is to scatter her effort and her reduced resources both in Europe and all her large colonial empire and in Asia Minor among peoples who have long welcomed her friendship, but abhor any domination?

"France would do the world an immense service by openly reverting to the war aims proclaimed by herself and her allies. Far from endangering, she would thus strengthen her traditional influence in the East; she would thus do more than by risky military operations to smother the ambitions and rebellions that might set on fire again the Balkan States, Anatolia, and even Mesopotamia.

"After five years of sacrifices that have brought us victory, to start on a would-be crusade against the Arabs and Turks in a remote country, in the middle of summer, would imply for France as well as for England, Italy, Greece, and Serbia, the beginning of a new war that might last for ever, to the benefit of anarchy.

"At any rate I ask that the intended treaty of peace with Turkey, which has not been signed yet, should not be presented to the French Parliament as an irremediable fact."

After a long debate on Eastern affairs and on the questions raised by M. Millerand's communications, the Commission for Foreign Affairs, seeing things were taking a bad turn, and the situation of France in Syria, Cilicia, and Constantinople was getting alarming, decided on June 15 to send a delegation to the East to make an inquiry on the spot.

At the first sitting of the French Chamber on June 25, 1920, M. Briand, who three months before had made a speech in favour of the 1916 agreements which were being threatened by English ambition, though he considered the Turkish bands "went too far," and our policy "played too much into their hands," felt it incumbent on him to say:

"When we leave a nation like Turkey, after a long war, for over a year, under what might be called a Scotch douche, telling her now 'Thou shalt live,' now 'Thou shalt not live,' we strain its nerves to the extreme, we create within it a patriotic excitement, a patriotic exasperation, which now becomes manifest in the shape of armed bands. We call them bands of robbers; in our own country we should call them 'bands of patriots.'"

In the course of the general discussion of the Budget, during a debate which took place on July 28 in the Senate, an amendment was brought in by M. Victor Bérard and some of his colleagues calling for a reduction of 30 million francs on the sums asked for by the Government, which already amounted, as a beginning, to 185 million francs.

M. d'Estournelles de Constant then expressed his fear that this Eastern expedition might cause France to make sacrifices out of proportion to her resources in men and money, and asked how the Government expected to recuperate the expenditure incurred in Syria.

M. Victor Bérard, in his turn, sharply criticised our Eastern policy.

M. Bompard, too, expressed his fears concerning our Syrian policy, and M. Doumergue asked the Government to consent to a reduction of the credits "to show it intended to act cautiously in Syria."

But after M. Millerand's energetic answer, and after M. Doumer, chairman of the Commission, had called upon the Senate to accept the figures proposed by the Government and the Commission, these figures were adopted by 205 votes against 84.

M. Romanos, interviewed by the *Matin*,[31] and soon after M. Venizelos, at the Lympne Conference, maintained that the treaty could be fully carried out, and the Greeks felt quite able to enforce it themselves.

As the Allied troops were not sufficient to take decisive action, and as a large part of the Ottoman Empire had been assigned to Greece, England herself soon asked why the latter should not be called upon to pay for the operation if she insisted upon carrying it out.

About June 20 the situation of the British troops became rather serious, as General Milne did not seem to have foreseen the events and was certainly unable to control them.

The Nationalist troops, which met with but little resistance, continued to gain ground, and after marching past Ismid occupied Guebze. The Government forces were retreating towards Alemdagh.

By this time the Nationalists occupied the whole of Anatolia, and the English held but a few square miles near the Dardanelles. The Nationalists, who had easy access to both coasts of the Gulf of Ismid, attempted to blow up the bridges on the Haïdar-Pasha-Ismid railway line. Though the English were on the lookout, four Turkish aeroplanes started from the park of Maltepe, bound for Anatolia. One of them was piloted by the famous Fazil Bey, who had attacked English aeroplanes during their last flight over Constantinople a few days before the armistice in October, 1918.

Indeed, the Government forces only consisted of 15,000 specialised soldiers, artillerymen or engineers, with 6 light batteries of 77 guns and 2 Skoda batteries; in addition to which 20,000 rifles had been given to local recruits. The Nationalists, on the contrary, opposed them with 35,000 well-equipped men commanded by trained officers. Besides, there was but little unity of command among the Government forces. Anzavour Pasha, who had been sent with some cavalry, had refused to submit to headquarters, and at the last moment, when ordered to outflank the enemy and thus protect the retreat of the Government forces, he had flatly refused to do so, declaring he was not going to be ordered about by anybody.

So, considering how critical the situation of the British troops was in the zone of the Straits, England immediately made preparations to remedy it and dispatched reinforcements. The 2nd battalion of the Essex Regiment was held in readiness at Malta, and the light cruiser *Carlisle* kept ready to set off at a few minutes' notice. All available destroyers had already left Malta for the Eastern Mediterranean, where the first and fourth squadrons had already repaired. Besides, the cruiser *Ceres*, which had left Marseilles for Malta, received orders on the way to steam straight on to the Ægean Sea. All the Mediterranean fleet was concentrated in the East, while in the Gulf of Ismid the English warships, which were already there, carefully watched the movements of the Turkish Nationalist forces.

Such a state of things naturally brought about some anxiety in London, which somewhat influenced Mr. Lloyd George's decisions.

During the Hythe Conference, after some conversations on the previous days with Mr. Lloyd George, Lord Curzon, and Mr. Philip Kerr, in which he had offered to put the Greek Army at the disposal of the Allies, M. Venizelos, accompanied by Sir John Stavridi, a rich Greek merchant of London, who had been his intimate adviser for several years, went on Saturday evening, June 18, to the Imperial Hotel at Hythe, where were met all the representatives and experts whom Sir Philip Sassoon had not been able to accommodate at his mansion at Belcair, to plead the cause of Greek intervention with them.

M. Venizelos, on the other hand, in order to win over the British Government to his views, had secured the most valuable help of Sir Basil Zaharoff, who owns most of the shares in the shipbuilding yards of Vickers and Co. and who, thanks to the huge fortune he made in business, subsidises several organs of the British Press. He, too, has been a confidential adviser of M. Venizelos, and has a great influence over Mr. Lloyd George, owing to services rendered to him in election time. So it has been said with reason that M. Venizelos' eloquence and Sir Basil Zaharoff's wealth have done Turkey the greatest harm, for they have influenced Mr. Lloyd George and English public opinion against her.

According to M. Venizelos' scheme, which he meant to expound before the Conference, the Turkish Nationalist army, concentrated in the Smyrna area, could be routed by a quick advance of the Greek forces, numbering 90,000 fully equipped and well-trained men, who would capture the railway station of Afium-Karahissar. This station, being at the junction of the railway line from Smyrna and the Adana-Ismid line, via Konia, the only line of lateral communication Mustafa Kemal disposed of, would thus be cut off, and the Nationalist leader would have to withdraw towards the interior. His resistance would thus break down, and the British forces on the southern coast of the Sea of Marmora that M. Venizelos offered to reinforce by sending a Greek division would be at once freed from the pressure brought to bear on them, which, at the present moment, they could hardly resist.

The next day the Allies decided to accept M. Venizelos' offer, as the Greek troops were on the spot and no other force could arrive soon enough to relieve the British forces, which were seriously threatened.

Mr. Lloyd George declared that the British Government was sending to the spot all the ships it had at its disposal, but that this naval intervention could not affect the situation much without the help of the Greek Army.

"Without the Greek help," he said, "we may be driven to an ignominious evacuation of that region of Asia Minor before Kemal's forces, which would certainly have a terrible repercussion throughout the East and would pave the way to endless possibilities."

This was also the view held by Sir Henry Wilson, Chief of the Imperial General Staff.

Marshal Foch, too, was asked his advice about the Greek co-operation. He had already declared at San Remo, in agreement with Marshal Wilson, that an army of 300,000 or 400,000 well-equipped men would be needed to conquer Asia Minor. Now, after making full reserves in regard to the political side of the question, he merely remarked that from a strictly military point of view, Greek co-operation might be a decisive element of success; moreover, in a report he had drawn up a few months before, he had pointed out the advantage that an active co-operation of the Greek Army was sure to bring, from a military point of view.

M. Millerand, while admitting these advantages, is said to have raised some serious objections to the scheme.

Finally, as the question could not be solved definitely without Italy's consent, it was adjourned till the Boulogne Conference met.

Mr. Lloyd George accepted this solution the more readily as he only seemed to look upon M. Venizelos' scheme as an experiment; and he wanted to gain time, in order to know whether he was to pursue it, till facts had proved that M. Venizelos was right and the Turkish Nationalists' resistance could be overcome in a short time. If after some time things did not turn out as he expected, he would merely resort to another policy, as is usual with him. But England, meanwhile, was in an awkward situation, since, while accepting the help of an ally, she hinted at the same time that she would not stand by the latter if things turned out wrong. On the other hand, it was surprising that the Supreme Council should take such decisions before receiving Turkey's answer and knowing whether she would sign the treaty.

When the decisions taken at Hythe in regard to the part to be entrusted to Greece were made known on June 21 at the Boulogne Conference, they brought forth some remarks on the part of Count Sforza, who refused to engage Italy's responsibility in the policy that was being recommended. He thought it his duty to make reservations in regard to the timeliness of these decisions and the consequences that might ensue, referring to the technical advice given at San Remo by Marshal Foch and Marshal Wilson as to the huge forces they thought would be needed to enforce the treaty against the Nationalists' wish.

Soon after—on July 13—M. Scialoja, in the long speech he delivered before the Senate to defend the attitude of Italy in the Peace Congress, declared that Italy could not be held responsible for the serious condition of things now prevailing in Asia Minor and the East, for she had attempted, but in vain, to secure a more lenient treatment for Turkey. Finally, in spite of all the objections raised against the treaty, and the difficulties that would probably ensue, it was decided at the few sittings of the Boulogne Conference that the Ottoman delegation should be refused any further delay in giving their answer, which averted any possibility of revision of the treaty. The Powers represented in the Conference gave a free hand to Greece in Asia Minor, because they had not enough soldiers there themselves—let us add that none of them, not even England probably, cared to rush into a new Eastern adventure. The Greeks had none but themselves to blame; their landing at Smyrna had started the Nationalist movement, and now they bore the brunt of the fight.

This new decision implied the giving up of the policy of conciliation which might have been expected after the three weeks' armistice concluded on May 30 between the French Staff and the Nationalists, which seemed to imply that the French military authorities intended to evacuate the whole of Cilicia, left by the treaty to Turkey. Owing to the serious consequences and infinite repercussions it might have through the Moslem world, the new decision heralded a period of endless difficulties.

Even the Catholic Press did not much appreciate the treaty, and had been badly impressed by recent events. The Vatican, which has always sought to prevent Constantinople from falling into the hands of an Orthodox Power, might well dread the treaty would give the Phanar a paramount influence in the East, if Greece became the ruling Power both at Stambul and Jerusalem. In the first days of the war, when at the time of the Gallipoli expedition Constantinople seemed doomed to fall, the Holy See saw with some anxiety that the Allies intended to assign Constantinople to Russia, and it then asked that at least Saint Sophia, turned into a mosque by the Turks, should be given back to the Catholic creed. This fear may even have been one of the reasons which then induced the Holy See to favour the Central States. M. René Johannet, who was carrying on a campaign in the newspaper *La Croix*[32] for the revision of the treaty, wrote as follows:

"But then, if Asia Minor is deprived of Smyrna and thus loses at least half her resources, we ask with anxiety where France, the chief creditor of Turkey, will find adequate financial guarantees? To give Smyrna to Greece is to rob France. If the Turks are stripped of everything, they will give us nothing.

"Lastly, the fate of our innumerable religious missions, of which Smyrna is the nucleus, is to us a cause of great anxiety. After the precedents of Salonika and Uskub, we have everything to fear. The Orthodox Governments hate Catholicism. Our religious schools—that is to say, the best, the soundest part of our national influence—will soon come to nothing if they are constantly worried by the new lords of the land. How can we allow this?"

According to the account given by the Anatolian newspapers of the sittings of the Parliament summoned by Mustafa Kemal to discuss the conditions of peace, very bitter speeches had been delivered. The Assembly had passed motions denouncing the whole of the treaty, and declaring the Nationalists were determined to oppose its being carried out, supposing it were signed by Damad Ferid Pasha, or any venal slave of the foreigner, and to fight to the bitter end.

Mustafa Kemal was said to have declared, in a conversation, that he had not enough soldiers to make war, but he would manage to prevent any European Power establishing dominion in Asia Minor. And he is reported to have added: "I don't care much if the Supreme Council ejects the Turks from Europe, but in this case the Asiatic territories must remain Turkish."

The Greek Army, which, according to the decisions of the Conference, had started an offensive on the Smyrna front, after driving back the Nationalists concentrated at Akhissar, occupied the offices of the captainship of the port of Smyrna and the Ottoman post-office.

On June 20, at Chekmeje, west of Constantinople on the European coast of the Marmora, a steamer had landed a detachment of Kemalist troops, which the British warships had immediately bombarded at a range of eight miles.

On June 21 and 22 two battalions, one English and the other Indian, landed on the Asiatic coast and blew up the eighty guns scattered all along the Straits, on the Asiatic shore of the Dardanelles.

On June 23 the 13th Greek division attacked Salikili and occupied it. A column of cavalry advanced towards Kula.

On June 24 the Greek troops carried on their advance in four directions and the Nationalists withdrew, fighting stoutly all the time.

On June 25 the Greeks overcame their resistance and captured Alashehr, formerly called Philadelphia, an important town on the Smyrna-Konia line, about 100 miles from Smyrna, took some prisoners and captured material.

On July 1 the Greeks occupied Balikesri, an important station on the Smyrna-Panderma line, nearly fifty miles to the north of Soma, in spite of the Nationalists' energetic resistance.

On July 3 a landing of Greek troops hastened the fall of Panderma. Some detachments which had landed under the protection of the fleet marched southwards, and met the enemy outposts at Omerkeui, fifteen miles to the north-west of Balikesri.

Then on July 7 M. Venizelos stated at the Spa Conference that the Greek offensive against Mustafa Kemal's forces which had begun on June 22 and whose chief objective was the capture of the Magnesia-Akhissar-Soma-Balikesri-Panderma line, had ended victoriously on July 2, when the forces coming from the south and those landed at Panderma had effected a junction, and that the scheme of military operations drawn up at Boulogne, which was to be carried out in two weeks, according to General Paraskevopoulos' forecast, had been brought to a successful end in eleven days.

On July 8 Brusa was occupied by the Greek army, and Mudania and Geumlek by British naval forces. Before the Greek advance began every wealthy Turk had fled to the interior with what remained of the 56th Turkish division, which had evacuated Brusa on July 2. Brusa had been occupied by the Greeks without any bloodshed. A good number of railway carriages and a few steam-engines belonging to a French company had been left undamaged by the Turks on the Mudania line. The British naval authorities, under the pretext that some shots had been fired from the railway station, had had it shelled, together with the French manager's house, and all that was in these two buildings had been looted by British sailors and the Greek population of Mudania.

Some misleading articles in the Greek and English Press, which were clearly unreliable, extolled the correct attitude of the Greek troops towards the inhabitants during their advance in Asia Minor. According to the Greek communiqué of July 17, "the Nationalists, now deprived of any prestige, were being disarmed by the Moslem population which earnestly asked to be protected by the Greek posts," and "the Turks, tired of the vexatious measures and the crushing taxes enforced by the Kemalists, everywhere expressed their confidence and gratitude towards the Greek soldiers, whom they welcomed as friends and protectors."

At the same time political circles in Athens openly declared that the Greek operations in Asia Minor had now come to an end, and that Adrianople and Eastern Thrace would soon be occupied—this occupation being quite urgent as the Turks already evinced signs of resistance, and the Bulgarians were assuming a threatening attitude. Moreover, as might have been foreseen, the Greeks already began to speak of territorial compensations after their operations in Asia Minor and of setting up a new State.

General Milne, whose forces had been reinforced by Greek elements, also undertook to clear all the area lying between Constantinople and Ismid from the irregular Turkish troops that had made their way into it.

On July 7 it was officially notified by the British Headquarters that "military movements were going to take place in the direction of Ismid, and so the Asiatic shore of the Bosphorus was considered as a war zone." Accordingly troops quartered in that district, and soldiers employed in the various services, were to be recalled to the European shore at once, and the next day any Turkish soldier found within that zone would be treated as an enemy.

The great Selimie barracks, at Skutari, were therefore evacuated by the Turks, who thus had no troops left on the Asiatic shore of the Straits.

At Pasha Bagtche Chiboukli, on the Asiatic shore of the Bosphorus, Greek soldiers helped to disarm the population, and searched everybody who landed at that village.

At Stambul, on the great bridge of Karakeui, British agents halted all officers and soldiers wearing the Turkish uniform, and directed them to the buildings of the English gendarmerie to be examined.

The Alemdagh district was occupied, and General Milne had all the Government troops disarmed, on the pretext of their questionable attitude and the weakness of the Turkish Government. Yet the latter had, of its own accord, broken up the Constantinople army corps, and replaced it by one division that was to be dissolved, in its turn, after the signature of the Peace Treaty, as according to the terms of peace only 700 Turkish soldiers had a right to reside in Constantinople as the Sultan's guard.

In an article of *Le Matin*, July 7, 1920, under the title, "A New Phase of the Eclipse of French Influence in the East," M. André Fribourg pointed out the encroachment of the British Commander in Constantinople.

The decision taken by the Allies at Boulogne not to grant any further delay had placed the Turks in a difficult situation. The Grand Vizier, who had come to Paris in the hope of negotiating, handed his answer on the 25th, in order to keep within the appointed time.

The Supreme Council examined this answer on Wednesday, July 7, at Spa. After hearing the English experts, who advised that any modification should be rejected, the Council refused to make any concessions on all the chief points mentioned in the Turkish answer, and only admitted a few subsidiary requests as open to discussion. It deputed a Commission of political experts to draw up an answer in collaboration with the military experts.

Meanwhile the Minister of the Interior, Reshid Bey, chairman of the Ottoman delegation, who had left Constantinople on the 25th, and had arrived in Paris with Jemil Pasha only at the beginning of July, sent a note to the Secretary of the Peace Conference to be forwarded to M. Millerand at Spa. This note, which came to hand on July 11, completed the first answer. It included the decisions taken in Constantinople during Damad Ferid's stay at Versailles.

The remarks offered by the Ottoman delegation about the peace conditions presented by the Allies made up a little book of forty pages with some appendices, which was handed to the Conference on the 25th. The answer, which had been revised in Constantinople, and consisted of forty-seven pages, was delivered a few days after; it differed but little from the first.

This document began with the following protest against the conditions enforced on Turkey:

"It was only fair—and it was also a right recognised by all nations nowadays—that Turkey should be set on an equal footing with her former allies. The flagrant inequality proffered by the draft of the treaty will be bitterly resented not only by 12 million Turks, but throughout the Moslem world.

"Nothing, indeed, can equal the rigour of the draft of the Turkish treaty. As a matter of fact, it is a dismemberment.

"Not only do the Allies, in the name of the principle of nationalities, detach important provinces from the Ottoman Empire which they erect to the rank of free, independent States (Armenia and the Hejaz), or independent States under the protection of a mandatory Power (Mesopotamia, Palestine, and Syria); not only do they wrench from it Egypt, Suez, and Cyprus, which are to be ceded to Great Britain; not only do they require Turkey to give up all her rights and titles to Libya and the States of the Ægean Sea: they even mean to strip her, notwithstanding the said principle of nationalities, of Eastern Thrace and the zone of Smyrna, which countries, in a most iniquitous way, would be handed over to Greece, who wants to be set on an equal footing with the victors, though she has not even been at war with Turkey.

"Further, they are preparing to take Kurdistan and in an indirect way to slice the rest of the country into zones of influence.

"In this way more than two-thirds of the extent of the Ottoman Empire would already be taken from it. With regard to the number of inhabitants, it would be at least two-thirds. If we consider the economic wealth and natural resources of the country, the proportion would be greater still.

"But that is not all. To this spoliation, the draft of the treaty adds a notorious infringement on the sovereignty of the Ottoman State. Even at Constantinople Turkey would not be her own mistress. Side by side with His Imperial Majesty the Sultan and the Turkish Government—or even above them in some cases—a 'Commission of the Straits' would rule over the Bosphorus, the Sea of Marmora, and the Dardanelles. Turkey would not even be represented in this Commission, whereas Bulgaria would send a representative to it.

"In addition to these two powers, there would be a third one—the military power exercised by the troops of occupation of three States, whose headquarters would have the upper hand even of the Ottoman gendarmerie.

"Any possibility of mere defence against an attack would thus be taken away from Turkey, whose capital would henceforth be within the range of her enemies' guns.

"The sovereignty of the State would also be deeply infringed upon in all matters relating to legislation, international treaties, finance, administration, jurisdiction, trade, etc., so that finally the crippled Ottoman Empire would be stripped of every attribute of sovereignty both at home and abroad, but would be held responsible all the same for the execution of the Peace Treaty and the international obligations pertaining to every State.

"Such a situation, which would be an utter denial of justice, would constitute both a logical impossibility and a judicial anomaly. For, on the one hand, it is impossible to maintain a State and at the same time divest it of all that is an essential judicial condition of its existence; and, on the other hand, there cannot be any responsibility where there is no liberty.

"Either the Allied Powers are of opinion that Turkey should continue to exist, in which case they should make it possible for her to live and fulfil her engagements by paying due regard to her rights as a free, responsible State.

"Or the Allied Powers want Turkey to die. They should then execute their own sentence themselves, without asking the culprit—to whom they did not even give a hearing—to append his signature to it and bring them his co-operation."

After these general considerations and some remarks as to the responsibility of Turkey, the fundamental rights of the State, and the right of free disposal of peoples, the Ottoman Government made counter-proposals which were quite legitimate, and at the same time bore witness to its goodwill.

This document, to which we refer the reader for further particulars, may be summed up as follows: The Turkish Government recognises the new States of Poland, Serbia-Croatia-Slovenia, and Czecho-Slovakia. It confirms the recognition made by Turkey in 1918 of Armenia as a free, independent State. It also recognises the Hejaz as a free, independent State. It recognises the French protectorate over Tunis. It accepts all economic, commercial, and other consequences of the French protectorate over Morocco, which was not a Turkish province. It renounces all rights and privileges over Libya and the isles and islets of the Ægean Sea. It recognises Syria, Mesopotamia, Palestine, as independent States. It recognises the British protectorate over Egypt, the free passage of the Suez Canal, the Anglo-Egyptian administration of the Soudan, the annexation of Cyprus by Great Britain.

In regard to Constantinople and the régime of the zone of the Straits, the Ottoman delegation remarked that according to the terms of the treaty there would be together in that town—

"First, His Imperial Majesty the Sultan and the Turkish Government, whose rights and titles shall be maintained.

"Secondly, the Commission of the Straits.

"Thirdly, the military powers of occupation.

"Fourthly, the diplomatic representatives of France, Britain, and Italy, deliberating in a kind of council with the military and naval commanders of the Franco-Anglo-Italian forces."

With them would be—

"Fifthly, the Inter-Allied Commissioners of Control and Military Organisation.

"Sixthly, the Commission of Finance.

"Seventhly, the Council of the Ottoman Public Debt.

"Eighthly, the consuls' jurisdictions."

After going over all the objections raised by the coexistence of these various bodies, whose powers would encroach upon each other or would be exactly similar, and the impossibility that foreign agents accredited to the Sultan should hold such functions, the memorandum opposed the following reasons to the decisions of the Conference:

"First, the draft of the treaty does not in any way institute *an international judicial and political organisation* of the Straits.

"Secondly, it institutes a political and military power on behalf of *some* States, attended with all the international risks pertaining to it.

"Thirdly, with regard to Turkey it would constitute *a direct and deep infringement on her rights of sovereignty, preservation, and security, which infringements are not necessary to safeguard the freedom of passage* of the Straits.

"Fourthly, from an international point of view the intended régime would create a kind of *international moral person by the side of the States, which would not represent the League of Nations.*

"Fifthly, the new international condition of Turkey would in some respects be inferior to that of the new States consisting of territories detached from Turkey, for these new States would be placed under the mandate of a Power *appointed by the League of Nations* mainly in accordance with *the wishes of the populations concerned*, and bound to give a periodical account to the League of Nations of the exercise of its mandate.

"Sixthly, far from ensuring the internationalisation of the Straits, which was aimed at by the Powers, the régime instituted by the draft of the treaty would *favour their nationalisation by another State.*

"The internationalisation of the Straits could only be realised by means of an international organisation—viz., *a judicial organisation representing all the Powers.*"

Therefore, the Government allows the free passage of the Straits, but asks that they should be controlled only by the League of Nations, and that the Straits zones mentioned in the scheme of internationalisation "should be reduced territorially to what is necessary to guarantee the free passage of the Straits." Turkey declares herself ready to accept "this scheme, if restricted to the Straits zone, whose frontiers were fixed as follows":

"(*a*) In Europe the Sharkeui-Karachali line, thus including all the Gallipoli Peninsula.

"(*b*) In Asia a line passing through Kara-Bigha (on the Sea of Marmora), Bigha, Ezine, and Behramkeui."

She thus agrees to "all restrictions to her sovereignty over the Straits that are necessary to control the navigation and ensure their opening to all flags on a footing of complete equality between the States."

Further,

"As regards all matters concerning the region of the Straits and the Sea of Marmora, the Ottoman Government is willing to discuss a convention instituting for these waters a régime of the same kind as the one established for the Suez Canal by the Constantinople treaty of October 29, 1888, the very régime advocated by Great Britain (Art. 109)."

The Ottoman Government—this article, together with the one concerning the Hejaz that will be mentioned later on, was the most important addition in the revised answer drawn up at Constantinople—wishes the islands of Lemnos, Imbros, Tenedos, lying before the entrance to the Dardanelles, to be included in the zone of the Straits—that is to say, to remain Ottoman territories under inter-Allied occupation. The Allies intended to give these islands to Greece, and it was feared in Constantinople the latter might hand them over to another Power—England, for instance—that would cede her Cyprus in exchange.

Among a great many measures intended for ensuring the security of Constantinople, the Ottoman Government chiefly asks for the limitation of the number of foreign warships allowed to stay in Turkish waters.

It wants to maintain, under Ottoman sovereignty, Eastern Thrace within its pre-war boundaries, and Smyrna with the surrounding area, which shall be evacuated by Hellenic troops, and may be occupied for three years at the utmost by troops of the chief Allied Powers.

The Ottoman Government asks for an international inquiry to fix the frontiers of Kurdistan according to the principle of nationalities, in case the Kurds—who, it firmly believes, are "indissolubly attached to His Majesty the Sultan," and who "have never wished, and will never have the least desire, to be completely independent or even to relax the bonds that link them with the Turkish people"—should express the wish to enjoy local autonomy. The intended frontier between Syria and Mesopotamia should also be altered, for otherwise it would cut off from the Ottoman Empire a predominantly Turkish population; "an international commission should make a thorough inquiry with a view to ascertan facts from an ethnic point of view."

It also wants the King of the Hejaz to pledge himself to respect the titles and prerogatives of the Sultan as Caliph over the holy cities and places of Mecca and Medina.

Lastly, it declares itself ready to accept, without asking for reciprocity, the clauses concerning the protection of minorities.

Meanwhile the Greeks seemed eager to carry on their campaign in Asia Minor, without even waiting for the definite settlement of the treaty. According to information sent from Greece,[33] the Hellenic army, having reached all its objectives, was waiting for the decisions of the Spa Conference, and if the latter wished her to carry on her operations in Asia Minor, her fourth objective would probably be Eskishehr, the nucleus of the Anatolian railways, which commands all the traffic and revictualling of Asia Minor, and whose fall would perhaps bring the war to an end.

The Allied answer to the Turkish request for further delays and to the Turkish remarks was handed to the Ottoman delegation on July 17.

In this answer, the main lines or perhaps even the very words of which had been settled at Spa, the Allies only repeated their previous arguments—some of which were ineffective and others unfounded; and both the letter and the spirit of the answer were most unconciliatory.

The assertion that "Turkey entered into the war without the shadow of an excuse or provocation," recurred again in it and was fully enlarged upon. The events that had taken place lately and the character they had assumed since the end of hostilities did not seem to have taught the writers or instigators of the answer anything at all. We do not wish here to mitigate in any way the responsibilities of Turkey or her wrongs to the Allies; yet we should not overlook the most legitimate reasons that drove her to act thus, and we must own she had a right to mistrust the promises made to her. For the policy that the Allies pursued at that time and that they have not wholly repudiated obviously proved that they would give a free hand to Russia to carry out her ambitious schemes on Constantinople and Turkey-in-Asia, as a reward for her energetic share in the war.

Besides, a fact helps us to understand how Turkey was driven to enter into the war and accounts for her apprehension of England and the Anglo-Hellenic policy pursued by England in relation with her later on, both in the working out of the Sèvres treaty and after the signature of this treaty; it is the proposition made by England to Greece to attack Turkey. According to the letter that M. Venizelos addressed to King Constantine on September 7, 1914, sending in his resignation, which was not accepted by the King, Admiral Kerr, the very man whom later on, in 1920, the British Government was to entrust with a mission to the Hellenic King while he was at Lucerne, formally waited upon the latter to urge him to attack Turkey. The King is said to have laid down as a necessary condition to his consent that Britain should guarantee the neutrality of Bulgaria and should contrive to bring Turkey to afford him a pretext for opening hostilities. Admiral Kerr, speaking on behalf of the British Government, is reported to have given him full guarantee on the first point; but with reference to the second point he hinted that he thought it unnecessary to seek for a pretext or wait for a provocation as the Hellenic policy constantly evinced a feeling of hostility towards Turkey.[34]

In this answer the Allies again reproached the Turks with their atrocities—without mentioning the atrocities committed by the Armenians against the Turks; and yet at that time Mr. Lloyd George seemed to have wholly forgotten the German atrocities, for he did not say a word about the punishment of the war criminals, and seemed ready to make concessions as to the reparations stipulated in the treaty with Germany. Why should the Turks be chastised—as was said at the time—if the other criminals were not punished? Was it merely because they were weaker and less guilty than the Germans?

Though it was a palpable falsehood, it was asserted again in this document that in Thrace the Moslems were not in a majority.

The Powers also gravely affirmed they contemplated for Smyrna "about the same régime as for Dantzig," which could not greatly please either the Greeks or the Turks, judging from the condition of the Poles in the Baltic port; but they did not add that perhaps in this case too England would finally control the port.

"With regard to the control of the Straits," said the document, "the Powers must unhesitatingly take adequate measures to prevent the Turkish Government from treacherously trampling upon the cause of civilisation." It seemed to be forgotten that Turkey insisted upon keeping them in order to prevent Russia from seizing them; and at the very time when the note was drawn up some newspapers declared—which might have sufficed to justify the Turkish claim—that the passage of the Straits must be free in order to allow the Allies to send munitions to Wrangel's army.

The Allies, however, decided to grant to "Turkey, as a riparian Power and in the same manner and on the same conditions as to Bulgaria, the right to appoint a delegate to the Commission and the suppression of the clause through which Turkey was to surrender to the Allied Governments all steamers of 1,600 tons upwards." These were the only two concessions made to Turkey.

The Allies' answer laid great stress upon the advantages offered by the organisation of a financial control of Turkey, which, to quote the document itself, "was introduced for no other purpose than to protect Turkey against the corruption and speculation which had ruined her in the past." As a matter of fact, that corruption and speculation had been let loose in Turkey by the Great Powers themselves, under cover of the privileges given by the Capitulations.

Judging from the very words of the clause which left Constantinople in the hands of the Turks, the Allies seemed to allow this merely out of condescension, and even alleged that the territory left to Turkey as a sovereign State was "a large and productive territory."

Finally, the note concluded with the following threat:

"If the Turkish Government refuses to sign the peace, still more if it finds itself unable to re-establish its sovereignty in Anatolia or to give effect to the treaty, the Allies, in accordance with the terms of the treaty, may be driven to reconsider the arrangement by ejecting the Turks from Europe once and for all."

These lines plainly show that some Powers had not given up the idea of ejecting the Turks from Europe, and were only awaiting an opportunity that might warrant another European intervention to carry out their plans and satisfy their ambition; and yet this policy, as will be seen later on, went against their own interests and those of Old Europe.

The idea that the British Premier entertained of the important strategic and commercial consequences that would ensue if the Near East were taken away from Turkish sovereignty was obviously contradictory to the historical part played by Turkey; and by disregarding the influence of Turkey in European affairs in the past and the present, he made a grievous political mistake. If one day Germany, having become a strong nation again, should offer her support to Turkey, cut to pieces by England, all the Turks in Asia might remember Mr. Lloyd George's policy, especially as M. Venizelos might then have been replaced by Constantine or the like.

Turkey was granted a period of ten days, expiring on July 27 at 12 midnight, to let the Allies definitely know whether she accepted the clauses of the treaty and intended to sign it.

This comminatory answer did not come as a surprise. Mr. Lloyd George openly said he was convinced the Greeks would be as successful in Thrace as they had been in Asia Minor, which was easy to foresee but did not mean much for the future; and he thought he was justified in declaring with some self-satisfaction before the Commons on July 21, 1920—

"The Great Powers had kept the Turk together not because of any particular confidence they had in him, but because they were afraid of what might happen if he disappeared.

"The late war has completely put an end to that state of things. Turkey is broken beyond repair, and from our point of view we have no reason to regret it."

The Greek troops, supported by an Anglo-Hellenic naval group, including two British dreadnoughts, effected a landing in the ports of Erekli, Sultan Keui (where they met with no resistance), and Rodosto, which was occupied in the afternoon.

The Hellenic forces landed on the coasts of the Marmora reached the Chorlu-Muradli line on the railway, and their immediate objective was the occupation of the Adrianople-Constantinople railway in order to cut off all communications between Jafer Tayar's troops and the Nationalist elements of the capital, and capture Lule Burgas. From this position they would be able to threaten Jafer Tayar and Huhi ed Din on their flanks and rear in order to compel them to withdraw their troops from the Maritza, or run the risk of being encircled if they did not cross the Bulgarian frontier.

The Greek operations against Adrianople began on July 20. The Turkish Nationalists had dug a network of trenches on the right bank of the Tunja, which flows by Adrianople; they offered some resistance, and bombarded the bridgeheads of Kuleli Burgas and of the suburbs of Karagatch, three miles from Adrianople, where the Greeks had taken their stand for over a month. But on Saturday, July 24, the confident spirit of the Turkish civilians and officers suddenly broke down when it was known that the Greeks had landed on the shores of the Marmora, had reached Lule Burgas, and threatened to encircle the troops that defended Adrianople. In the absence of Jafer Tayar, who had repaired to the front, the officers suddenly left the town without letting it be known whether they were going to Northern Thrace or withdrawing to Bulgaria, and the soldiers, leaving the trenches in their turn, scattered all over Adrianople. The white flag was hoisted during the night, and the next day at daybreak a delegation, including Shevket Bey, mayor of the town, the mufti, the heads of the Orthodox and Jewish religious communities, repaired to the Hellenic outposts, at Karagatch, to ask the Greeks to occupy the town at once. At 10 o'clock the troops marched into the town, and by 12 they occupied the Konak, the prefect's mansion, where the Turks had left everything—archives, furniture, carpets, and so on.

Meanwhile, it was reported that 12,000 Turks who had refused to surrender and accept Greek domination crossed the Bulgarian frontier.

As soon as the Grand Vizier came back to Constantinople a conflict arose between the latter, who maintained Turkey was compelled to sign the treaty, and some members of the Cabinet. As the Grand Vizier, who was in favour of the ratification, hesitated to summon the Crown Council, the Minister of Public Works, Fakhr ed Din, Minister of Public Education, Reshid, Minister of Finance and provisional Minister of the Interior, and the Sheik-ul-Islam, who all wanted the Council to be summoned, are said to have offered their resignation, which was not accepted by the Sultan—or at any rate was no more heard of.

On July 20 the Sultan summoned a Council of the Imperial Family, including the Sultanas, and on July 22 the Crown Council, consisting of fifty-five of the most prominent men in Turkey, among whom were five generals, a few senators, the members of the Cabinet, and some members of the former Government. The Grand Vizier spoke first, and declared Turkey could not do otherwise than sign the treaty. All the members of the Council supported the Government's decision, with the exception of Marshal Fuad, who had already used his influence with the Sultan in favour of the Nationalists and who said the Turks should die rather than sign such a peace, and of Riza Pasha, who had commanded the artillery before the war, who said Turkey did not deserve such a grievous punishment and refused to vote. Turkey had been at war for ten years, which partly accounts for the decision taken. Therefore the order to sign the treaty of peace was officially given, and, as had already been announced, General Hadi Pasha, of Arabian descent, Dr. Riza Tewfik Bey, and Reshad Halis Bey, ambassador at Berne, were appointed Turkish plenipotentiaries.

The Grand Vizier in an appeal to Jafer Tayar, the Nationalist leader in Thrace, begged of him "to surrender at once and leave Thrace to the Greek army." He concluded with these words: "We fully recognise your patriotism, but protracting the war would be detrimental to the interests of the nation. You must submit."

Then the question arose how the treaty—which now admitted of no discussion—after being enforced and carried out by arms, before the delay for acceptance granted to the Ottoman Government had come to an end, against all rules of international law and diplomatic precedents, could solve the Eastern question.

Of course it was alleged that the Greek offensive in Anatolia had nothing to do with the treaty of peace presented to Turkey, that it only constituted a preventive measure in support of the treaty and it was not directed against the Stambul Government, but against Mustafa Kemal's troops, which had broken the armistice by attacking the British troops on the Ismid line. Yet this was but a poor reason, and how was it possible to justify the Greek attack in Thrace, which took place immediately after? The fact was that England and Greece, being afraid of losing their prey, were in a hurry to take hold of it, and neither Mr. Lloyd George nor M. Venizelos shrank from shedding more blood to enforce a treaty which could not bring about peace.

Now that the Allies had driven a Government which no longer represented Turkey to accept the treaty, and the latter had been signed, under English compulsion, by some aged politicians, while the Greeks and the British partitioned the Ottoman Empire between themselves, was it possible to say that all the difficulties were settled? The signature of the treaty could but weaken the tottering power of the Sultan. Moreover, England, eager to derive the utmost benefit from the weakness of Turkey, raised the question of the Caliphate; it was learned from an English source that the title of Caliph had been offered to the Emir of Afghanistan, but the latter had declined the offer. On the other hand, how could Mustafa Kemal be expected to adhere to the decisions taken in Constantinople? It was to be feared, therefore, the agitation would be protracted, for an Anatolian campaign would offer far greater difficulties than those the Greek army had had to overcome on the low plains along the sea; and at Balikesri, standing at an altitude of 400 feet, begin the first slopes of the Anatolian uplands. As a matter of fact, Turkey was not dead, as Mr. Lloyd George believed, but the policy of the British Premier was doomed to failure—the same policy which the Soviets were trifling with, which was paving the way to the secession of Ireland, and may one day cost Great Britain the loss of India and Egypt.

It has even been said the Bolshevists themselves advised Turkey to sign the treaty in order to gain time, and thus organise a campaign in which the Bolshevist forces and the Nationalist forces in Turkey and Asia Minor would fight side by side.

The Ottoman delegation, consisting of General Hadi Pasha, Riza Tewfik Bey, a senator, and the Turkish ambassador at Berne, Reshad Halis Bey, arrived in Paris on Friday, July 30. The signature of the treaty, which was first to take place on July 27 and had been put off till the next Thursday or Saturday because the delegates could not arrive in time, was at the last moment postponed indefinitely.

Some difficulties had arisen between Italy and Greece concerning the "Twelve Islands," or Dodecanese, and this Italo-Greek incident prevented the signature of the treaty. For it was stipulated in Article 122 of the treaty:

"Turkey cedes to Italy all her rights and titles to the islands of the Ægean Sea—viz., Stampalia, Rhodes, Calki, Scarpanto, Casos, Piscopis, Nisyros, Calimnos, Leros, Patmos, Lipsos, Symi, and Cos, now occupied by Italy, and the islets pertaining thereunto, together with the Island of Castellorizzo."

The thirteen islands mentioned here constitute what is called the Dodecanese, and Italy had taken possession of them in 1912, during the war with the Ottoman Empire. But in July, 1919, an agreement, which has already been mentioned, had been concluded between the Italian Government, represented by M. Tittoni, and the Greek Government, represented by M. Venizelos, according to which Italy ceded to Greece the Dodecanese, except Rhodes, which was to share the fate of Cyprus, and pledged herself not to object to Greece setting foot in Southern Albania. Of course, Italy in return was to have advantages in Asia Minor and the Adriatic Sea.

At the meeting of the Supreme Council held in London before the San Remo Conference to draw up the Turkish treaty, M. Venizelos had stated that Greece could not accept Article 122, if the Italo-Greek agreement did not compel Italy to cede the Dodecanese to Greece. M. Scialoja, the Italian delegate, had answered that on the day of the signature of the Turkish treaty an agreement would be signed between Italy and Greece, through which Italy transferred to Greece the sovereignty of the aforesaid islands.

Now Italy, in 1920, considered that the agreement which was binding on both parties had become null and void, as she had not obtained any of the compensations stipulated in it, and so she thought she had a right now not to cede the islands—Castellorizzo, though inhabited by 12,000 Greeks, not being included in the agreement. As to Rhodes, that was to share the fate of Cyprus: England did not seem willing now to cede it to Greece; so that was out of the question for the moment. Moreover, the Italian Government insisted upon keeping the Island of Halki, or Karki, lying near Rhodes. Lastly, as Italy, after the solemn proclamation of the autonomy and independence of Albania, had been obliged to evacuate nearly the whole of Albania, the cession to Greece of part of Southern Albania could not be tolerated by Italian public opinion and had now become an utter impossibility.

Under such circumstances the Greek Government had stated it was no longer willing to sign the Turkish treaty, which, if the previous agreement alone is taken into account, assigns the Dodecanese to Italy. This incident at the last moment prevented the signature of the treaty which had been so laboriously drawn up, and put the Powers in an awkward situation since the regions occupied by the Greek armies in Asia Minor were five times as large as the Smyrna area assigned to Greece, and obviously could not be evacuated by the Greeks before a state of peace was restored between them and Turkey.

The signature of the treaty, which had been put off at first, as has just been mentioned, till the end of July, was, after various delays, arranged for Thursday, August 5, then postponed till the next Saturday, and finally took place only three days later.

Meanwhile, the Armenian delegation raised another objection, and informed the Allies that as their president, Nubar Pasha, had been admitted by the Allied Governments to the signature of the Peace Treaty, as representing the Armenians of Turkey and the Armenian colonies, they thought it unfair not to let him sign the Turkish treaty too, merely because he represented the Turkish Armenians. The Allies advised the Armenians for their own sake not to insist, in order to avoid an official protest of Turkey against the treaty after its signature, under the pretext that it had not been signed regularly.

In the House of Lords the treaty was sharply criticised by Lord Wemyss, especially in regard to the condition of Smyrna and the cession of Eastern Thrace to Greece.

In the speech he delivered on Friday, August 6, at Montecitorio, Count Sforza, coming to the question of the Dodecanese, summed up the Tittoni-Venizelos agreement of July 29, 1919, as follows:

"Italy pledged herself to support at the Conference the Greek claims on Eastern and Western Thrace; she even pledged herself to support the Greek demand of annexing Southern Albania. Greece, in return for this, pledged herself to give Italy a free zone in the port of Santi Quaranta, and to give Italian industry a right of preference for the eventual building of a railway line beginning at this port.

"Greece pledged herself to support at the Conference the Italian mandate over Albania, to recognise Italian sovereignty over Valona, and confirm the neutralisation of the Corfu Canal already prescribed by the London

Conference in 1913-14, when Greece had promised not to build any military works on the coast between Cape Stilo and Aspriruga.

"Greece pledged herself, in case she should have satisfaction in Thrace and Southern Albania, to give up, in favour of Italy, all her territorial claims in Asia Minor which hindered Italian interests.

"The Italian and Greek Governments promised to support each other at the Conference concerning their claims in Asia Minor.

"Italy had already pledged herself to cede to Greece the sovereignty of the isles of the Ægean Sea, except Rhodes, to which the Italian Government promised to grant a liberal administrative autonomy.

"Italy also pledged herself to respect the religious liberty of the Greeks who were going to be more under her rule in Asia Minor, and Greece took a similar engagement with respect to the Italians.

"Article 7 dealt with what would happen if the two countries wished to resume their full liberty of action.

"Italy pledged herself to insert a clause in the treaty, in which she promised to let the people of Rhodes freely decide their own fate, on condition that the plebiscite should not be taken before five years after the signature of the Peace Treaty."

Count Sforza proceeded to say that on July 22, after coming back from Spa, he had addressed M. Venizelos a note to let him know that the Allies' decisions concerning Asia Minor and the aspirations of the Albanian people compelled the Italian Government to alter their policy in order to safeguard the Italian interests in those regions:

"Under the circumstances, the situation based on the agreement of July 29, 1919, as to the line of conduct to be followed at the Conference was substantially modified.

"Therefore Italy, in conformity with Article 7 of the agreement, now resumes her full liberty of action. Yet the Italian Government, urged by a conciliatory spirit, intends to consider the situation afresh, as it earnestly wishes to arrive at a satisfactory and complete understanding.

"The desire to maintain friendly relations with Greece is most deeply felt in Italy. Greece is a vital force to the East. When I tried to get better conditions of peace for Turkey, I felt convinced I was safeguarding the independence and the territorial integrity which the Turkish people is entitled to, and at the same time I was serving the true interests of Hellenism."

In an interview published by the *Stampa*, M. Tittoni on his side declared, concerning the Dodecanese and the arrangement he had negotiated with M. Venizelos, that, as circumstances had changed, the clauses of the agreement had become null and void.

Alluding to the note handed by him on coming to Paris to M. Clémenceau and Mr. Lloyd George and recently read to the Senate by M. Scialoja, he complained that the Allies supported the Greek claims in Asia Minor, and overlooked the Italian interests in the same region. As Greece had got all she wanted and Italy's hopes in Asia Minor had been frustrated, the agreement with M. Venizelos was no longer valid, according to him, and he concluded thus: "The agreement became null and void on the day when at San Remo the draft of the Turkish treaty was definitely drawn up." Finally, on August 9 Greece and Italy came to an agreement, and a protocol was signed. The Dodecanese, according to the Tittoni-Venizelos agreement, were given up to Greece, with the exception of Rhodes, which, for the present, remained in the hands of Italy. In case England should cede Cyprus to Greece, a plebiscite was to be taken at Rhodes within fifteen years, instead of five years as had been settled before. There was no reason why Italy should give up Rhodes if England, which had ruled over Cyprus since 1878, did not hand it over to Greece. The League of Nations was to decide in what manner this plebiscite was to be taken; meanwhile Italy would grant Rhodes a wide autonomy. According to the account given of the Italo-Greek agreement, it includes some stipulations concerning Smyrna, and at the request of the Italian Government the Italian schools, museums, and subjects enjoy a special treatment. Italy keeps her privilege for the archæological excavations at Kos.

Not a word was said of Albania, though there had been some clauses about it in the 1919 agreement. Italy and Greece were to make separate arrangements with the Albanians.

Yugo-Slavia in its turn protested in regard to the share of the Turkish debt that was assigned to her and complained that the charges inherent in the Turkish territories she had received in 1913 were too heavy.

King Hussein too was dissatisfied with the Syrian events and the attitude of France. So he refused to adhere to the treaty, though it indirectly acknowledged the independence of his States and his own sovereignty. He thus showed he really aimed at setting up a huge Arabian Kingdom where his sons would have only been his lieutenants in Syria and Mesopotamia. Besides, King Hussein earnestly begged that the Kingdom of Mesopotamia, which had hitherto been promised to his son Abdullah, should be given to the Emir Feisal as a compensation for Syria, and a hint was given that England would not object to this.

Then the Turkish delegates, seeing the Allies at variance, raised objections to the treaty, and on the morning of August 10 Hadi Pasha informed the Conference he could not sign the treaty if the Allies could not agree together. However, at the earnest request of a high official of the Foreign Office and after he had been repeatedly urged to do so, he consented to sign the treaty in the afternoon at Sèvres.

Together with the Turkish treaty seven treaties or agreements were also signed—namely:

"A treaty in regard to Thrace; sanctioning the cession to Greece of some territories given up by Bulgaria in accordance with the Versailles treaty, and giving Bulgaria a free outlet to the sea at the port of Dedeagatch.

"A tripartite convention between England, France, and Italy, settling the zones of economic influence of France and Italy in the Ottoman territory of Asia Minor.

"A Greco-Italian convention assigning the 'Twelve Islands' to Greece—a plebiscite was to be taken in regard to the sovereignty over Rhodes.

"A treaty between Armenia and the Great Powers, settling the question of the minorities in the future Armenian State.

"A treaty in regard to the Greek minorities, ensuring them protection in the territories that had newly been occupied by Greece.

"A treaty concerning the New States, settling administrative questions between Italy and the States which occupied territories formerly belonging to Austria-Hungary.

"A treaty fixing various frontiers in Central Europe at some places where they had not yet been definitely laid down."

According to the terms of the agreement concerning the protection of minorities, Greece pledged herself to grant to Greek subjects belonging to minorities in language, race, or religion the same civil and political rights, the same consideration and protection as to the other Greek subjects, on the strength of which France and Great Britain gave up their rights of control over Greece, established by the London treaty of 1832, their right of control over the Ionian Islands established by the London treaty of 1864, and their right of protection of religious freedom conferred by the London Conference of 1830.

Greece pledged herself also to present for the approval of the League of Nations within a year a scheme of organisation of Adrianople, including a municipal council in which the various races should be represented. All the clauses of the treaty for the protection of minorities were under the guarantee of the League of Nations. Greece also pledged herself to give the Allies the benefit of the "most favoured nation" clause till a general commercial agreement had been concluded, within five years, under the patronage of the League of Nations.

All these delays and incidents bore witness to the difficulty of arriving at a solution of the Eastern question in the way the Allies had set to work, and to the frailty of the stipulations inserted in the treaty.

They also testified to the lack of skill and political acuteness of Mr. Lloyd George. Of course, the British Premier, owing to the large concessions he had made to Greece, had managed to ensure the preponderance of British influence in Constantinople and the zone of the Straits, and by seeking to set up a large Arabian Empire he had secured to his country the chief trunk of the Baghdad Railway.

But the laborious negotiations which had painfully arrived at the settlement proposed by the Conference did not seem likely to solve the Eastern question definitely. It still remained a burning question, and the treaty signed by the Ottoman delegates was still most precarious. Accordingly Count Sforza, in the Chamber of Deputies in Rome, made the following statement with regard to Anatolia:

"Everybody asserts the war has created a new world; but practically everybody thinks and feels as if nothing had occurred. The Moslem East wants to live and develop. It, too, wants to have an influence of its own in to-morrow's world. To the Anatolian Turks it has been our wish to offer a hearty and earnest collaboration on economic and moral grounds by respecting the independence and sovereignty of Turkey."

The signatures of plenipotentiaries sent by a Government which remained in office merely because its head, Damad Ferid, was a tool in the hands of England, were no guarantee for the future, and the failure of the revolutionary movement indefinitely postponed the settlement of the Eastern question which for half a century has been disturbing European policy.

Islam remains, notwithstanding, a spiritual force that will survive all measures taken against the Sublime Porte, and the dismemberment of the Ottoman Empire does not solve any of the numerous questions raised by the intercourse of the various races that were formerly under the Sultan's rule. Russia has not given up her ambitious designs on the Straits, and one day or another she will try to carry them out; and it is to be feared that German influence may benefit by the resentment of the Turkish people. These are some of the numerous sources of future conflicts.

On the day that followed the signature of the treaty all the Turkish newspapers in Constantinople were in mourning and announced it as a day of mourning for the Turkish nation.

At Stambul all public entertainments were prohibited, all shops and public buildings were closed. Many Turks went to the mosques to pray for the welfare of the country, the people who seek nothing but peace and quietude looked weary and downcast.

A few organs of the Turkish Press violently attacked the delegates who had signed "the death-warrant of Turkey and laid the foundations of a necessary policy of revenge."

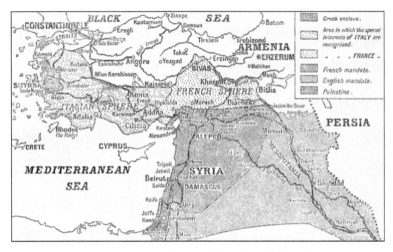

TURKEY UNDER THE TREATY OF SÈVRES.

(201 kB)

SCHEMATIC MAP OF THE TERRITORIES LOST BY TURKEY SINCE 1699, AND OF THE TERRITORIES LEFT TO TURKEY BY THE SÈVRES TREATY.

(204 kB)

Others hoped the Great Powers would take into account the goodwill of Turkey, and would gradually give up some of their intolerable demands.

Others, finally, bewailing the direful downfall of the Turkish Empire and insisting upon the lesson taught by this historical event for the future, hoped that the future would forcibly bring on a revision of that "iniquitous and impracticable" treaty of peace.

In France, M. Pierre Loti devoted one of his last articles to the treaty, which he called "the silliest of all the silly blunders of our Eastern policy."[35]

The map on p. 269 shows the area left to the Turks in Europe and in Asia Minor by the Treaty of Sèvres. There will be seen the territories of Mesopotamia under English mandate, those of Syria under French mandate, and those which have been added to Palestine and are practically under English control. There will also be seen the regions on which France and Italy, in virtue of the tripartite agreement signed on August 10, 1920, enjoy preferential claims to supply the staff required for the assistance of the Porte in organising the local administration and the police. The contracting Powers in that agreement have undertaken not to apply, nor to make or support applications, on behalf of their nationals, for industrial concessions in areas allotted to another Power.

The map on p. 270 is a scheme of the territories lost by Turkey from 1699 down to the Sèvres Treaty; it shows that, by completing the dismemberment of Turkey, the treaty aimed at her annihilation.

Footnotes:

26 *The Times*, March 26, 1920.

27 *The Times*, March 27, 1920: "Mesopotamia and the Mandate."

28 The very words of this agreement were given by M. Pierre Loti in his book, *La Mort de notre chère France en Orient*, p. 153.

29 *Journal des Débats*, May 26, 1920.

30 *Daily Telegraph*, June 12, 1920.

31 *Matin*, June 12, 1920.

32 *La Croix*, July 14, 1920.

33 *Le Temps*, July 17, 1920.

34 Cf. *Ex-King Constantine and the War*, by Major J. M. Melas, p. 239.

35 The *Œuvre*, August 20, 1920.

VII

THE DISMEMBERMENT OF THE OTTOMAN EMPIRE

THE condition of affairs in the East now seemed all the more alarming and critical as the Allies, after dismembering Turkey, did not seem to have given up their plan of evicting the Turks. This policy, which had taken Armenia from Turkey, but had not succeeded in ensuring her a definite status, could only hurry on the Pan-Turkish and Pan-Arabian movements, drive them to assert their opposition more plainly, and thus bring them closer together by reinforcing Pan-Islamism.

Of course it had been said at the beginning of January, 1920, that the Turks were downhearted, that Mustafa Kemal was short of money, that he had to encounter the opposition of the other parties, and that his movement seemed doomed to failure. It was also asserted that his army was only made up of bands which began to plunder the country, and that anarchy now prevailed throughout Turkey-in-Asia. Yet the Nationalist generals soon managed to intercept the food-supply of Constantinople, and when the conditions of the Peace Treaty were made known the situation, as has just been seen, underwent a complete change. They held in check the English till the latter had called the Greeks to their help, and though at a certain stage it would have been possible to negotiate and come to terms with Mustafa Kemal, now, on the contrary, it was impossible to do so, owing to the amplitude and strength gained by the Nationalist movement.

It was soon known that many a parley had been entered into between Turkish and Arabian elements, that some Turkish officers had gone over to the Arabian Nationalists of Syria and had taken command of their troops, and though a political agreement or a closer connection between the two elements did not ensue, yet the Turks and the Arabs, dreading foreign occupation, organised themselves and were ready to help each other to defend their independence.

We should bear in mind what Enver Pasha, who was playing a questionable part in the East, and Fethy Bey had once done in Tripoli. Turkish officers might very well, if an opportunity occurred, impart to these bands the discipline and cohesion they lacked and instil into them a warlike spirit; or these bands might side with the Bolshevists who had invaded the Transcaspian isthmus; they would have been able to hinder the operations that the Allies had once seemed inclined to launch into, but had wisely given up, and they could always raise new difficulties for the Allies.

Lastly, the idea, once contemplated and perhaps not definitely given up, to send back to Asia the Sultans and viziers who, after their centuries-old intercourse with the West, had become "Europeanised" and to whom the ways and manners of our diplomacy had grown familiar, could only modify their foreign policy to our disadvantage, and give it an Asiatic turn; whereas now, having long associated Ottoman affairs with European affairs, they have thus been brought to consider their own interests from a European point of view. The influence of this intercourse with Europe on the Constantinople Government naturally induced it to exercise a soothing influence over the Mussulmans, which was to the advantage of both Europe and Turkey. It is obvious that, on the contrary, the eviction of the Sultan, at a time when the Arabian world and the Turkish world were being roused, would have left the Allied Powers face to face with anarchist elements which, being spurred on by similar religious and nationalist passions, would have grouped together; and one day the Powers would have found themselves confronted with the organised resistance of established governments. Even as things are now, who can foresee what will be all the consequences in the East of the clauses enforced on Turkey by the Sèvres Treaty?

1. THE TURCO-ARMENIAN QUESTION.

The Armenian question, which has convulsed Turkey so deeply and made the Eastern question so intricate, originated in the grasping spirit of Russia in Asia Minor and the meddling of Russia in Turkish affairs under pretence of protecting the Armenians. This question, as proved by the difficulties to which it has given rise since the beginning, is one of the aspects of the antagonism between Slavs and Turks, and a phase of the everlasting struggle of the Turks to hinder the Slavs from reaching the shores of the Mediterranean Sea, to which the Russians have always striven to get access either through Asia Minor or through Thrace, or through both countries at once.

Yet Mohammed II, after taking Constantinople, had in 1461 instituted a patriarchate in favour of the Armenians. Later on various rights were granted to them at different times by Imperial firmans.

Some Armenian monks of Calcutta, availing themselves of the liberty they enjoyed in India, founded at the beginning of the eighteenth century the *Aztarar* (the Newsmonger), the first newspaper published in the Armenian language; and at the end of the same century the Mekhitharists published in Venice *Yeghanak Puzantian* (the Byzantine Season). About the middle of the nineteenth century, the same monks edited a review of literature and information, *Pazmareb*, which still exists. The Protestant Armenians too edited a review of propaganda, *Chtemaran bidani Kidehatz*, at Constantinople.

Finally, in 1840, the first daily paper printed in the Armenian language, *Archalouis Araradian* (the Dawn of Ararat), was published at Smyrna.

In 1857, in the monastery of Varag, near Van, Miguirditch Krimian, who later on became Patriarch and Catholicos, established printing-works. Under the title of *Ardziv Vaspourakani* (the Eagle of Vaspourakan) he edited a monthly review to defend the cause of Armenian independence, and at the same time a similar review, *Ardziv Tarono* (the Eaglet of Taron), was published at Mush. About the same time the Armenians in Russia too began to publish various periodicals, such as *Hussissapail* (the Aurora Borealis), a review printed at Moscow in 1850, and several newspapers at Tiflis and Baku. In 1860 the Armenians were allowed to hold an Armenian National Assembly to discuss and settle their religious and national affairs.

From the fourteenth century till about 1860, the Armenian element lived on good terms with the Moslem element, and some Armenians persecuted in Russia even sought refuge in Turkey. The Turks, on their coming, had found Armenians, but no Armenia, for the latter country, in the course of a most confused history, had enjoyed but short periods of independence with ever-changing frontiers; and the Armenians who had successively been under Roman, Seljuk, Persian, and Arabian dominion lived quietly with the Turks for six centuries.

But in 1870 a group of young men revived and modified a movement which had been started and kept up by Armenian monks, and wrote books in Constantinople in favour of the Armenians.

In 1875, Portokalian established the first revolutionary Armenian Committee, and edited a newspaper, *Asia*. Soon afterwards the *Araratian* committee was formed, aiming at establishing a close connection between Turkish and Russian Armenians, followed by other committees such as *Tebrotssassiranz, Arevelian*, and *Kilikia*.

Other committees with charitable or economic purposes, such as "The Association of Kindness" and "The Association of Benevolence," which were started in 1860 with a large capital to develop the natural resources of Cilicia, also played a part in the Armenian movement.

The Armenian question began really to arise and soon grew more and more acute in 1878, after the Turco-Russian war, at a time when Turkey had to face serious domestic and foreign difficulties. This question was dealt with in Article 16 of the San Stefano treaty of July 10, 1878, and Article 61 of the Berlin treaty. Article 16 of the San Stefano treaty, drawn up at the Armenians' request, and supported by the Russian plenipotentiaries, stated that "the Sublime Porte pledges itself to realise without any more delay the administrative autonomy rendered necessary by local needs in the provinces inhabited by Armenians." The Turks raised an objection to the words "administrative autonomy" and wanted them to be replaced by "reforms and improvements," but the Russians then demanded the occupation of Armenia by the Tsar's troops as a guarantee. The Berlin Congress did away with this clause of guarantee, and instead of the words proposed by Russia adopted those asked for by Turkey.

In order to acquire a moral influence over the Armenians living in Turkey and play a prominent part among them, the Orthodox Christians who were devoted to the Tsar endeavoured to get themselves recognised as a superior power by the patriarchate of Constantinople, and with the help of Russian political agents they succeeded in their endeavours. It was soon observed that the new connection between the Catholicos and the Constantinople Patriarchate aimed at, and succeeded in, starting an anti-Turkish movement within the Armenian populations of Russia and Asia Minor.

When the Russians arrived close to Constantinople, at the end of the Turco-Russian war, Nerses Varzabedian, who had succeeded Krimian, was received by the Grand Duke Nicholas, and handed him a memorandum, in which, after stating all the Armenian grievances against the Ottoman Government, he asked "that the Eastern provinces of Asia Minor inhabited by Armenians should be proclaimed independent or at least should pass under the control of Russia." Four prelates were sent separately to Rome, Venice, Paris, and London to make sure of the Powers' support, and met together at the Berlin Congress. Though they strongly advocated the maintenance of Article 16 of the San Stefano treaty, they only succeeded in getting Article 61 of the Berlin treaty.

It was not until about 1885 that what was afterwards called the Armenian movement began to be spoken of, and then some Armenian revolutionaries who had sought shelter in England, France, Austria, and America began to edit periodicals, form committees, inveigh against the would-be Turkish exactions, and denounce the violation of the Berlin treaty.

These ideas of independence soon made more and more headway and the prelates who, after Nerses' death, were known for their pro-Turkish feelings, as Haroutian Vehabedian, Bishop of Erzerum, made Patriarch in 1885, were forsaken by the Armenian clergy and soon found themselves in opposition to the committees.

In 1888 Khorene Achikian, who succeeded Vehabedian, was also accused of being on friendly terms with the Turks, and the committees strove to have him replaced by Narbey, who had been a member of the delegation sent to Europe for the Berlin Congress.

This Armenian movement naturally caused some incidents between the various elements of the population, which were magnified, brought by the bishops and consuls to the knowledge of the European Powers, and cited as the outcome of Turkish cruelty.

After the Turco-Russian war, the revolutionary agitation which stirred up Russia and the Caucasus had its repercussion among the Armenians, and the harsh measures of the Tsar's Government only strengthened the agitation by increasing Armenian discontent.

Miguirditch Portokalian, a teacher living at Van, came to Marseilles, where in 1885 he edited a newspaper, *Armenia*. At the same time Minas Tscheraz started another newspaper in Paris under the same title. These publicists, both in their journals and in meetings, demanded that Article 61 of the Berlin treaty should be carried out.

In 1880 some revolutionary committees were formed in Turkey. In 1882 "The Association of the Armed Men" was founded at Erzerum; some of its members were arrested, and the association itself was dissolved in 1883.

A rising took place at Van in 1885 on the occasion of the election of a bishop, and some insurrectionist movements occurred at Constantinople, Mush, and Alashehr under various pretexts.

Next year, in 1886, one Nazarbey, a Caucasian by birth, and his wife Maro, formed in Switzerland the *Huntchag* (the Bell), a social-democrat committee that aimed at getting an autonomous administration for the Armenians, and published in London a monthly periodical bearing the same name. This committee meant to achieve its object not through the intervention or mediation of the European Powers—to which it thought it useless to make another appeal, as their individual interests were so much at variance—but solely by the action of its organisations throughout the country, which were to raise funds, equipment, foment troubles, weaken the Government, and take advantage of any opportunity that might occur.

The *Huntchag* committee found representatives in every great town—Smyrna, Aleppo, Constantinople, etc.—and its organisation was completed in 1889.

In 1890, at the instigation of the Huntchagists, a rebellion broke out at Erzerum, and incidents occurred in various places. At Constantinople a demonstration of armed men, headed by the Patriarch Achikian, repaired to the Sublime Porte to set forth their grievances, but were scattered; and the Patriarch, who was reproached with being too moderate, and whose life was even attempted, had to resign.

In fact the *Huntchag* committee, which enlisted the effective and moral support of the representatives of the Powers, especially those of Russia and

England, carried on its intrigues without intermission, and increased its activity.

On Sunday, March 25, 1894, at Samsun, in the ground adjoining the church, one Agap, living at Diarbekir, who had been chosen by the *Huntchag* committee to kill the Patriarch Achikian because he was accused of being on friendly terms with the Ottoman Government, fired at the prelate with a revolver, but missed his mark. After this criminal attempt, Achikian resigned his office, and Mathew Ismirlian, supported by the committees, was elected Patriarch, owing to the pressure brought to bear on the National Assembly. The new Patriarch immediately became chairman of the *Huntchag* committee, which he developed, and soon after appointed President of the Ecclesiastical Council of the Patriarchate and later on Catholicos of Cilicia a certain priest, Kirkor Alajan, who had been dismissed and sent to Constantinople for insulting the Governor of Mush.

A few Armenians, dissatisfied with the programme of the Huntchagists, founded a new association in 1890 under the name of *Troshak*, which later on was called *Tashnaktsutioun*, and edited the *Troshak* newspaper. The members of this committee often resorted to threats and terror to get the funds they needed, and did not shrink from assassinating whoever refused to comply with the injunctions of the committee.

In 1896 the committees attempted to seize the Ottoman Bank. Some armed komitadjis, who had come from Europe with Russian passports, rushed into the Ottoman Bank, but were driven back by Government troops. But the promoters of the raid were not arrested, owing to their being protected by the Russian and French authorities. Attended by Maximof, an Armenian by birth, first dragoman of the Russian embassy, and Rouet, first dragoman of the French embassy, they were brought by the dispatch-boat of the latter embassy on board the *Gironde*, a packet-ship of the Messageries Maritimes. The adherents of the *Troshak*, entrenched in the churches of Galata, Samatra, and the Patriarchate, begged for mercy, while Armene Aktoni, one of the leaders of the committee, committed suicide after waiting for the coming of the English fleet on the heights of Soulou-Monastir, at Samatra.

The bishops continued to solicit, and to some extent obtained, the support of the Russian, English, and French consuls; yet Mgr. Ismirlian, who had sent an ultimatum to the Imperial Palace and never ceased to intrigue, was finally dismissed in 1896 and sent to Jerusalem.

At that time many Armenians set off to Europe and America, and the Catholicos of Etchmiadzin sent some delegates to the Hague Conference to lay before it the Armenian plight in Turkey. These committees, which displayed so much activity in Turkey, did not attempt anything on behalf of their fellow-countrymen in Russia.

The committees which had been founded during or before Nerses' patriarchate under the names of *Ararat*, *The Orient*, *The Friends of Education*, *Cilicia*, were all grouped, in 1890, into one called *Miatzal Anikeroutioun Hayotz*, which association continued to organise committees even in the smallest villages, taking advantage of the tolerance of the Ottoman Government and its benevolence to the Armenians to carry on an active anti-Turkish propaganda.

This propaganda was supported by the Armenian bishops in the eastern provinces, where they endeavoured to bring about European intervention. On the other hand the Russians, as eager as ever to domineer over both the Orthodox Church and Armenia, incited the Armenians against the Turks by all possible means and urged them to fulfil their national aspirations, as they knew full well they would thus bring them more easily under Russian sovereignty.

The influence of these committees, as will be seen later on, had a very important bearing on the events that took place in Asia Minor at that time.

Risings, which may be traced back to 1545 and lasted till the proclamation of the 1908 constitution, were continually taking place in the mountainous area of Zeitun. They were partly brought about by the feudal system of administration still prevailing in that region. Each of the four districts of Zeitun was governed by a chief who had assumed the title of "ishehan" or prince, a kind of nobleman to whom Turkish villages had to pay some taxes collected by special agents. The action of the committees, of course, benefited by that state of things, to which the Ottoman Government put an end only in 1895.

The Armenians had already refused to pay the taxes and had rebelled repeatedly between 1782 and 1851, at which time the Turks, incensed at the looting and exactions of the Armenian mountaineers, left their farms and emigrated. Till that time the rebellions of Zeitun could be partly accounted for by the administration of the "ishehan." But the leaders of the Armenian movement soon took advantage of these continual disturbances and quickly gave them another character. The movement was spurred on and eagerly supported by Armenians living abroad, and in 1865, after the so-called Turkish exactions, the Nationalist committees openly rebelled against the Government and demanded the independence of Zeitun. Henceforth rebellion followed rebellion, and one of them, fomented by the Huntchagists, lasted three months.

In 1890 the *Huntchag* and *Tashnaktsutioun* committees stirred up riots at Erzerum, and in 1894 at Samsun, where the Patriarch Ashikian was fired at, as has just been seen. In 1905 the Tashnakists started a new insurrection. The rebellion extended to Amasia, Sivas, Tokat, Mush, and Van, and the committees endeavoured to spread and intensify it. In 1905-06 the manœuvres of the Armenian committees succeeded in rousing hostile feelings between Kurds and Armenians, which no reform whatever seemed able to soothe. And in 1909-10, when new troubles broke out, the revolutionary leaders openly attacked the Government troops.

Two years after the confiscation and handing over to the Ottoman Government of the Armenian churches on June 21, 1903, massacres took place at Batum on February 6, 1905, and later on at Erivan, Nakhitchevan, Shusha, and Koshak. In 1908 the Tsar's sway in the whole of Caucasus became most oppressive, and a ukase prescribed the election of a new catholicos to succeed Mgr. Krimian, who had died in October, 1907. Mgr. Ismirlian was appointed in his stead in 1908. By that time the Russian sway had become so oppressive that the Tashnakists took refuge in Constantinople, where the Young Turks openly declared in favour of the Russian Armenians.

It might have been expected that after the proclamation of the Constitution the committees, who had striven to hurry on the downfall of the Empire through an agitation that might have brought about foreign intervention, would put an end to their revolutionary schemes and turn their activity towards social and economic questions. Sabah-Gulian, a Caucasian by birth, president of the *Huntchag*, at a meeting of this committee held in 1908 in Sourp-Yerourtoutioun church at Pera, speaking of the Huntchagists' programme and the constitutional régime, declared: "We, Huntchagists, putting an end to our revolutionary activity, must devote all our energy to the welfare of the country." On the other hand Agnoni, a Russian by birth, one of the presidents of the *Tashnaktsutioun*, stated that "the first duty of the Tashnakists would be to co-operate with the Union and Progress Committee in order to maintain the Ottoman Constitution and ensure harmony and concord between the various elements."

The union of the committees did not last long, as they held widely different views about the new condition of the Turkish Empire; but soon after the *Tashnaktsutioun*, the *Huntchag*, and the *Veragaznial-Huntchag* committees were reorganised and new committees formed throughout Turkey. The *Ramgavar* (the Rights of the People) committee was instituted in Egypt by M. Boghos Nubar after the proclamation of the Constitution, and displayed the greatest activity. This committee, in March, 1914, agreed to work on the same lines with the *Huntchag*, the *Tashnaktsutioun*, and the *Veragaznial-Huntchag*. Another committee, the *Sahmanatragan*, was also constituted. They made sure of the support of the Patriarchate and the bishops to reassert their influence and spread a network of ramifications all over the country in order to triumph at the elections. They carried on an active propaganda to conciliate public opinion, by means of all kinds of publications, school books, almanacs, postcards, songs, and so on, all edited at Geneva or in Russia.

As early as 1905 the Armenian committees had decided at a congress held in Paris to resort to all means in order to make Cilicia an independent country. Russia, on the other hand, strove hard to spread orthodoxy in the districts round Adana, Marash, and Alexandretta, in order to enlarge her zone of influence on this side and thus get an outlet to the Mediterranean. At the same time, the Bishop of Adana, Mosheg, did his best to foment the rebellion which was to break out soon after.

In this way the Armenian Christians contributed to the extension of the Russian Empire. In 1904-05, the Nestorians asked for Russian priests and expressed their intention to embrace the Orthodox Faith. The Armenians of Bitlis, Diarbekir, and Kharput in 1907 handed the Russian consul a petition bearing over 200,000 signatures, in which they asked to become Russian subjects.

The Huntchagist leader, Sabah-Gulian, even owned in the *Augah Hayassdan* (Independent Armenia) newspaper that the members of the committee had taken advantage of the Turks' carelessness to open shops, where rifles were being sold at half-price or even given away.

The Armenian committees took advantage of the new parliamentary elections to stir up a new agitation. They increased their activity, and, contrary to their engagements, corresponded with the members of the opposition who had fled abroad.

During the Balkan war in 1913 the Tashnakist committees issued manifestoes against the Ottoman Government and the Union party. The Russian consuls at Erzerum and Bitlis did not conceal their sympathy, and at Van the Russian consul threatened to the vali to ask Russian troops to come through Azerbaïjan under the pretext of averting the fictitious dangers the Armenians were supposed to run, and of restoring order.

Now, whereas Russia at home unmercifully stifled all the attempts of the Armenian committees, she encouraged and energetically supported the agitators in Turkey. Moreover, in the report addressed by the Russian consul at Bitlis to the Russian ambassador in Constantinople, dated December 24, 1912, and bearing number 63, the Russian Government was informed that the aim of the Tashnakists was, as they expressly said, "to bring the Russians here," and that, in order "to reach this end, the Tashnakists are resorting to various means, and doing their best to bring about collisions between

Armenians and Moslems, especially with Ottoman troops." In support of this statement he mentioned a few facts that leave no doubt about its veracity.

This report contained the following lines, which throw considerable light on the Allies' policy:

"Your Excellency will understand that the future collisions between Armenians and Moslems will partly depend on the line of conduct and activity of the *Tashnaktsutioun* committee, on the turn taken by the peace negotiations between Turkey and the Slavonic States of the Balkans, and on the eventuality of an occupation of Constantinople by the Allies. If the deliberations of the London Conference did not bring about peace, the coming downfall of the Ottoman capital would certainly influence the relations between Moslems and Armenians at Bitlis.

"Both in towns and in the country the Armenians, together with their religions leaders, have always displayed much inclination and affection for Russia, and have repeatedly declared the Turkish Government is unable to maintain order, justice, and prosperity in their country. Many Armenians have already promised to offer the Russian soldiers their churches to be converted into orthodox places of worship.

"The present condition of the Balkans, the victory of the Slav and Hellenic Governments over Turkey, have delighted the Armenians and filled their hearts with the cheerful hope of being freed from Turkey."

Of course, the coming to Bitlis of a mixed Commission of Armenians and Turks under the presidency of an Englishman, in order to carry out reforms in the Turkish provinces near the Caucasus, did not please the Armenians and Russians who had sacrificed many soldiers to get possession of these regions.

Taking advantage of the difficulties experienced by the Ottoman Government after the Balkan war, the committees agreed together to raise anew the question of "reforms in the Eastern provinces." A special commission, presided over by M. Boghos Nubar, was sent by the Catholicos of Etchmiadzin to the European Governments to uphold the Armenian claims. At the same time a campaign was started by the Armenian newspapers of Europe, Constantinople, and America, especially by the *Agadamard*, the organ of the *Tashnaktsutioun* committee, which had no scruple in slandering the Turks and announcing sham outrages.

In 1913 Russia proposed a scheme of reforms to be instituted in Armenia. It was communicated by M. de Giers to the Six Ambassadors' Conference, which appointed a commission to report on it. As the German and Austrian representatives raised objections to the Russian scheme before that Commission of Armenian Reforms, which met from June 20 to July 3, 1913, at the Austrian embassy at Yeni Keui, Russia, after this defeat, strove to bring over Germany to her views.

In September, 1913, M. de Giers and M. de Wangenheim came to terms on a programme to which the Porte opposed a counter-proposal. Yet the Russian representatives succeeded in concluding a Russo-Turkish agreement, January 26 to February 8, 1914.

When the scheme of reforms was outlined, and the powers and jurisdiction of the inspectors and their staff were settled, the Catholicos sent a telegram of congratulation to M. Borghos Nubar and the latter sent another to M. Sazonov, for the Armenian committees considered the arrangement as a first step towards autonomy. Encouraged by this first success, the committees exerted themselves more and more. The *Tashnaksutioun* transferred its seat to Erzerum, where it held a congress. The *Huntchag* committee sent to Russia and Caucasus several of its most influential members to raise funds in order to foment a rising to attack the Union and Progress party especially, and to overthrow the Government. Such was the state of things when war broke out.

The Patriarch, who passed himself off as representing the Armenian people, gathered together under his presidency the leaders of the *Tashnaktsutioun*, the *Huntchag*, the *Ramgavar*, and the *Veragaznial-Huntchag*, and the members of the National Assembly who were affiliated to these committees to decide what attitude they were to take in case the Ottoman Government should enter into the war. No decision was taken, the Huntchagists declining to commit themselves and the Tasknakists stating they preferred waiting to see how things would turn out. Yet these committees carried on their activities separately, and sent instructions to the provinces that, if the Russians advanced, all means should be resorted to in order to impede the retreat of the Ottoman troops and hold up their supplies, and if, on the contrary, the Ottoman army advanced, the Armenian soldiers should leave their regiments, form themselves into groups, and go over to the Russians.

The committees availed themselves of the difficulties of the Ottoman Government, which had recently come out of a disastrous war and had just entered into a new conflict, to bring about risings at Zeitun, in the sandjaks of Marash and Cesarea, and chiefly in the vilayet of Van, at Bitlis, Talori, and Mush in the vilayet of Bitlis, and in the vilayet of Erzerum.

In the sandjaks of Erzerum and Bayazid, as soon as the decree of mobilisation was issued, most of the Armenian soldiers went over to the Russians, were equipped and armed anew by them, and then sent against the

Turks. The same thing occurred at Erzindjan, where three-fourths of the Armenians crossed the Russian frontier.

The Armenians of the vilayet of Mamouret' ul Azig (Kharput), where the Mussulmans were also attacked and where depots of arms had been concealed, provided with numerous recruits the regiments dispatched by Russia to Van and the Persian frontier. Many emissaries had been sent from Russia and Constantinople to Dersim and its area to raise the Kurds against the Ottoman Government. So it was in the vilayet of Diarbekir, though the Armenians were in a minority. Depots of arms of all descriptions were discovered there, together with many refractory soldiers.

In the Karahissar area, where several revolutionary movements had broken out during and after the Balkan war, the Armenians refused to obey the decree of mobilisation and were only waiting for the coming of the Russians to rebel.

Similar incidents—such as mutinous soldiers, attacks against the Turks, threats to families of mobilised Ottomans—occurred in the vilayet of Angora.

In the vilayet of Van, when the Russians, reinforced by Armenian volunteers, started an offensive, some Armenian peasants gathered together and prepared to attack the Ottoman officials and the gendarmerie. At the beginning of 1915 rebellions took place at Kevash, Shatak, Havassour, and Timar, and spread in the kazas of Arjitch and Adeljivaz. At Van over five thousand rebels, seven hundred of whom attacked the fortress, blew up the military and Government buildings, the Ottoman Bank, the offices of the Public Debt, the excise office, the post and telegraph offices, and set fire to the Moslem quarter. When this insurrection subsided about the end of April, numerous Armenian bands, led by Russian officers, attempted to cross the Russian and Persian frontiers.

After the capture of Van, the Armenians gave a great dinner in honour of General Nicolaiev, commander-in-chief of the Russian army in Caucasus, who made a speech in which he said: "Since 1826, the Russians have always striven to free Armenia, but political circumstances have always prevented their success. Now, as the grouping of nations has been quite altered, we may hope Armenians will soon be free." Aram Manoukian, known as Aram Pasha, soon after appointed provisional Governor of Van by General Nicolaiev, replied: "When we rose a month ago, we expected the Russians would come. At a certain moment, our situation was dreadful. We had to choose between surrender and death. We chose death, but when we no longer expected your help, it has suddenly arrived."[36]

The Armenian bands even compelled the Ottoman Government to call back troops from the front to suppress their revolutionary manœuvres in the vilayet of Brusa and the neighbourhood. At Adana, as in the other provinces, all sorts of insurrectionary movements were smouldering.

Under such circumstances, the Turkish Government tried to crush these revolutionary efforts by military expeditions, and the repression was merciless. A decree of the Government about changes of residence of the Armenian populations included measures for the deportation of Armenians. As the Turks are generally so listless, and as similar methods had been resorted to by the Germans on the Western front, these measures may have been suggested to the Turks by the Germans.

Tahsin Pasha, Governor of Van, was replaced by Jevdet Bey, Enver's brother-in-law, and Khalil Pasha, another relation of Enver, had command of the Turkish troops in the Urmia area. Talaat sent Mustafa Khalil, his brother-in-law, to Bitlis.

The revolutionary manœuvres of the Armenians and the repressive measures of the Turks, with their mutual repercussions, could not but quicken the old feuds; so the outcome was a wretched one for both parties.

One cannot wonder that under such conditions continuous conflicts arose between the two elements of the population, that reprisals followed reprisals on either side, first after the Turco-Russian war, again after the events of 1895-96, then in the course of the Adana conflict, during the Balkan war, and finally during the late war. But it is impossible to trust the information according to which the number of the Armenians slaughtered by the Turks rose to over 800,000 and in which no mention is made of any Turks massacred by the Armenians. These figures are obviously exaggerated,[37] since the Armenian population, which only numbered about 2,300,000 souls before the war throughout the Turkish Empire, did not exceed 1,300,000 in the eastern provinces, and the Armenians now declare they are still numerous enough to make up a State. According to Armenian estimates there were about 4,160,000 Armenians in all in 1914—viz., 2,380,000 in the Ottoman Empire, 1,500,000 in Russia, 64,000 in the provinces of the Persian Shah and in foreign colonies, and about 8,000 in Cyprus, the isles of the Archipelago, Greece, Italy, and Western Europe.

The best answer to the eager and ever-recurring complaints made by the Armenians or at their instigation is to refer the reader to a report entitled "Statistics of the Bitlis and Van Provinces" drawn up by General Mayewsky, who was Russian consul first at Erzerum for six years and later on at Van, and in this capacity represented a Power that had always showed much hostility to Turkey. It was said in it:

"All the statements of the publicists, which represent the Kurds as doing their best to exterminate the Armenians, must be altogether rejected. If they were reliable, no individual belonging to an alien race could have ever lived in the midst of the Kurds, and the various peoples living among them would have been obliged to emigrate bodily for want of bread, or to become their slaves. Now nothing of the kind has occurred. On the contrary, all those who know the eastern provinces state that in those countries the Christian villages are at any rate more prosperous than those of the Kurds. If the Kurds were only murderers and thieves, as is often said in Europe, the prosperous state of the Armenians till 1895 would have been utterly impossible. So the distress of the Armenians in Turkey till 1895 is a mere legend. The condition of the Turkish Armenians was no worse than that of the Armenians living in other countries.

"The complaints according to which the condition of the Armenians in Turkey is represented as unbearable do not refer to the inhabitants of the towns, for the latter have always been free and enjoyed privileges in every respect. As to the peasants, owing to their perfect knowledge of farmwork and irrigation, their condition was far superior to that of the peasants in Central Russia.

"As to the Armenian clergy, they make no attempt to teach religion; but they have striven hard to spread national ideas. Within the precincts of mysterious convents, the teaching of hatred of the Turk has replaced devotional observances. The schools and seminaries eagerly second the religious leaders."

After the collapse of Russia, the Armenians, Georgians, and Tatars formed a Transcaucasian Republic which was to be short-lived, and we have dealt in another book with the attempt made by these three States together to safeguard their independence.[38]

The Soviet Government issued a decree on January 13, 1918, stipulating in Article 1 "the evacuation of Armenia by the Russian troops, and the immediate organisation of an Armenian militia in order to safeguard the personal and material security of the inhabitants of Turkish Armenia," and in Article 4, "the establishment of a provisional Armenian Government in Turkish Armenia consisting of delegates of the Armenian people elected according to democratic principles," which obviously could not satisfy the Armenians.

Two months after the promulgation of this decree, the Brest-Litovsk treaty in March, 1918, stipulated in Article 4 that "Russia shall do her utmost to ensure the quick evacuation of the eastern provinces of Anatolia. Ardahan, Kars, and Batum shall be evacuated at once by the Russian troops."

The Armenians were the more dissatisfied and anxious after these events as they had not concealed their hostile feelings against the Turks and their satisfaction no longer to be under their dominion; they now dreaded the return of the Turks, who would at least make an effort to recover the provinces they had lost in 1878.

In April of the same year fighting was resumed, and Trebizond, Erzinjan, Erzerum, Mush, and Van were recaptured by the Turks. After the negotiations between the Georgians and the Turks, and the arrangements that supervened, the Armenians constituted a Republic in the neighbourhood of Erivan and Lake Sevanga (Gokcha).

After the discussion of the Armenian question at the Peace Conference and a long exchange of views, Mr. Wilson, in August, 1919, sending a note direct to the Ottoman Government, called upon it to prevent any further massacre of Armenians and warned it that, should the Constantinople Government be unable to do so, he would cancel the twelfth of his Fourteen Points demanding "that the present Ottoman Empire should be assured of entire sovereignty"—which, by the by, is in contradiction with other points of the same message to Congress, especially the famous right of self-determination of nations, which he wished carried out unreservedly.

The Armenians did not give up the tactics that had roused Turkish animosity and had even exasperated it, for at the end of August they prepared to address a new note to the Allied High Commissioners in Constantinople to draw their attention to the condition of the Christian element in Anatolia and the dangers the Armenians of the Republic of Erivan were beginning to run. Mgr. Zaven, Armenian Patriarch, summed up this note in a statement published by *Le Temps*, August 31, 1919.

Mr. Gerard, former ambassador of the United States at Berlin, in a telegram[39] addressed to Mr. Balfour on February 15, 1920, asserted that treaties for the partition of Armenia had been concluded during Mr. Balfour's tenure of the post of Secretary for Foreign Affairs and at a time when the Allied leaders and statesmen had adopted the principle of self-determination of peoples as their principal war-cry. He expressed distress over news that the Allies might cut up Armenia, and said that 20,000 ministers, 85 bishops, 250 college and university presidents, and 40 governors, who had "expressed themselves in favour of unified Armenia, will be asked to join in condemnation of decimation of Armenia." He added that Americans had given £6,000,000 for Armenian relief, and that another £6,000,000 had been asked for. Americans were desirous of aiding Armenia during her formative period. "Ten members of our committee, including Mr. Hughes and Mr. Root, and with the approval of Senator Lodge, had telegraphed to the President that America should aid Armenia. We are earnestly anxious that Britain should seriously consider American opinion on the Armenian case. Can you not postpone consideration of the Turkish question until after ratification of the treaty by the Senate, which is likely to take place before March?"

Mr. Balfour, in his reply dispatched on February 24, said:

"In reply to your telegram of February 16, I should observe that the first paragraph seems written under a misapprehension. I concluded no treaties about Armenia at all.

"I do not understand why Great Britain will be held responsible by 20,000 ministers of religion, 85 bishops, 250 university professors, and 40 governors if a Greater Armenia is not forthwith created, including Russian Armenia on the north and stretching to the Mediterranean on the south.

"Permit me to remind you of the facts.

"1. Great Britain has no interests in Armenia except those based on humanitarian grounds. In this respect her position is precisely that of the United States.

"2. I have always urged whenever I had an opportunity that the United States should take its share in the burden of improving conditions in the pre-war territories of the Turkish Empire and in particular that it should become the mandatory in Armenia. Events over which Great Britain had no control have prevented this consummation and have delayed, with most unhappy results, the settlement of the Turkish peace.

"3. There appears to be great misconception as to the condition of affairs in Armenia. You make appeal in your first sentence to the principle of self-determination. If this is taken in its ordinary meaning as referring to the wishes of the majority actually inhabiting a district, it must be remembered that in vast regions of Greater Armenia the inhabitants are overwhelmingly Mussulman, and if allowed to vote would certainly vote against the Armenians.

"I do not think this conclusive; but it must not be forgotten. Whoever undertakes, in your own words, to aid Armenia during her formative period must, I fear, be prepared to use military force. Great Britain finds the utmost difficulty in carrying out the responsibilities she has already undertaken. She cannot add Armenia to their number. America with her vast population and undiminished resources, and no fresh responsibilities thrown upon her by the war, is much more fortunately situated. She has shown herself most generous towards these much oppressed people; but I greatly fear that even the most lavish charity, unsupported by political and military assistance, will prove quite insufficient to deal with the unhappy consequences of Turkish cruelty and misrule.

"If I am right in inferring from your telegram that my attitude on the question has been somewhat misunderstood in America, I should be grateful if you would give publicity to this reply."

On February 28 Mr. Gerard telegraphed to Mr. Balfour that in referring to treaties made during Mr. Balfour's period of office he had in mind the Sykes-Picot compact. After saying that "Great Britain and France could not be justified in requiring American aid to Armenia as a condition precedent to their doing justice to Armenia," he declared that "Armenia's plight since 1878 is not unrelated to a series of arrangements, well meant, no doubt, in which Great Britain played a directive rôle," and he concluded in the following terms:

"Our faith in chivalry of Great Britain and France and our deliberate conviction in ultimate inexpediency of allowing Turkish threat to override concerted will of Western civilisation through further sacrifice of Armenia inspire us to plead with you to construe every disadvantage in favour of Armenia and ask you to plan to aid her toward fulfilment of her legitimate aspirations, meanwhile depending on us to assume our share in due time, bearing in mind imperative necessity of continued concord that must exist between our democracies for our respective benefit and for that of the world."

Soon after, Lord Curzon said in the House of Lords: "It must be owned the Armenians during the last weeks did not behave like innocent little lambs, as some people imagine. The fact is they have indulged in a series of wild attacks, and proved blood-thirsty people." *The Times* gave an account of these atrocities on March 19.

At the beginning of February, 1920, the British Armenia Committee of London had handed to Mr. Lloyd George a memorandum in which the essential claims of Armenia were set forth before the Turkish problem was definitely settled by the Allies.

In this document the Committee said they were sorry that Lord Curzon on December 17, 1919, expressed a doubt about the possibility of the total realisation of the Armenian scheme, according to which Armenia was to stretch from one sea to the other, especially as the attitude of America did not facilitate the solution of the Armenian question. After recalling Lord Curzon's and Mr. Lloyd George's declarations in both the House of Lords and the House of Commons, the British Armenia Committee owned it was difficult, if the United States refused a mandate and if no other mandatory could be found, to group into one nation all the Ottoman provinces which they believed Armenia was to include; yet they drafted a programme which, though it was a minimum one, aimed at completely and definitely freeing these provinces from Turkish sovereignty. It ran as follows;

"An Ottoman suzerainty, even a nominal one, would be an outrage, as the Ottoman Government deliberately sought to exterminate the Armenian people.

"It would be a disgrace for all nations if the bad precedents of Eastern Rumelia, Macedonia, and Crete were followed, and if similar expedients were resorted to, in reference to Armenia. The relations between Armenia and the Ottoman Empire must wholly cease, and the area thus detached must include all the former Ottoman provinces. The Ottoman Government of Constantinople has for many years kept up a state of enmity and civil war among the various local races, and many facts demonstrate that when once that strange, malevolent sovereignty is thrust aside, these provinces will succeed in living together on friendly, equable terms."

The British Armenia Committee asked that the Armenian territories which were to be detached from Turkey should be immediately united into an independent Armenian State, which would not be merely restricted to "the quite inadequate area of the Republic of Erivan," but would include the former Russian districts of Erivan and Kars, the zone of the former Ottoman territories with the towns of Van, Mush, Erzerum, Erzinjan, etc., and a port on the Black Sea. This document proclaimed that the Armenians now living were numerous enough "to fortify, consolidate, and ensure the prosperity of an Armenian State within these boundaries, without giving up the hope of extending farther." It went on thus:

"The economic distress now prevailing in the Erivan area is due to the enormous number of refugees coming from the neighbouring Ottoman provinces who are encamped there temporarily. If these territories were included in the Armenian State, the situation would be much better, for all these refugees would be able to return to their homes and till their lands. With a reasonable foreign support, the surviving manhood of the nation would suffice to establish a National State in this territory, which includes but one-fourth of the total Armenian State to be detached from Turkey. In the new State, the Armenians will still be more numerous than the other non-Armenian elements, the latter not being connected together and having been decimated during the war like the Armenians."

Finally, in support of its claim, the Committee urged that the Nationalist movement of Mustafa Kemal was a danger to England, and showed that only Armenia could check this danger.

"For if Mustafa Kemal's Government is not overthrown, our new Kurdish frontier will never be at peace; the difficulties of its defence will keep on increasing; and the effect of the disturbances will be felt as far as India. If, on the contrary, that focus of disturbance is replaced by a stable Armenian State, our burden will surely be alleviated."

Then the British Armenia Committee, summing up its chief claims, asked for the complete separation of the Ottoman Empire from the Armenian area, and, in default of an American mandate, the union of the Armenian provinces of the Turkish Empire contiguous to the Republic of Erivan with the latter Republic, together with a port on the Black Sea.

In the report which had been drawn up by the American Commission of Inquiry sent to Armenia, with General Harboor as chairman, and which President Wilson had transmitted to the Senate at the beginning of April, 1920, after the latter assembly had asked twice for it, no definite conclusion was reached as to the point whether America was to accept or refuse a mandate for that country. The report simply declared that in no case should the United States accept a mandate without the agreement of France and Great Britain and the formal approbation of Germany and Russia. It merely set forth the reasons for and against the mandate.

It first stated that whatever Power accepts the mandate must have under its control the whole of Anatolia, Constantinople, and Turkey-in-Europe, and have complete control over the foreign relations and the revenue of the Ottoman Empire.

Before coming to the reasons that tend in favour of the acceptance of the mandate by the United States, General Harboor made an appeal to the humanitarian feelings of the Americans and urged that it was their interest to ensure the peace of the world. Then he declared their acceptance would answer the wishes of the Near East, whose preference undeniably was for America, or, should the United States refuse, for Great Britain. He added that each Great Power, in case it could not obtain a mandate, would want it to be given to America.

The report valued the expenditure entailed by acceptance of the mandate at 275 million dollars far the first year, and $756,140,000 for the first five years. After some time, the profits made by the mandatory Power would balance the expenses, and Americans might find there a profitable investment. But the Board of Administration of the Ottoman Debt should be dissolved and all the commercial treaties concluded by Turkey should be cancelled. The Turkish Imperial Debt should be unified and a sinking fund provided. The economic conditions granted to the mandatory Power should be liable to revision and might be cancelled.

Further, it was observed that if America refused the mandate the international rivalries which had had full scope under Turkish dominion would assert themselves again.

The reasons given by the American Commission against acceptance of the mandate were that the United States had serious domestic problems to deal with, and such an intervention in the affairs of the Old World would weaken the standpoint they had taken on the Monroe doctrine. The report also pointed out that the United States were in no way responsible for the awkward situation in the East, and they could not undertake engagements for the future—for the new Congress could not be bound by the policy pursued by the present one. The report also remarked that Great Britain and Russia and the other Great Powers too had taken very little interest in those countries, though England had enough experience and resources to control them. Finally, the report emphasised this point—that the United States had still more imperious obligations towards nearer foreign countries, and still more urgent questions to settle. Besides, an army of 100,000 to 200,000 men would be needed to maintain order in Armenia. Lastly, a considerable outlay of money would be necessary, and the receipts would be at first very small.

On the other hand, the British League of Nations Union asked the English Government to give instructions to its representatives to support the motion of the Supreme Council according to which the protection of the independent Armenian State should be entrusted to the League of Nations.

According to the terms of the Treaty of Peace with Turkey, President Wilson had been asked to act as an arbiter to lay down the Armenian frontiers on the side of the provinces of Van, Bitlis, Erzerum, and Trebizond.

Under these circumstances the complete solution of the Armenian problem was postponed indefinitely, and it is difficult to foresee how the problem will ever be solved.

2. The Pan-Turanian and Pan-Arabian Movements.

The attempts at Russification made immediately after the 1877 war by means of the scholastic method of Elminski resulted in the first manifestations of the Pan-Turanian movement. They arose, not in Russia, but in Russian Tatary. The Tatars of the huge territories of Central Asia, by reason of their annexation to the Russian Empire and the indirect contact with the West that it entailed, and also owing to their reaction against the West, awoke to a consciousness of their individuality and strength.

A series of ethnographic studies which were begun at that time by M. de Ujfalvi upon the Hungarians—all the peoples speaking a Finno-Ugrian idiom descending from the same stock as those who speak the Turkish, Mongol, and Manchu languages—and were continued by scholars of various nationalities, gave the Pan-Turanian doctrine a scientific basis; the principles of this doctrine were laid down by H. Vambéry,[40] and it was summed up by Léon Cahun in his *Introduction a l'histoire de l'Asie*.[41] This Turco-Tartar movement expanded, and its most authoritative leaders were Youssouf Ahtchoura Oglou; Ahmed Agayeff, who was arrested at the beginning of the armistice by the English as a Unionist and sent to Malta; and later Zia Geuk Alp, a Turkish poet and publicist, the author of *Kizil-Elma* (The Red Apple), who turned the Union and Progress Committee towards the Pan-Turanian movement though he had many opponents on that committee, and who was arrested too and sent to Malta.

Islam for thirteen centuries, by creating a religious solidarity between peoples of alien races, had brought about a kind of religious nationality under its hegemony. But the ambitious scheme of Pan-Islamism was jeopardised in modern times by new influences and widely different political aspirations. It was hoped for some time that by grouping the national elements of Turkey and pursuing a conciliatory policy it would be possible to give a sound basis to that religious nationality. But that nationality soon proved unable to curb the separatist aspirations of the various peoples subjected to the Turkish yoke, and then, again, it wounded the pride of some Turkish elements by compelling them to obey the commandments of Islam, to which all the Turanian populations had not fully adhered. The Pan-Islamic movement later on grew more and more nationalist in character, and assumed a Pan-Turkish tendency, though it remained Pan-Turanian—that is to say, it still included the populations speaking the Turkish, Mongol, and Manchu languages.

Without in any way giving up the Pan-Islamic idea, Turkish Nationalism could not but support the Pan-Turanian movement, which it hoped would add the 18 million Turks living in the former Russian Empire, Persia, and Afghanistan, to the 8 million Turks of the territories of the Ottoman Empire.

Owing to its origin and the character it has assumed, together with the geographical situation and importance of the populations concerned, this movement appears as a powerful obstacle to the policy which England seems intent upon pursuing, and to which she seeks to bring over Italy and France. It also exemplifies the latent antagonism which had ever existed between the

Arabian world and the Turkish world, and which, under the pressure of events, soon asserted itself.

Indeed, the mutual relations of the Arabs and the Turks had been slowly but deeply modified in the course of centuries.

After the great Islamic movement started by Mohammed in the seventh century, the Arabs who had hitherto been mostly confined within the boundaries of the Arabian peninsula spread to the west over the whole of Northern Africa as far as Spain, and to the east over Mesopotamia and a part of Persia. In the twelfth century Arabian culture reached its climax, for the Arabian Caliphs of Baghdad ruled over huge territories. At that time Arabic translations revealed to Europe the works of Aristotle and of the Chaldean astronomers, and the Arabs, through Spain, had an important influence on the first period of modern civilisation.

In 1453, when the Turks, who had extended their dominion over all the shores of the Mediterranean, settled at Constantinople, which became the capital of the Islamic Empire, the influence of Arabia decreased; yet the Arabs still enjoyed in various parts political independence and a kind of religious predominance.

For instance, the Arabs settled in the north of Western Africa, after losing Spain, became quite independent, and formed the Empire of Morocco, which was not under the suzerainty of Constantinople.

The Arabian tribes and Berber communities of Algeria and Tunis, which had more or less remained under the suzerainty of the Sultan, were no longer amenable to him after the French conquest. The Pasha of Egypt, by setting up as an independent Sovereign, and founding the hereditary dynasty of the Khedives, deprived the Ottoman dominion of Egypt, where the Arabs were not very numerous, but had played an important part in the development of Islam. The Italian conquest took away from Turkey the last province she still owned in Africa. Finally, when the late war broke out, England deposed the Khedive Abbas Hilmi, who was travelling in Europe and refused to go back to Egypt. She proclaimed her protectorate over the Nile valley, and, breaking off the religious bond that linked Egypt with the Ottoman Empire, she made Sultan of Egypt, independent of the Sultan of Constantinople, Hussein Kamel, uncle of the deposed Khedive, who made his entry into Cairo on December 20, 1914.

The Turks, however, kept possession of the Holy Places, Mecca and Medina, which they garrisoned and governed. This sovereignty was consolidated by the railway of the pilgrimage. The investiture of the Sherif of Mecca was still vested in them, and they chose the member of his family who was to succeed him, and who was detained as a hostage at Constantinople. But after the failure of the expedition against the Suez Canal during the late war, and at the instigation of England, the Sherif, as we shall see, proclaimed himself independent, and assumed the title of Melek, or King of Arabia.

On the other hand, the province of the Yemen, lying farther south of the Hejaz, has always refused to acknowledge the authority of Constantinople, and is practically independent. Lastly, at the southern end of the Arabian peninsula, the English have held possession of Aden since 1839, and have extended their authority, since the opening of the Suez Canal in 1869, over all the Hadramaut. All the sheiks of this part of Arabia along the southern coast, over whom the authority of Turkey was but remotely exercised and was practically non-existent, naturally accepted the protectorate of England without any difficulty, in return for the commercial facilities she brought them and the allowances she granted them, and in 1873 Turkey formally recognised the English possession of this coast.

On the eastern coast of the Arabian peninsula the territory of the Sultan of Oman, or Maskat, lying along the Persian Gulf, has been since the beginning of the nineteenth century under the authority of the Viceroy of India. This authority extends nowadays over all the territories lying between Aden and Mesopotamia, which are in consequence entirely under English sway.

Moreover, the English have proclaimed their protectorate over the Sheik of Koweit.

Koweit had been occupied by the British Navy after the Kaiser's visit to Tangier, and thus Germany had been deprived of an outlet for her railway line from Anatolia to Baghdad. The Rev. S. M. Zwemer, in a book written some time ago, *Arabia, the Birthplace of Islam*, after showing the exceptional situation occupied by England in these regions, owned that British policy had ambitious designs on the Arabian peninsula and the lands round the Persian Gulf.

Since the outbreak of the war, Ottoman sovereignty has also lost the small Turkish province of Hasa, between Koweit and Maskat, inhabited entirely by Arabian tribes.

The rebellion of the Sherif of Mecca against the temporal power of the Sultans of Mecca shows how important was the change that had taken place within the Arabian world, but also intimates that the repercussions of the war, after accelerating the changes that were already taking place in the relations between the Arabs and the Turks, must needs later on bring about an understanding or alliance between these two elements against any foreign dominion. In the same way, the encroachments of England upon Arabian territories have brought about a change in the relations between the Arabs and the English; in days of yore the Arabs, through ignorance or because they were paid to do so, more than once used English rifles against the Turks; but the recent Arabian risings against the British in Mesopotamia seem to prove that the Arabs have now seen their mistake, and have concluded that the English were deceiving them when they said the Caliphate was in danger.

Finally, in order to pave the way to a British advance from Mesopotamia to the Black Sea, England for a moment contemplated the formation of a Kurdistan, though a long existence in common and the identity of feelings and creed have brought about a deep union between the Kurds and the Turks, and a separation is contrary to the express wishes of both peoples.

It is a well-known fact that the descendants of Ali, the Prophet's cousin, who founded the dynasty of the Sherifs, or Nobles, took the title of Emirs—*i.e.*, Princes—of Mecca, and that the Emir of the Holy Places of Arabia had always to be recognised by the Sherif to have a right to bear the title of Caliph. This recognition of the Caliphs by the Sherifs was made public by the mention of the name of the Caliph in the Khoutba, or Friday prayer.

In consequence of political vicissitudes, the Emirs of Mecca successively recognised the Caliphs of Baghdad, the Sultans of Egypt until the conquest of Egypt by Selim I in 1517, and the Sultans of Turkey, whose sovereignty over the Holy Places has always been more or less nominal, and has hardly ever been effective over the Hejaz.

When the Wahhabi schism took place, the Wahhabis, who aimed at restoring the purer doctrines of primitive Islam, and condemned the worship of the holy relics and the Prophet's tomb, captured Mecca and Medina.

Mehmet Ali, Pasha of Egypt, was deputed by the Porte to reconquer the Holy Places, which he governed from 1813 to 1840. Since that time the Ottoman Government has always appointed a Governor of the Hejaz and maintained a garrison there, and the Porte took care a member of the Sherif's family should reside in Constantinople in order to be able to replace the one who bore the title of Sherif, should the latter ever refuse to recognise the Caliph.

Long negotiations were carried on during the war between the British Government and Hussein, Sherif of Mecca, the Emir Feisal's father, concerning the territorial conditions on which peace might be restored in the East. These views were set forth in eight letters exchanged between July, 1915, and January, 1916.

In July, 1915, the Sherif offered his military co-operation to the British Government, in return for which he asked it to recognise the independence of the Arabs within a territory including Mersina and Adana on the northern side and then bounded by the thirty-seventh degree of latitude; on the east its boundary was to be the Persian frontier down to the Gulf of Basra; on the south the Indian Ocean, with the exception of Aden; on the west the Red Sea and the Mediterranean as far as Mersina.

On August 30, 1915, Sir Henry MacMahon, British resident in Cairo, observed in his answer that discussion about the future frontiers was rather premature.

In a letter dated September 9, forwarded to the Foreign Office on October 18 by Sir Henry MacMahon, the Sherif insisted upon an immediate discussion. As he forwarded this letter, Sir Henry MacMahon mentioned the following statement made to him by the Sherif's representative in Egypt:

"The occupation by France of the thoroughly Arabian districts of Aleppo, Hama, Homs, and Damascus would be opposed by force of arms by the Arabs: but with the exception of these districts, the Arabs are willing to accept a few modifications of the north-western frontiers proposed by the Sherif of Mecca."

On October 24, 1915, by his Government's order, Sir Henry MacMahon addressed the Sherif the following letter:

"The districts of Mersina and Alexandretta and the parts of Syria lying to the west of the districts of Damascus, Homs, Hama, and Aleppo cannot be looked upon as merely Arabian, and should be excluded from the limits and frontiers that are being discussed. With these modifications, and without in any way impairing our present treaties with the Arabian chiefs, we accept your limits and frontiers. As to the territories within these limits, in which Great Britain has a free hand as far as she does not injure the interests of her ally, France, I am desired by the British Government to make the following promise in answer to your letter.

"'With the reservation of the above-mentioned modifications, Great Britain is willing to recognise and support Arabian independence within the territories included in the limits and frontiers proposed by the Sherif of Mecca.'"

On November 5, 1915, the Sherif, in his answer, agreed to the exclusion of Mersina and Adana, but maintained his claims on the other territories, especially Beyrut.

On December 13 Sir Henry MacMahon took note of the Sherif's renunciation of Mersina and Adana.

On January 1, 1916, the Sherif wrote that, not to disturb the Franco-British alliance, he would lay aside his claims to Lebanon during the war; but he would urge them again on the conclusion of hostilities.

On January 30, 1916, Sir Henry MacMahon took note of the Sherif's wish to avoid all that might be prejudicial to the alliance between France and England, and stated that the friendship between France and England would be maintained after the war.

On June 10, 1916, a rebellion broke out at Mecca. At daybreak the barracks were encircled by Arabs. Hussein ibn Ali, who was at the head of the movement, informed the Turkish commander that the Hejaz had proclaimed its independence. On June 11 the Arabs captured the Turkish fort of Bash-Karacal, and on the 12th Fort Hamadie. Soon after Jeddah surrendered, and on September 21 El Taif.

In a proclamation dated June 27, 1916, the Sherif Hussein ibn Ali stated the political and religious reasons that had induced him to rebel against the Ottoman Government. He declared the latter was in the hands of the Young Turk party, that the Committee of Union and Progress had driven the country to war, was destroying the power of the Sultan, and had violated the rights of the Caliphate.

On October 5 the Sherif Hussein formed an Arabian Cabinet, convened an Assembly, and on November 6 caused himself to be proclaimed King of the Arabs.

In November, 1916, he issued a second proclamation, not so lofty in tone, but more wily in its wording, which seemed to lack personality in its inspiration. It began thus: "It is a well-known fact that the better informed people in the Moslem world, Ottomans and others, saw with much misgiving Turkey rush into the war." He then stated that—

"The Ottoman Empire is a Moslem empire, whose wide territories have a considerable sea-frontage. So the policy of the great Ottoman Sultans, inspired by this twofold consideration, has always aimed at keeping on friendly terms with the Powers that rule over the majority of Moslems and at the same time hold the mastery of the seas."

He went on as follows:

"The one cause of the downfall of the Ottoman Empire and the extermination of its populations was the short-sighted tyranny of the leaders of the Unionist faction—Enver, Jemal, Talaat, and their accomplices; it is the giving up of the political traditions established by the great Ottoman statesmen and based on the friendship of the two Powers that deserve most to be glorified—England and France."

He shared the opinion of those who reproached the Turks with the "atrocities committed by Greeks and Armenians"; he called upon them "the reprobation of the world"; and he wound up his proclamation with these words:

"Our hatred and enmity go to the leaders who are responsible for such doings—Enver, Jemal, Talaat, and their accomplices. We will not have anything to do with such tyrants, and in communion with all believers and all unprejudiced minds in the Ottoman Empire and Islam throughout the world we declare our hatred and enmity towards them, and before God we separate our cause from their cause."

Great Britain later on insisted upon this point—that the question of the territorial conditions with a view to restoring peace had not been dealt with since the beginning of 1916, except in the above-mentioned exchange of notes. In September, 1919, in a semi-official communication to the Press, she emphatically declared that it followed from these documents:

(1) That in the letter dated October 24, 1915, which formulates the only engagement between Great Britain and the Sherif, the British Government had not pledged itself to do anything contrary to the Anglo-French treaty of 1916.

(2) That no fresh engagement had been entered into by Great Britain with the Sherif since the beginning of the negotiations that M. Georges Picot had been directed to carry on in London to pave the way to the treaty of 1916. For the negotiators had met for the first time on November 23, 1915, and the last two letters exchanged in January, 1916, added nothing to the engagements made with King Hussein in the letter of October 24 of the previous year.

Finally, on March 5, 1917, Hussein, now King of the Hejaz, sent an appeal to all the Moslems of Turkey against the Ottoman Government, which he charged with profaning the tomb of the Prophet in the course of the operations of June, 1916.

On October 1, 1918, Feisal entered Damascus at the head of his own victorious troops, but not with the Allied armies, after fighting all the way from Maan to Aleppo, a distance of above 400 miles. By his military and political activity, he had succeeded in quelling the private quarrels between tribes, and grouping round him the Arabian chiefs, between whom there had been much rivalry not long before, at the same time protecting the right flank of the British army, which was in a hazardous position.

Without giving up his favourite scheme, he was thus brought face to face with the Syrian question.

Though the Arabian movement cannot be looked upon merely as the outcome of the arrangements concluded in regard to Syria between the Allies during the war, the latter seem at least to have brought about a state of things which reinforced the Syrian aspirations and encouraged them to assert themselves.

The Syrians had once more taken advantage of the events which had convulsed Europe, and had had their after-effects in Asia Minor, to assert their determination to be freed from Ottoman sovereignty; and now they hoped to bring the Peace Conference to recognise a mode of government consistent with their political and economic aspirations.

The suppression of the autonomy of Lebanon, the requisitions, the administrative measures and prosecutions ordered in 1916 by Jemal Pasha against the Syrians, who wanted Syria to be erected into an independent State, had not succeeded in modifying the tendency which for a long time had aimed at detaching Syria from the Ottoman Empire, and at taking advantage of the influence France exercised in the country to further this aim.

In 1912 M. R. Poincaré, then Minister of Foreign Affairs, clearly stated before the French Chamber that the French and British Governments shared exactly the same views concerning the Syrian question. Yet later facts soon proved that the English policy would necessarily conflict with French influence and try to destroy it after turning it to her own advantage. Simultaneously the Turks saw that the time had come to modify the existing régime.

M. Defrance, who is now French High Commissioner in Turkey, but was then French Consul-General at Cairo, informed the French Government that the Ottoman Committee of decentralisation was of opinion that Syria should become an autonomous country, governed by a Moslem prince chosen by the people, and placed under the protection of France.

On March 11, 1914, M. Georges Leygues again raised the Syrian question before the French Parliament. He maintained that the axis of French policy lay in the Mediterranean—with Algeria, Tunis, and Morocco on one side and on the other side Syria and Lebanon, the latter being the best spheres open to French action on account of the economic interests and moral influence France already exercised there. And the French Parliament granted the sums of money which were needed for developing French establishments in the East.

About the same time the Central Syrian Committee expressed the wish that the various regions of Syria should be grouped into one State, under French control. Fifteen Lebano-Syrian committees established in various foreign countries expressed the same wish; the Manchester committee merely asked that Syria should not be partitioned. A Syrian congress, held at Marseilles at the end of 1918 under the presidency of M. Franklin Bouillon, declared that for various economic and judicial reasons France could be of great use to Syria, in case the direction of the country should be entrusted to her.

But the establishment of a Syrian State, whether enjoying the same autonomy as Lebanon has had since 1864 under the guarantee of France, England, Russia, Austria, Prussia, and later on Italy, or being governed in another way, was in contradiction to the arrangements made by France and England in 1916. Though the agreement between these two Powers has never been made public, yet it is well known that it had been decided—contrary to the teaching of both history and geography—that Syria should be divided into several regions. Now, the centre of Syria, which stretches from the Euphrates to the sea, happens to be Damascus, and this very town, according to the British scheme, was to be included in an Arabian Confederation headed by the Hejaz.

At the beginning of 1916, the Emir Feisal came to Paris, and, after the conversations held in France, a satisfactory agreement seemed to have been reached.

The Emir Feisal was solemnly received in January, 1919, at the Hôtel de Ville in Paris, and in the course of a reception at the Hôtel Continental, the Croix de Guerre of the first class was presented to the Arab chief on February 4, with the following "citation":

"As early as 1916, he resolutely seconded the efforts of his father, the King of the Hejaz, to shake off the Turkish yoke and support the Allied cause.

"He proved a remarkable, energetic commander, a friend to his soldiers.

"He planned and carried out personally several important operations against the Damascus-Medina railway, and captured El-Ouedjy and Akaba.

"From August, 1917, till September, 1918, he led numerous attacks north and south of Maan, capturing several railway stations and taking a great number of prisoners.

"He helped to destroy the 4th, 7th, 8th, and 9th Turkish armies by cutting off their communications to the north, south, and west of Deraa, and after a very bold raid he entered Damascus on October 1, and Aleppo on the 26th with the Allied troops."

On February 6, 1919, he asked the Committee of the Ten on behalf of his father, Hussein ibn Ali, to recognise the independence of the Arabian peninsula, and declared he aimed at grouping the various regions of Arabian Asia under one sovereignty. He did not hesitate to remind the members of the Conference that he was speaking in the name of a people who had already reached a high degree of civilisation at a time when the Powers they represented did not even exist; and at the end of the sitting in the course of which the scheme of a League of Nations was adopted, he asked that all the secret treaties about the partition of the Asiatic dominion of the Ottoman Empire between the Great Powers should be definitely cancelled.

In March, 1919, the Emir went back to Syria, under the pretext of using his influence in favour of a French collaboration. He was given an enthusiastic greeting; but the supporters of the Arabian movement, which was partly his own work, declared their hostility to any policy that would bring about a mandate for Syria.

On March 7 it was announced that a National Syrian Congress, sitting at Damascus, had just proclaimed Syria an independent country, and the Emir Feisal, son of the Grand Sherif of Mecca, King of Syria.

It was reported that a declaration, issued by a second congress that was held in the same town and styled itself Congress of Mesopotamia, had been read at the same sitting, through which the latter congress solemnly proclaimed the independence of Irak—Mesopotamia—with the Emir Abdullah, the Emir Feisal's brother, as King under the regency of another brother of his, the Emir Zeid.

All this, of course, caused a good deal of surprise in London, though something of the kind ought to have been expected.

In the above-mentioned document, after recalling the part played by the Arabs in the war and the declarations made by the Allies about the right of self-determination of peoples, the Congress declared the time had come to proclaim the complete independence and unity of Syria, and concluded as follows:

"We, therefore, the true representatives of the Arabian nation in every part of Syria, speaking in her name and declaring her will, have to-day unanimously proclaimed the independence of our country, Syria, within her natural boundaries, including Palestine, which independence shall be complete, without any restriction whatsoever, on the basis of a civil representative government.

"We will take into account every patriotic wish of all the inhabitants of Lebanon concerning the administration of their country and maintain her pre-war limits, on condition Lebanon shall stand aloof from any foreign influence.

"We reject the Zionists' claim to turn Palestine into a national home for the Jews or a place of immigration for them.

"We have chosen His Royal Highness the Emir Feisal, who has always fought for the liberation of the country, and whom the nation looks upon as the greatest man in Syria, as constitutional King of Syria under the name of H.M. Feisal I.

"We hereby proclaim the military governments of occupation hitherto established in the three districts have now come to an end; they shall be replaced by a civil representative government, responsible to this Council for anything relating to the principle of the complete independence of the country, till it is possible for the government to convene a Parliament that shall administer the provinces according to the principles of decentralisation."

The Congress then asked the Allies to withdraw their troops from Syria, and stated that the national police and administration would be fully able to maintain order.

To some extent the Emir Feisal resisted the suggestions, or at least refused to comply with the extreme demands, of the Nationalists of Damascus and Palestine—whose club, the Nadi El Arabi, played in these regions the same part as the Committee of Union and Progress—for after forming a Government of concentration, he had merely summoned one class of soldiers, whereas the Nationalists in his absence had decreed the mobilisation of several classes, and in agreement with General Gouraud he had appointed administrator of the disputed region of Bukaa his cousin, the Emir Jemil, who was a moderate man. Yet, whether he wished to do so or not, whether he was an accomplice of the leaders or not, the fact is that, after being the agent of England, he became the agent of the Nationalists, who had succeeded in having the independence of the Arabian countries of Asia Minor proclaimed under the leadership of the Hejaz.

Thus it turned out that the foundation of an Arabian State assumed a capital importance at the very time when the future condition of the Ottoman Empire was under discussion.

In the course of the interview between M. Mohammed Ali and Mr. Lloyd George, as the Prime Minister asked him whether he was averse to the action of the Syrian Moslems, who had acknowledged the Emir Feisal as King of Arabia and proclaimed an independent Moslem State unconnected with the

Caliphate, the leader of the Indian delegation, after hinting that "this matter can well be left for settlement amongst Muslims," made the following statement:

"Just as we have certain religious obligations with regard to the Khilafat that have brought us here, we have other religious obligations, equally solemn and binding, that require us to approach the Turks and Arabs. 'All Muslims are brothers, wherefore make peace between your brethren,' is a Quranic injunction. We have come here in the interests of peace and reconciliation, and propose going to the Arabs and Turks for the same purpose.

"Quite apart from the main claim for preservation of the Khilafat with adequate temporal power, the Muslims claim that the local centre of their Faith—namely, the 'Island of Arabia'—should remain inviolate and entirely under Muslim control. This is based on the dying injunction of the Prophet himself. The Jazirat-ul-Arab, as its name indicates, is the 'Island of Arabia,' the fourth boundary being the waters of the Tigris and Euphrates. It therefore includes Syria, Palestine, and Mesopotamia, as well as the region commonly known to European geographers as the Arabian peninsula. Muslims can acquiesce in no form of non-Muslim control, whether in the shape of mandates or otherwise, over any portion of this region. Religious obligations, which are absolutely binding on us, require that there at least there shall be exclusively Muslim control. It does not specify that it should be the Khalifa's own control. In order to make it perfectly clear, I may say the religious requirements, sir, will be satisfied even if the Emir Feisal exercises independent control there.

"But, since we have to provide sufficient territories and resources and naval and military forces for the Khalifa, the necessity for the utmost economy which has to rule and govern all our claims in these matters suggests that both these requirements may easily be satisfied if the Jazirat-ul-Arab remains, as before the war, under the direct sovereignty of the Khalifa. We have great hopes that if we have opportunities of meeting our co-religionists we shall bring about a reconciliation between them and the Turks. After all, it cannot be said that Turkish rule in Arabia has been of such a character that other Powers are bound to interfere."

Moreover, he added:

"With regard to the Arabs, about whom you asked me a little while ago, the delegation are not apprehensive with regard to the feasibility of an adjustment between the Khalifa and the Arabs. As I have already pointed out, there is the Quranic injunction: 'All Muslims are brothers, wherefore make peace between your brethren.' That is a duty laid upon us, and recently, at the Bombay Session, the All-India Khilafat Conference passed a resolution authorising a delegation to proceed to the Hejaz and other parts of Arabia to reconcile the Arabs and the Turks. Our interest is in the Khilafat as Mussulmans. No population and no territory could be so dear to the Muslim as the Arabs and Arabia. The Turks could not win such affection from us as the Arabs do. This is the land that we want to keep purely under Muslim control. Even if the Arabs themselves want a mandate in that country we will not consent. We are bound by our religious obligations to that extent. Therefore, it cannot be through antipathy against the Arabs or because of any particular sympathy for the Turks that we desire the Khalifa's sovereignty over the Island of Arabia. The Turks are much farther removed from us. Very few of us know anything of the Turkish language; very few of us have travelled in the Turkish Empire. But we do go in large numbers to Mecca and Medina. So many of us want to die there. So many Mussulmans settle down and marry in Arabia; one of my own aunts is an Arab lady. Wherever we have met Arabs on our journey—we have had no opportunity, of course, of discussing the subject with well-educated people, but—we have asked the class of people we have met what they thought of the action of the King of the Hejaz—'King' in a land where God alone is recognised as a king: nobody can ever claim kingship there. They said his was an act that they condemned, it was an act they did not in the least like. They considered it to be wrong; the Arabs spoke disparagingly of it. I do not know to what extent it may be true, but there are a number of people who now come forward as apologists for the Arabs. They say that what Emir Feisal and the Sherif did was to save something for Islam; it was not that they were against the Turks, but they were for Islam. Whether this was or was not the fact, it is very significant that such apologies should be made now. Honestly, we have no apprehensions that could not reconcile the Arabs and the Turks. This is a question which I think the Allied Council, the Peace Conference, could very well leave the Mussulmans to settle amongst themselves. We do not want British bayonets to force the Arabs into a position of subservience to the Turks."

Resuming the idea he had already expressed, he concluded his speech thus:

"That can be very easily arranged, and if such a Federation as we dream of becomes a reality—and I do not see why it should not—the Arabs would have all the independence they require. They may claim national independence, but they cannot forget that Islam is something other than national, that it is supernational, and the Khilafat must be as dear to them as it is to us. Even now the King of the Hejaz does not claim to be the Khalifa. When people began to address him as such, he rebuked them, and he published in his official organ, *Al-Qibla*, that he wanted to be called King of the Hejaz, and not Amir-ul-Mumineen, a title reserved only for the Khalifa."

M. Syud Hossain declared in his turn:

"We are not opposed to the independence of Arabia. We are opposed to Emir Feisal's declaration of independence only for this reason—that Arabia, throughout the history of Islam, has up till now remained under the direct control of the Khalifa. This is the first time in the history of Islam that anyone who is not the Khalifa has set up any claim over Arabia. That is why there is, from the Muslim point of view, a conflict of religious obligations with actual facts. We are not opposed to Arabian independence. On the contrary, we wish very much for complete autonomy in that region, but we want it to be in harmony and not in conflict with the Khilafat and its claims. The idea is not unrealisable, as both Arabs and Turks are Muslims."

Naturally the concentration of the French troops, during the Cilician troubles, had made the action of the Syrian Nationalists popular among the Moslem masses. On the other hand, an anti-Zionist agitation had gained ground in Palestine and quickly developed into a propaganda in favour of the union of Palestine and Syria under one sovereign. All these facts, which point to the existence in Syria of a movement in favour of an independent State, explain how it turned out that the Emir Feisal, who favoured the scheme of a confederate Arabian Empire, was proclaimed King.

General Noury Pasha, sent by the Emir Feisal to London at the beginning of April, handed to the Foreign Office and to the representative of the French Foreign Office who happened to be in that city, three letters written in the Emir's own hand in which he is said to have asked both Governments to recognise and support the independence of his country, and informed them that the measures taken by the Damascus Congress concerning Mesopotamia merely aimed at putting an end to Turkish anarchy and the riots of Mosul.

The proclamation of the Emir Feisal as King of Syria brought about much discontent in Lebanon.

A meeting was held on March 22 at Baabda, where the General Government of Lebanon resided, to protest against the decision of the Damascus Congress. About a thousand people were present, and the following motions were passed unanimously:

"1. The meeting enters a protest against the right the Syrian Congress has assumed of disposing of Lebanon, of laying down its frontiers, of restricting its independence, and of forbidding it to collaborate with France.

"2. The Congress asserts the independence of Lebanon. In the demarcation of its frontiers, allowance should be made for its vital necessities and the claims repeatedly expressed by the populations.

"3. The Congress considers as null and void the decisions taken by the Damascus Congress concerning Syria, as the latter Congress was never regularly constituted.

"4. The Congress confirms the mandate given to the delegates sent by Lebanon who are now in Paris.

"5. The Congress confirms the independence of Greater Lebanon with the collaboration of France.

"6. The Congress expresses the wish that a Commission consisting of inhabitants of Lebanon will lay the foundation of the future constitution of Lebanon, which is to replace the protocol of 1860.

"7. The Congress asserts the Union of Lebanon and France; the national emblem shall be the tricolour with a cedar on the white part."

This opposition was supported by the Maronite archbishops of the sanjak of Tripolis, Latakia, Hama, and Homs, who sent a telegram of protest from Tripolis to Syria on March 13. Thus the Arabian movement also met with Christian opposition.

Khyatin Saffita Tabez Abbas, chief of the Alawite tribe, sent the following protest from Tartus to the Peace Conference:

"Without the consent of the Alawite tribes, the Emir Feisal has had himself proclaimed King of Syria. We protest energetically against such illegal proceedings. We want an Alawite Confederation established under the direct and exclusive protectorate of France."

Of course, it was urged that the Assembly of the Syrian Congress at Damascus included only extremists who worked hand in hand with the Turkish Nationalists; it seems, nevertheless, that it represented the opinions of most Syrians, who wanted to restore the unity of Syria; and their wish was no doubt connected with the wish that was gaining ground to restore the unity of Arabia.

On the other hand, the Anglo-French treaty, which aimed at a partition of Ottoman Arabia so as to balance French and English interests, but disregarded the wishes of the peoples, could not but rouse a feeling of discontent. Moreover, some Anglo-Egyptian agents and some British officers had foolishly supported this movement in order to cripple French influence, feeling quite confident they could check this movement later on and put Syria under their own suzerainty. But they were soon thrust aside by the movement, which had been fostered by them in India and now logically was turning against them.

The Arabs of the interior of Arabia also addressed a proclamation to General Gouraud stating they welcomed the French as friends, but did not want them as masters and conquerors.

The Arabian opposition to France which made itself felt far beyond the boundaries of independent Syria, the difficulties raised by the Emir Feisal in the coast area, and the agitation stirred up by the Damascus Government in Syria since the French troops had relieved the English in those parts in October, 1919, induced General Gouraud to occupy the railway stations of Maalhakah and Rayak, the latter being at the junction of the railway line from Aleppo with the Beyrut-Damascus line leading to the Hejaz. At the same time, by way of reprisal for the capture of Mejel-Anjar in the plain of Bukaa lying between Libanus and Anti-Libanus by the Sherifian troops, he gathered his forces in the rear of that town at Zahleh and decided to occupy all this area, which was within the zone put under French control by the 1916 treaty.

On July 20 the Emir Feisal held a war council at Damascus and issued a decree of general mobilisation.

According to the Memoirs of Liman von Sanders, who commanded the Turkish troops in Syria-Palestine, doubts may be raised as to the Emir Feisal's straightforwardness in his dealings first with the Turks during the war, and later with both the English and the French after the cessation of hostilities.

"The commander of the fourth army, Jemal Pasha, informed me in the second half of August that the Sherif Feisal was willing to hold the front occupied by the fourth army along the Jordan on his own account and with his own troops, if guarantees were given him by the Turkish Government as to the creation of an Arabian State. According to the Sherif Feisal an important British attack was being prepared in the coast zone, and in this way it would be possible to reinforce the front between the sea and the Jordan with the troops of the fourth army. Through my Turkish brigadier-general I instructed General Jemal Pasha to enter into negotiations with the Sherif Feisal on this point, and I urged Enver to give the guarantees that were demanded.

"I never had any answer from either Enver or Jemal on this point. So I cannot say to what extent Feisal's offer could be relied upon. According to what I heard from my brigadier-general, I fancy the Turks mistrusted his offer, which they considered as a mere decoy to put our positions along the Jordan in the hands of the Arabs, while the main English attack was to take place in the coast zone or between the sea and the Jordan."[42]

As was pointed out by the *Journal des Débats*, which quoted the preceding lines on July 21, 1920, the opinion of Liman von Sanders was quite plausible; yet the recent events on the French front may also have had an influence on the Emir Feisal. Most likely, if we bear in mind the intrigues he carried on afterwards, his first proposal was a consequence of the German advance on the Western front in spring, 1918, but the Allies' victorious offensive on the Somme on August 8, 1918, caused him to alter his plans. It is noteworthy that in his proposals he disclosed where the first English attack was to take place. At any rate, both suppositions, which corroborate each other, increase the suspicions that might already be entertained about his sincerity; and, since then he has obviously taken advantage of every opportunity to play a double game, or at least to turn all the differences between the Powers to the advantage of Arabian independence.

We criticise him the more severely, as we fully understand the Arabs' aspirations. We disapprove of his policy and blame his attitude, because we believe Arabian aspirations cannot be lawfully fulfilled at the Turks' expense, and the Arabs cannot expect they will safeguard their liberty by supporting the English policy in the East in every particular, especially with regard to the Turks, at a time when India and Egypt are seeking to shake off that policy.

Let us add that the Pan-Arabian movement owes the development it has now taken to Colonel Lawrence's manœuvres, who diverted it from its original aim to make use of it, and became the Emir Feisal's counsellor in order to influence him in favour of England. Miss Bell, too, played an influential part in that movement.

Though the Emir was the leader of a movement which, on the whole, was hostile to Turkey, and though he asked for English support, he had no objection to co-operating with the Nationalists, who, being threatened by the Allies, offered their support in order to conciliate him. Thus things had come to a more and more confused state. According to the information given by *Le Temps* on July 20, 1920, it appeared that as early as January, 1919—

"The Sherifian agents, Noury Shalaan, Mohammed Bey, and the Emir Mahmoud Faour, are working hand in hand with the Turkish Nationalists. The Turkish Colonel Selfi Bey has several times travelled from Anatolia to Damascus and *vice versa* to carry instructions.

"At the beginning of February, Mustafa Kemal sent an appeal to the population of Anatolia in which he said: 'The Arabian Government relies or will rely on us.'

"The Sherifian authorities are constantly raising difficulties to prevent the French from sending reinforcements or supplies to Cilicia by rail."

In view of the exactions of all sorts the Emir Feisal indulged in, such as the capture of revenue lawfully belonging to the administration of the Ottoman debt and the proscription of French currency, to say nothing of such acts of aggression as attacks on French outposts and the closing of the railways, General Gouraud on Wednesday, July 14, addressed to the Arabian chief the following ultimatum, which expired on the 18th:

"Recognition of the French mandate for Syria.

"Liberty to make use of the Rayak-Aleppo railway.

"The occupation of Aleppo and the stations lying between Aleppo and Rayak.

"The immediate abolition of forced recruiting.

"Reduction of the Sherifian army to its effectives of December, 1919.

"Free circulation for the French-Syrian currency.

"Punishment of the authors of crimes against French soldiers.

"Acceptance of the above-mentioned conditions within four days. If these conditions are not complied with, they shall be enforced by arms."

Syria, too, was in quite a perturbed state, owing to the discontent prevailing among the population and the differences between the various factions which were striving to get the upper hand in the country. Two towns, Hasbeiya and Rashaya, situated on the slopes of Mount Hermon, had rebelled against the Sherifian Government and wanted to become parts of Lebanon.

An important debate began on July 19 in the House of Commons about the condition of affairs in Asia Minor and the possible consequences the French ultimatum addressed to the Emir Feisal might have for British interests in that region.

Mr. Ormsby-Gore (Stafford, C.U.) asked the Prime Minister whether he could give any information regarding the new military action of France in Syria; whether the twenty-four hours' ultimatum issued by the French to the Arab Government in Damascus was submitted to and approved by the Supreme Council; whether the terms of the mandate for Syria had yet been submitted to the Allied and Associated Powers; and whether His Majesty's Government would use their influence with the French and Arab Governments to secure the suspension of further hostilities pending the decision of the Council of the League of Nations on the terms of the Syrian mandate. To this Mr. Bonar Law answered:

"The ultimatum had not been submitted to the Supreme Council. The terms of the mandate for Syria have not yet been submitted to the Allied Powers. As regards the last part of the question, His Majesty's Government, who had for some time, but unsuccessfully, been urging the Emir Feisal to come to Europe to discuss the outstanding questions with the Supreme Council, do not consider that they can usefully act upon the information at present at their disposal, but they are in communication with the French Government on the matter."

Then Mr. Ormsby-Gore asked again:

"Is it a fact that severe casualties have already resulted from this, and that the French have advanced over the line agreed upon between the British and French Governments last year, and that they have advanced from Jerablus to Jisir-Shugr and from the junction at Rayak; and has he any information with regard to the progress of hostilities in another part of the Arab area on the Euphrates?"

Mr. Bonar Law having replied that he had not received the information, Lord Robert Cecil intervened in the discussion, and asked in his turn:

"Have the Government considered the very serious effect of these proceedings on the whole situation in Asia Minor, particularly with reference to Moslem feeling, and whether, in view of the fact that these proceedings were apparently in absolute contravention of Article 22 of the Treaty of Versailles, he would cause representations to be made to our French Allies on the subject?"

Of course, Mr. Bonar Law could only reply:

"We are in communication with the French Government, but I do not accept the statement of my noble friend that what has happened is against the Treaty of Versailles. It is very difficult for us here to judge action which is taken on the responsibility of the French Government."

Finally, to Lord Hugh Cecil's inquiry whether the British Government was bound by promises made to the Emir Feisal, Mr. Bonar Law answered:

"The Government are certainly bound by their pledge. In my opinion the fact that the mandate was given to France to cover that area was not inconsistent with that pledge."

Later on, Mr. Ormsby-Gore obtained leave to move the adjournment of the House in order to call attention to the immediate danger to British interests in the Middle East arising from the threatened new hostilities in Syria. He said that first—

"He wished to criticise vigorously the sins of omission and commission committed by the British Government, and more particularly by the British Foreign Office. Only by a frank and full statement by the British Government would bloodshed be prevented. The responsibility of this country was deeply involved in view of the pledges which had been given to the Arabs before they came into the war, while they were our allies, and above all since the armistice.... It was essential that both the French Government and the Arab Government in Damascus should know exactly what the demands of the British Government were, and how far we were committed and how far we intended to stand by those commitments. The British taxpayer, too, wanted to know how far we were committed. Our pledges to the French were less specific than those to the Arabs. We pledged ourselves to recognise the independence of the Arabs. The British Government were bound by their undertaking to Hussein to recognise the establishment of an independent Arab State comprising within its borders Damascus, Hama, Homs, and Aleppo. Did the British Government communicate these pledges frankly to the French Government? We were responsible for encouraging the Arabs to believe that we were going to stand by them. Were we going to stand by that pledge or not? If not, we ought to tell the Arabs so frankly. It was quite impossible for us to secure the pacification of Arabia, including Mesopotamia, unless Damascus was at peace. French, Arab, and British areas had been agreed upon to last until the permanent settlement was come to, and if there had been a breach of that agreement those who were responsible for the breach ought to be held responsible. Until the mandate for Syria had been approved by the Council of the League of Nations and the new Arab Government in Syria was established there should be no disturbance of the *status quo* without the willing agreement of all parties. For years the Arabs had been our greatest friends in the East and France our dearest ally in Europe. The outbreak of hostilities between them revealed the bankruptcy of British diplomacy."

Earl Winterton, like Mr. Ormsby-Gore, took up the defence of the Emir and suggested that Great Britain should act as mediator between France and the Arabs:

"As one who had fought with the Arabs during the war, he resented the idea contained in the suggestion that while it was all very well to use the Arabs during the war, it was not worth while now that the war was over having a row with France for their sake.... Prince Feisal had put his case before the Peace Conference, but the Government, following its usual practice of secrecy, had never allowed the House to hear a word of it or of the considered answer of the Supreme Council. He submitted that the claims that France had to the mandate in Syria were based, and could only be based, on the law of the League of Nations. He was amazed to see in a Northcliffe newspaper that day a reference to 'the great historical traditions of France in Syria.' If that suggested that France had any rights in Syria over and above those given by the League of Nations they were coming to a very dangerous argument. It was absurd to treat a people like the Arabs as an upstart people, to be treated in a condescending way by the Allies. The duty of the Government was to make representations at once to both the French and Arab Governments, asking that this matter should be submitted to arbitration, and that the whole case should be made public."

Finally, General Seely, a former Minister, rose, and owned that under the terms of the treaty with Turkey, France had got a force in Syria, but the whole difficulty lay in the French issuing an ultimatum without consulting Great Britain. According to the three speakers, England was interested in the question, owing to her engagements with the Emir Feisal, and the after-effects which French action might have in Syria and the neighbouring regions.

Mr. Bonar Law, feeling obliged to take into account both the section of public opinion on behalf of which the three speakers had spoken, and the feelings of an Allied country, reminded his opponents, who hardly concealed their unwillingness to approve the arrangements which had just been concluded, that France had the same mandate for Syria as Great Britain had for Mesopotamia, and endeavoured to prove that the situation of England in Mesopotamia was very much the same as the situation of France in Syria. He expressly said:

"The real question before the House was whether the British Government had a right to interfere in a country over which France had duly received a mandate. It was true that, in October, 1915, the British Government had declared they were prepared to recognise and support the independence of the Arabs within those portions of the territories claimed by the Emir Feisal in which Great Britain was free to act, but it was added, without detriment to the interests of her ally France.' ...

"It was said that the independence of the Arab people was incompatible with the mandate. If so, this part of the Treaty of the Covenant of the League of Nations ought not to have been in, and France ought not to have been allowed to obtain a mandate in Syria. It was also said that what the French were doing was uncalled for; that all that was necessary was to have the *status quo*. But British troops were in occupation of all the territories, and the British Government came to the conclusion that it was not fair that we should be called upon to bear the burdens of occupation of territories in which later we should have no interest. We gave notice that we intended to withdraw the British troops. The country had therefore to be occupied, and at the San Remo Conference the mandate for Syria was given definitely to the French Government. That was not done behind the back of the Emir Feisal. It was done with his knowledge, and when he was in Paris he himself agreed that there should be a French mandate for that territory.

"We had accepted a mandate in Mesopotamia. Supposing the French Government said to us, 'You are using force in Mesopotamia, and you are doing it without consulting the French Government. You are breaking the conditions of the proper homogeneity of the Allies, and you should not take steps to repulse the troops attacking you in Mesopotamia until you have come to an arrangement with the French Government.' The analogy was complete. We were in Mesopotamia for the purpose of setting up not a colony, but an independent Arab State, and, in spite of that, we were attacked by Arabs all through Mesopotamia. Our answer to the French would be that the mandate for Mesopotamia had been entrusted to us, and we claimed to deal with the country in the way we thought right. It was said that this action of the French Government was contrary to the whole spirit of the mandate and an independent Arab State. That was not so. In the ultimatum to which reference had been made a passage occurred which he would quote. Acceptance of the French mandate was one of the conditions. 'The mandate,' it is stated, 'will respect the independence of Syria and will remain wholly compatible with the principle of government by Syrian authorities properly invested with powers by the popular will. It will only entail on the part of the mandatory Power co-operation in the form of collaboration and assistance, but it will in no case assume the colonial form of annexation or direct administration.' The French Government told us they were acting on that principle, and was the House of Commons really going to ask the British Government to say, 'We do not accept your assurance, but we ask you to allow us to interfere with you in the exercise of your authority'?

"The mandate having been given, it was clearly no business of ours to interfere unless some action had been taken so outrageous that we had a right to say that it was not in accordance with the Peace Treaty and would not be accepted by the League of Nations or any other independent body....

"Had we that justification? He thought we had a right at least to assume that the French Government had something of a case for the action they were taking. He had the actual words in which the French described the necessity of their taking this action. They pointed out that a large number of French soldiers had been massacred by Arabs. They did not say that the Emir Feisal was responsible for that—he did not think the Emir was—but that whether it was due to his responsibility or want of power to prevent it the situation was one which the French Government could not allow to continue. With regard to the railway, on which they said they depended absolutely under present conditions for the support of their forces in dealing with the rebellion of Mustafa Kemal in Cilicia, they complained that they had tried over and over again to get from the Emir the use of that railway for the purpose of the supply of their troops, but had failed. They said that that was a condition of things which they could not allow to continue if they were to be responsible for the mandate. He thought that was a very good case."

On Lord Winterton exclaiming: "Then the French have a mandate for Damascus! But neither the Arabs nor the Supreme Council have ever admitted such a mandate," Mr. Bonar Law, on behalf of the Government, answered:

"They had been in communication with the French Government on that point, and their reply was to this effect: 'There is no intention of permanent military occupation. As soon as the mandate has been accepted and order has been restored the troops will be withdrawn.'

"A great deal had been said about the claims of Emir Feisal. No one would recognise them more readily than His Majesty's Government. They knew that he and his tribesmen did gallant service in the war, but he asked the House to remember that but for the sacrifices both of the French and ourselves, there would have been no possibility of King Hussein having any authority in his country....

"They met him over and over again in London and Paris, and when the question came of giving the mandate, on two occasions the British and French Governments sent a joint invitation to the Emir Feisal to come to Europe and discuss the question with them. The Emir Feisal was not able to come for one reason or another on either occasion; but he did say that no case of any ally or anyone in connection with the Peace Treaty was considered more thoroughly than his, or with more inclination to meet his wishes. The House must be under no misapprehension. There was great trouble in the Middle East. Arab fighting would add to that trouble, and what happened in Syria must have reflex action in Mesopotamia. If it was assumed, as some hon. members were ready to assume, that we in Mesopotamia were pursuing solely selfish aims with no other object, and if they assumed that the French were pursuing imperialistic aims in Syria with no other object, then, of course, the case was hopeless. There was no Frenchman who had shown a broader mind and a greater readiness to grasp the position of other people than General Gouraud. In any degree to reflect upon the French Government in this matter was a very serious thing."

The time seemed very badly chosen indeed for such a debate in the English Parliament, as Mr. Winston Churchill, War Secretary, had just informed the Commons that important reinforcements coming from India had recently been dispatched to Mesopotamia, and the Commander-in-Chief had been given full powers to take any measures the situation might require.

It was the policy of England in the East which stood responsible for such a state of things. Though the bulk of public opinion in France was averse to any military action in the East, either in Syria or in Turkey, yet France was driven to fight, as it were, by England—though both Governments were supposed to act jointly in the East—in order to prevent her ally from undermining her influence. Such was the outcome of England's ill-omened policy, who first had supported the Arabian movement and now seemed to forsake it, and thus had roused all the East against Europe through the resentment caused by her attitude towards Turkey and Persia. Perhaps England was not very sorry, after all, that France should divert against herself part of the Arabian forces from the Mesopotamian front, where the British effectives were insufficient in number.

M. Millerand corroborated Mr. Bonar Law's statements before the French Chamber, disclosed some of the agreements made with England, and apologised for being unable to say more; he also declared England had officially recognised she had no right to meddle with Syrian affairs; and finally declared that whoever should feel tempted—he meant the Emir who had just submitted to General Gouraud's ultimatum—to oppose France to Great Britain in Asia Minor would now know it would have France alone in front of him. And yet if one day Great Britain rules over Mesopotamia, she is not likely to give France a free hand in Syria.

Just at the same time—on July 20—the Cairo correspondent of *The Times* wrote that he understood the King of the Hejaz had telegraphed to Mr. Lloyd George how surprised and disappointed he was at the French policy in Syria, and asked him to interfere. King Hussein also declared he could not exert his influence on the Emir Feisal's brothers or prevent them from coming to his help.

The English Government circles, on the other hand, seemed at last inclined to favour a scheme that would put Syria and Mesopotamia, respectively under the sovereignty of the Emir Feisal and the Emir Abdullah, under a French mandate in Syria and a British one in Mesopotamia. But the *Daily Express* of July 17 seemed apprehensive lest the French expedition aimed at overthrowing the Emir Feisal and replacing him by the Emir Said, who had been expelled from Syria during the British occupation. Let it be said, incidentally, that the Arabs of the Emir Feisal possessed 100,000 rifles, the very arms taken from the Turks by the English and left by the latter in the hands of the Arabian leader.

General Gouraud's ultimatum had naturally been accepted by the Emir Feisal, but a few days after its expiration, and so military action had been started. General Gouraud, according to his communiqué, had, on July 22, at the Emir's request, stopped the column that was on its way from Zaleh to Damascus. Feisal had alleged that his answer had been sent in due time, but untoward circumstances had prevented it from coming to hand the appointed day.

The French General had consented to give him the benefit of the doubt and halt his troops on certain conditions, one of which was that his soldiers should not be attacked. Now the French column that guarded the country between Homs and Tripolis, some distance to the east of the post of Tel-Kelah, was attacked by Sherifian regulars. Under these circumstances, and to prevent another attack which seemed to be preparing between Damascus and Beyrut, the southern French column that guarded the railway in case of an attack coming from Damascus, dislodged the Sherifian troops whose headquarters were at Khan-Meiseloun, in the mountain range which divides the plain of the Bukaa from the plain of Damascus, and thus the way was open to the latter town.

France, who otherwise would not have been obliged to fight in order to maintain her influence in Syria, was compelled to do so by the policy in which she was involved. But this policy, which drove her to inaugurate a Syrian campaign at the very time when by the side of England she enforced on Turkey a treaty that no Turk could accept, might have brought about, as Pierre Loti said in an article of the *Œuvre*, July 22, "the death of France in the East."

Even the Christians[43]—the Armenians excepted—wished the French to leave Antioch in order to be able to come to an understanding with the Moslems who maintained order in the four great towns of Aleppo, Hama, Homs, and Damascus, occupied by the Sherifian troops. A delegation of eight members representing the Christian element wanted to go to France, but the Patriarch of Lebanon handed General Gouraud a protest to be forwarded to the French Government; he inveighed against what he called "the shameful conduct of some members of the administrative Council of Lebanon," and charged them, just as they were about to leave for Europe, with receiving important sums of money from the Emir Feisal to carry on an anti-French propaganda. After this protest, they were imprisoned by the French authorities: all of which shows the state of deep unrest then prevailing in Lebanon and our utter lack of reliable information from the East.

On July 23 a French column entered Aleppo, after a skirmish north of Muslemieh, and a reconnoitring body of cavalry which had pushed on as far as Homs bridge was greeted by some Sherifian officers, who informed them that the Sherifian troops had left the town. On the 25th, in the afternoon, the French troops entered Damascus without encountering any resistance. A new Government was formed after the downfall of the Sherifian Government, and General Gobet formally notified them on behalf of General Gouraud that the Emir Feisal was no longer King of the country. He demanded a war contribution of 10 million francs on account of the damage done by the war bands in the western zone; general disarmament should be proceeded with at once; the army should be reduced and converted into a body of police; all war material should be handed over to the French authorities, and the chief war criminals tried by military courts. All these conditions were, of course, assented to by the new Government, who expressed their sincere wish to collaborate with the French.

The Emir Feisal, who had come back to Damascus, was requested to leave the country with his family. He set off to England soon after and sought to meet Mr. Lloyd George at Lucerne.

Without considering the future relations between Lebanon and Syria or turning its attention to the future mode of government of Syria and its four great towns Damascus, Hama, Homs, and Aleppo, the French Government decided to restore Greater Lebanon. M. Millerand informed Mgr. Abdallah Kouri, Maronite Archbishop of Arca, president of the delegation of Lebanon, of this by a letter dated August 24, 1920. The new State was to extend from the Nahr-el-Litani, which flows along the frontier of Palestine, to another State, called "Territoire des Alaonites," or, in Arabic, Alawiya, coming between the Lebanon and Antioch, and to the crests of Anti-Libanus, including the Bukaa area, with the towns of Rayak and Baalbek. The ports of Beyrut and Tripolis in Syria were to enjoy local autonomy, but to keep in close connection with the new State. Beyrut was to be the seat of the new Government; Tripolis and its suburbs were to be grouped into a municipality. In this way Greater Lebanon would have recovered all its former territories, as it was before 1860, in conformity with the promises made by M. Clémenceau and confirmed by M. Millerand, and with the claims set forth in 1919 at the Peace Conference by the delegates of Lebanon.

Was it not a mistake in Syria, a country over which France had a mandate and where the proportion of Moslems is three to one, to start with a policy that favoured Lebanon and consequently the Christians? The question was all the more important as the discontent brought about by the Powers' decisions was far from subsiding in these and the neighbouring regions.

Indeed, the Ansarieh tribes, living in the mountainous regions to the east of Antioch and Alexandretta, and in the Jebel Ansarieh between Latakia and Tartus, which had persistently kept aloof from us in the past, made their submission after the downfall of the Emir Feisal, and several Ansarieh chiefs—Ismail Pasha, Inad, and Ismail Bey Yaouah—accepted the conditions imposed on them. Yet dissatisfaction was still rampant in the Hauran area, and the train in which ed Rubi Pasha, the Syrian Premier, and other Ministers were going to Deraa was attacked on Friday, August 20, at Kerbet-Ghazeleh by Arabian bands. Ed Rubi Pasha and Abdurrahman Youssef Pasha were murdered. The railway line was recaptured later on, but the contingents sent to Deraa had to fight with Arabian bands at Mosmieh.

Farther north, in the part of Cilicia entirely occupied by Kemalist troops, Colonel Brémond, commanding a group of 3,000 to 4,000 men consisting of French troops and native recruits, after being blockaded at Adana for six weeks, had to sign a truce in August because he was short of water, and the provisioning of Adana could only be ensured by establishing a base in the former Roman port of Karatash. Mersina, where the French had enlisted all the Armenian and Greek manhood, was also besieged and blockaded, except along the coast where a French warship overawed the rebels. Lastly, Tarsus, the third place occupied by French troops, was in the same predicament, and was cut off from the other two towns. Under these circumstances whoever could flee sailed to Cyprus, and the few boats which called at Mersina took away crowds of fugitives.

In Mesopotamia the situation was quite as bad, and everywhere the Arabs evinced much discontent. In the zone of the lower Euphrates and Lake Hamar, as well as in the Muntefik area, many disturbances occurred.

The *Sunday Times* of August 21, 1920, in an article in which the attitude of the British Government was severely criticised, wondered whether it was not too late to atone for the mistakes of England, even by expending large sums of money, and concluded thus:

"Would it not be wiser to confess our failure and give up meddling with the affairs of three million Arabs who want but one thing, to be allowed to decide their own fate? After all, Rome was not ruined when Hadrian gave up the conquests made by Trajan."

The *Observer* too asked whether a heavy expenditure of men and money could restore the situation, and added:

"The situation is serious; yet it is somewhat ludicrous too, when we realise that so much blood and money has been wasted for a lot of deserts and marshes which we wanted 'to pacify,' and when we remember that our ultimate aim is to impose our sovereignty on people who plainly show they do not want it."

The diversity of creeds among the various Moslem sects had also, from the beginning, imperilled the unity of the Arabian world within the Ottoman Empire by endangering its religious unity. By the side of the Sunnis, or Orthodox Moslems, the Shia—viz., the rebels or heretics, belonging to a schism which is almost as old as Islam itself—recognise nobody but Ali as the lawful successor of Mohammed. According to them, the title of Caliph should not go outside the Prophet's family, and his spiritual powers can only be conferred upon his descendants; so, from a religious point of view, they do not recognise the power of the other dynasties of Caliphs—for instance, that of the Ottoman Sultans. As Ali, the Prophet's son-in-law, was killed at Kufa in Mesopotamia, and as Ali's sons, Hassan and Hossein, were also massacred at Kerbela, near the ruins of Babylon, together with some of their descendants who had a lawful right to the title of Imam, Mesopotamia is looked upon by the Shia as their Holy Places.

Many wealthy Persians, to whom the worship of the members of Ali's family has become a symbol and who consider their death as a religious sacrifice, have their own coffins carried to Mesopotamia that their bodies may lie in the holy necropolis of Kerbela or of Nejef, to the north-east of Mecca and Medina; and as a great many Arabs of Mesopotamia are still Shia, this schism practically divides the Persian world from the Turkish world.

But though the Persians, who have never recognised any Caliph, and for the last thirteen hundred years have been waiting till the Khilafat should revert to the lineal descent of Ali, the Prophet's son-in-law, to acknowledge a Caliph's authority, do not recognise the Ottoman Caliphate, yet their monarchs do not seek to deprive the Sultan of his title of Caliph to assume it themselves.

So their case is entirely different from that of the people of Morocco, who do not recognise the Ottoman Caliphate because their own sovereigns, as descendants of the Prophet, profess they have an hereditary right to hold the office of Caliph within the frontiers of their State.

The Shia faith has even spread as far as India and the Sunda Isles; and so the opposition between Shia and Sunnis may play an important part in freeing Mesopotamia from the Turkish influence of Constantinople.

Yet the English occupation has been so bitterly resented in Mesopotamia that the Shia Mujtahids, or imams of Nejef and Kerbela, have lately asked for the restoration of Turkish sovereignty over these towns, where are the two famous holy shrines of Islam. Moreover, the controversy on the question whether the Sultans of Turkey have a right to the Caliphate, because they do not belong to the tribe of Koreish, in which the Prophet was born, seems to have come to an end among the Moslems, or at least to have been laid aside in view of the present events.

Moreover, the Prophet, when he advised the Faithful to choose his successor in the tribe of Koreish, does not seem at all, according to the best Moslem authorities, to have wished to confer the supreme spiritual power for ever upon a particular section of the community related to him by ties of blood, and to have reserved the Caliphate to this tribe. It seems more likely that, as Islam at that time had not yet given birth to powerful States, he chose this tribe because it was the best organised and the strongest, and thus considered it as the fittest to maintain the independence of the Caliphate and defend the interests of Islam. Besides, within half a century after the Prophet's death the Caliphate passed from Mohammed's four immediate successors to the Omayyids for the reason indicated above, and in contradiction to the theory of lineal descent. It is obvious that, had Mohammed been guided by family considerations, he would not have merely given the Faithful some directions about the election of his successor, but he would have chosen one of his relations himself to inherit his office, and would have made it hereditary in the latter's family.

The Wahhabis, who are connected with the Shia, are likewise a political and religious sect which was founded in the eighteenth century in Nejed, a region of Central Arabia conterminous with the north of Syria. The Wahhabi doctrine aims at turning Islam into a kind of deism, a rational creed, looking upon all the traditions of Islam as superstitions, and discarding all religious observances. Since the assassination of Ibn el Rashid in May, 1920, the present leaders of the Wahhabis are Abdullah ibn Mitah and Ibn Saud, over whom the Ottomans have a merely nominal power.

When King Hussein planned to join the Hejaz and Nejd to Syria, Ibn Saud refused to let Nejd fall under the suzerainty of the King of the Hejaz, who was powerful merely because he was supported by Europe and because Syria is a rich country. Most likely the religious question had something to do with this conflict. In August, 1919, the Wahhabis, who had asked the Emir Ibn Saud for his support, suddenly attacked the troops of the sons of the King of the Hejaz which were in the Taif area, and defeated them at Tarabad. The Wahhabi Emir gained a few more victories, and was about to threaten the Holy Cities when the rising of the Orthodox Moslem tribes compelled him to retreat.

So the hostility of the Wahhabis, whose independence was threatened by the Sunnis of the Hejaz, whom they look upon as heretics, still embittered the dissensions in the Arab world.

It has been asserted that this Wahhabi movement was at first started by the Turks, which would not have been unlikely at a time when it was Turkey's interest to divide Arabia in order to raise difficulties to the Allies after the Sherif's treason; but now it was no longer her interest—and it was beyond her power—to stir up an agitation.

The Ishmaelites, who laid waste Persia and Syria in the eighth century, and played an important part in the East till the twelfth century, have also broken off with the Shia.

Lastly, the Druses, who inhabit the slopes of Lebanon and the greater part of Anti-Lebanon between Jebeil and Saida along the Mediterranean, profess the creed of the Caliph Al-Hakem, who lived at the beginning of the eleventh century. They had withdrawn to Lebanon and long repelled the attacks of the Turks, whose suzerainty they acknowledged only in 1588. In 1842 the Porte gave them a chief, but practically they have remained almost independent. They have often fought with the Maronite Christians living to the north, especially in 1860, and there is still much hostility between them.

Moreover, all Moslem communities, without exception—whether the communities governed by independent national sovereigns such as Afghanistan; or by sovereigns owing allegiance to non-Moslem Powers such as Egypt, India, Tunis, Khiva, Bokhara; or the communities living under a non-Moslem rule, as is the case with those of Algeria, Russia, and also India and China—give their allegiance to the Sultan as Caliph, though they are always at liberty to refuse it. Even the Moslem communities of Algeria and Tunis, which are connected with those of Morocco by their common origin and language, and live close by them, do not deem it a sufficient reason to recognise the Emir of Morocco as Caliph that he is a descendant of the Prophet.

An even more striking argument is that the community of the Hejaz, which rebelled against Turkish sovereignty during the war and has made itself politically independent, still maintains its religious allegiance to the Sultan; and the present King, Hussein, who is the most authentic descendant of the Prophet, and who rules over the two holiest towns of Islam, Mecca and Medina, soon after the armistice addressed the Sultan a telegram of religious allegiance drawn up in the most deferential terms. The possession of Mecca and Medina being one of the attributes of the Caliph, and these towns having a great religious and political importance owing to the great annual pilgrimage, King Hussein might have taken advantage of this to dispute with the Sultan the title of Caliph. England had strongly urged him to do so, but King Hussein obstinately refused. Then the British Government, giving up all hope of bringing about the transference of the Caliphate from the Ottoman dynasty to another sovereign, concluded a secret alliance with Vahid ed Din.

Considering the intricate situation in the East due to the variety of races and religions, and the movements of all sorts by which the populations of those countries are swayed, it seems most unwise to increase the general restlessness by a vain intervention of the Powers, and to dismember what remains of Turkey in Europe and Aria Minor, a dismemberment which would necessarily have violent repercussions throughout the deeply perturbed Moslem world. Though the recent movements of emancipation in the East to a certain extent meet the legitimate wishes of the peoples and have somewhat cleared the situation in Asia Minor, yet it is obviously most perilous to infringe upon the Sultan's sovereignty, to endeavour to drive away the Turks into Asia, and to set up a kind of fictitious official Islam by compelling the Moslem peoples of the East to give up their cherished independence and submit to an Arab imperialism which would soon become British imperialism. At the present moment all the Moslem elements are determined to unite together against any enemy of their liberty; and all Moslems, without any distinction of creed or race, might very well one day flock to the standard of a bold leader who should take up arms in the name of Islam, in order to safeguard their independence.

These movements, and many other similar ones, were encouraged and strengthened by the development of the principle of nationalities and the support given to it by Mr. Wilson, who was bent upon carrying it out to its strictly logical consequences, without paying heed to the limitations imposed by the present material and political conditions. But we do not think it is true to say, as has been urged, that the assertion of the right of self-determination of peoples was the initial cause of these movements. The movement in favour of the rights of nationalities originated long before Mr. Wilson's declarations, which merely hurried on this powerful movement, and also caused it to swerve somewhat from its original direction.

This movement, on the whole, seems chiefly to proceed—though other factors have intervened in it—from a kind of reaction against the standardising tendency, from a material and moral point of view, of modern Western civilisation, especially the Anglo-Saxon civilisation, and also from a reaction against the extreme unification aimed at by russifying the numerous peoples living within the Russian Empire. Modern civilisation, having reached its present climax, has aimed—and its political and social repercussions have had the same influence—at doing away with all differences between human minds and making the world homogeneous; thus all men would have been brought to live in the same way, to have the same manners, and their requirements would have been met in the same way—to the very great advantage of its enormous industrial development. Of course, all this proved an idle dream; human nature soon asserted itself, amidst the commotions and perturbations experienced by the States, and a reaction set in among those who hitherto only aimed at enslaving various human groups, or linked them together politically in a most artificial way. Then the same feeling spread among all those peoples.

All this enables us to see to what extent this movement is legitimate, and to know exactly what proportions of good and evil it contains.

It rightly asserts that various peoples have different natures, and by protecting their freedom, it aims at ensuring the development of their peculiar abilities. For let us not forget that the characters of peoples depend on physical conditions, that even the features we may not like in some peoples are due to the race, and that if, by blending and mixing populations nowadays these features are modified, they are generally altered only from bad to worse.

But this principle is true only so far as it frees and enables to shape their own destinies peoples who have distinctive qualities of their own and are able to provide for themselves. It cannot be extended—as has been attempted in some cases—to States within which men descending from various races or having belonged in the course of centuries to different nationalities have long been united, and through a long common history and a centuries-old co-operation have formed one nation. This is one of the erroneous aspects of Mr. Wilson's conception, and one of the bad consequences it has entailed.

The eviction of the Turks from Constantinople, which the British wished for but which they dared not carry into effect, does not thwart the scheme of the Turkish Nationalists; it can only bring about a reaction of the Moslem populations against foreign intervention, and thus strengthen the Pan-Turanian movement. Though this movement cannot carry out all its aims, the eviction of the Turks obviously must urge those populations to constitute a State based both on the community of religion and the community of race of its various elements, and from which all alien ethnic elements would be expelled—viz., Slavs, Armenians, Greeks, and Arabs, who were all an inherent source of weakness to the Turkish Empire. This new State would include Anatolia, Russian Azerbaïjan, and Persian Azerbaïjan, the Russian territories in Central Asia—viz., Russian Turkistan, Khiva, Bokhara—the whole of the region of the Steppes; and towards it the Tatar populations of the Volga, Afghanistan, and Chinese Turkistan would necessarily be attracted.

As to the Arabs, the Turks have never been able to gain their friendship, though they have done their best to do so, and have drawn but little profit from the money squandered plentifully in their vast deserts. And the Russians have always stood in the way of an understanding between Turkey and the Arabian territories, because it would have benefited the cause of Islam and therefore would have hindered both their own designs on the territories of Asia Minor and the ambitions of the Orthodox Church. Yet to the Turks as well as the Arabs—and even to the Europeans—it would be a great advantage not to injure the understanding and goodwill that Islam engenders among these peoples, since its creed has both a religious and a political aspect.

The maintenance of this Islamic union has been wrongly called—in the disparaging sense of the word—Pan-Islamism. Yet its ideal has nothing in common with such doctrines as those of Pan-Germanism, Pan-Slavism, Pan-Americanism, Pan-Polism, Pan-Hellenism, etc., which are all imperialistic doctrines aiming at territorial conquests by military or economic means, and also by the diffusion of their own religious creeds and the extension of the influence of their Churches. While Pan-Germanism aims at the hegemony of the world; while Pan-Americanism wants to control the whole of America; while Pan-Slavism wishes to gather together all the Slavonic elements—which is defensible—but also means to supplant the old civilisation of Western Europe, which it considers as "rotten," and to renovate the world; while Pan-Polism, which has not such ambitious aims, merely seeks, like Pan-Hellenism, to conquer wider territories in order to restore Greater Poland or Greater Greece—Islam, which does not try to make any proselytes, has no other ambition than to group all Moslem elements according to the commandments of the Koran. Yet, Islam having both a political and a religious purpose, a Pan-Islamic concept might be defensible, and would be legitimate from the Moslem point of view, whereas it cannot be so from the Christian point of view. Pan-Catholicism, on the contrary, is an impossible thing, because Christianity does not imply a political doctrine, and is distinct from temporal power—though such a doctrine has sometimes been advocated. For in the doctrine of monarchy, especially in France, religion has always been held merely as a help, a support, and the monarch, though he has often been a defender of the Faith, has never looked upon his power as dependent on the Papacy or bound up with it. Islam, however, does not want to assert itself in, and give birth to, a huge political movement—a Pan-Islamic movement in the imperialistic sense of the word—aiming at constituting a huge theocratic State, including all the 300 million Moslems who are now living. But there is between all Moslems a deep moral solidarity, a mighty religious bond which accounts for their sympathetic feeling towards Turkey, and owing to which even the Moslem inhabitants of countries which have lost their independence still earnestly defend and jealously maintain the privileges and dignity of the Caliph.

So it is a mistake to speak of the ambitious designs of Islam, and the mistake has been made wilfully. Those who profess such an opinion are Pan-Slavic Russians who want to deceive public opinion in the world as to their true intent, and thus prepare for territorial annexations, because Pan-Slavism is the enemy of Islamism. As this Pan-Slavism has always been, and is still more than ever, a danger to Europe, it is the interest of the latter, in order to defend its civilisation, not to fight against Islamism, but even to support it. This necessity has been understood by many Catholics who have always been favourable to Turkey and by the Mussulmans, which accounts for the long friendly intercourse between Moslems and Catholics, and the Moslems' tolerance toward the devotees of a religion which, on the whole, is in complete contradiction to their own faith. On the other hand, Islam appears as counterbalancing Protestantism in the East, and it seems the future of thought and morality and of any culture would be endangered if the 60 million Indian Moslems and the 220 million Indian Brahminists, Buddhists, and the members of other sects ever listened to Mr. Lloyd George and were connected with Protestantism.

Moreover, King Hussein, in the course of the audience that he granted in July, 1920, to Prince Ruffo, the leader of the Italian mission to Arabia, before his departure, after saying that the Moslem world resented the hostile attitude of the Powers towards the Sultan of Constantinople, declared that the Moslems are not actuated by any feeling of conquest or proselytism, but simply claim the right to preserve their independence.

Footnotes:

36 *Hayassdan*, July 6, 1915; No. 25.

37 We are the more anxious to correct these figures as in 1916, at a time when it was difficult to control them, we gave about the same figures in a note to the Société d'Anthropologie as to the demographic consequences of the war. We then relied upon the documents that had just been published and on the statements of the Rev. Harold Buxton.

38 *Le Mouvement pan-russe et les Allogènes* (Paris, 1919).

39 *The Times*, March 15, 1920.

40 H. Vambéry. *Cagataische Sprachstudien* (Leipzig, 1867); *Etymologisches Wörterbuch der Turko-Tatarischen Sprachen* (Leipzig, 1875); *Das Turkenvolk* (1885).

41 Léon Cahun, *Introduction à l'histoire de l'Asie, Turcs et Mongols, des origines à 1405* (Paris, 1896).

42 Liman von Sanders, *Fünf Jahre Türkei*, pp. 330-331.

43 *Le Temps*, July 21, 1920.

VIII

THE MOSLEMS OF THE FORMER RUSSIAN EMPIRE AND TURKEY

THE Supreme Council, in the course of one of its last sittings, decided in January, 1920, practically to recognise the independence of Georgia,[44] Azerbaïjan, and Armenia.

It is deeply to be regretted that this decision came so late, for, considering the circumstances under which it was taken, it seemed to have been resorted to *in extremis* and under the Bolshevist threat.

It was even announced, then denied, that the Allies were going to send contingents to the Caucasus in order to check the Bolshevist advance towards Armenia, Turkey, Persia, and possibly towards Mesopotamia and India. But under the present circumstances, the Allies were not likely now to get all the benefit they might have derived from this measure if it had been taken long ago; and, on the other hand, this measure was not likely to produce any effect if the new States were not recognised definitely and could not rely on the Allies' moral and material support.

Since Georgia, Azerbaïjan, and Armenia seemed to have been recognised as independent States, in order to incite them to check the Reds' advance, how was it that the Republic of Northern Caucasus had not been treated similarly? The reason given by the Supreme Council was that, as the greater part of this State was occupied by Denikin's forces, it did not think it proper to take a decision about it. The true reason was that the Supreme Council wanted to favour the Pan-Russian general, and it was even rumoured that Koltchak and Denikin had demanded this rich country to be set aside for the Tsar, whom they wanted to restore to the throne.

Out of the 25 or 30 million Moslems living in the whole of Russia, 6 or 8 millions were scattered in the region of the Volga (Orenburg, Kazan) and in the Crimea; they were about 6 millions in Turkistan and 7 millions in the Caucasus region; about 2 millions in Northern Caucasus, 300,000 to 500,000 in Kuban, 600,000 in Georgia, 3,500,000 in Azerbaïjan. Half the population is Moslem in the new Armenian State, for only in two districts are the Armenians in a majority, the Tatars being in a majority in the others. It should be borne in mind that all these Moslems, after the downfall of Tsardom, had turned their hopes towards the Allies, especially England, to safeguard their political independence. Unfortunately neither Great Britain nor France paid any heed to the repeated entreaties of M. Haidar Bammate, then Minister of

Foreign Affairs of the Republic of Northern Caucasus, or later on to the appeals of the Georgian statesmen.

This omission appears all the more unaccountable if we remember that the Allies, by settling the fate of Armenia on this occasion, encroached upon the Turkish question and confused it with the Russian question, which was already intricate enough; and as it is clear that another obvious reason for the Allies' decision was to befriend the Moslem populations of those regions, that they might not join the Bolshevist cause, why then had Christian Armenia been included in the aforesaid settlement, while Northern Caucasus had been excluded from it? Of course, it is not to be regretted that Armenia benefited by the Allies' decision, but it is impossible logically to explain how it came to be included in their measure on account of its close relations with Georgia and Azerbaïjan, when, as a matter of fact, the latter republics want to form a close union with Caucasus. It was quite as urgent, therefore, to recognise the Republic of Northern Caucasus as the other three countries.

Moreover, as the Allies wanted to keep Bolshevism out of Transcaucasia, it seemed obvious that their first measure, from a military point of view, should have been to hold a strong position in the Caucasus Range, whose slopes were being lapped by the Red tide, and to organise its defence.

Indeed, the key to the defence of Transcaucasia lies to the north of the Caucasus Range. Four passes, crossing the mountains from the north to the south, give access to it: the defile of Sukhum; the road leading from Alatyr to Kutaris; the Georgian military road from Vladikavkaz to Tiflis; lastly, the gates of Derbent, along the Caspian Sea. Only the first of these defiles was held by the Georgians; the other three were in the hands of the mountaineers, "the Gortsy"—viz., the Chechens, the Ossetes, the Ingushes, the Kabardians, and the Daghestanians, who make up the Republic of Northern Caucasus. It was easy for the mountaineers to set up a first line of defence on the Rivers Terek and Malka, which constitute a good strategic position, a second line before the defiles, and, should some detachments venture across the latter, they would be quickly stopped by the mountaineers. If, on the contrary, nothing was done, the Bolshevists could easily cross the defiles and destroy the Batum-Baku railway. These tribes, who had displayed so much energy sixty years ago for the conquest of their liberty, had fought against the Bolshevists from November, 1917, till February, 1919; so they had a right to expect the Allies would support their claims.

Unfortunately, French policy resorted again to the same manœuvre to which it was indebted for its failure on the Baltic coast, and which repeatedly deferred a solution of the Russian question. For the Allies refused to settle the condition of the Baltic States definitely, and even tried to restore Russia to its former state; they even urged the Baltic States, till Yudenitch, Denikin, and Koltchak had been defeated, to carry on the onerous struggle they had undertaken and to make all sacrifices of men and money to capture Petrograd, which they were not eager to do, as they would have merely paved the way to the coming of the Pan-Russian generals.

The Allies made a similar mistake when they indirectly asked the mountaineers of Caucasus, who wanted to be independent, to attack the Bolshevists, but gave them no guarantee they would recognise their independence. Of course, the mountaineers refused to play such a part, for they risked finding themselves confronted one day or another with a Russia that would despise their national aspirations and would oppress them.

The situation could have been saved and the balance between the States on the confines of the Russian Empire could have been restored only by a close understanding of all the Caucasian peoples, after their independence should have been recognised; the representatives of Georgia and Azerbaïjan agreed on this point with the representatives of Northern Caucasus, and these peoples were ready to help each other mutually.

In the course of the last sitting of the Supreme Council to which the delegates of Georgia and Azerbaïjan had been invited, the latter declared "that the mountaineers were brave, that they had constituted some of the best units of the former Russian army, and were bent upon stopping the Bolshevists, but they lacked arms and ammunition."

Under such circumstances it seemed the Allies could not possibly ignore these peoples' determination and turn a deaf ear to their earnest request, yet they took no decision.

With regard to the Moslem question this attitude of the Conference, which seemed bent upon ignoring Northern Caucasus, was equally strange, for it was bound to bring about discontent among these Moslem populations. It was the more unaccountable as the Bolshevists, who set up as protectors of these populations, had sent many emissaries among them, who could not but derive profit from the Allies' attitude. The Bolshevists had, of course, immediately recognised Daghestan a Moslem State.

Nor had the Republic of Northern Caucasus any reason to be satisfied with the attitude assumed by the British mission sent to Baku, for this mission had constantly supported General Denikin, and seemed to endeavour to destroy the economic and political Caucasian union it had formed with Georgia and Azerbaïjan. The only theory which accounts for the British attitude is that the English meant to remain masters of Baku, and to leave the Russians the oil-field of Groznyi in Northern Caucasus, the output of which was already important before the war, and would certainly increase. But they were mistaken in thinking that the petroleum of Groznyi, which was partly used as fuel by the Vladikavkaz railway and partly sent to the Black Sea ports to be sold to Western Europe, was utilised in Central Russia; it is chiefly the petroleum of the Baku area, lying farther south, which is easily conveyed to Russia across the Caspian Sea and up the Volga.

Again, the Allies ought to have taken into account that the troublous state into which the Moslem world had been thrown by the settlement of the Turkish question as it was contemplated by the Peace Conference might have most important reactions in all directions on the populations of the former Russian Empire which now wanted to be independent.

Yet the claims which the delegations of the Republics of Georgia and Azerbaïjan—together with Northern Caucasus—had set forth in January in the course of their reception by the Supreme Council concerning the support they might expect from the Great Powers in case they should be attacked by the Soviets, brought forth no answer; and the Allies adjourned both the question of the defence of the Transcaucasian Republics and the question of their independence.

In consequence of all this, Northern Caucasus soon fell a prey to Bolshevism, and some insurrections broke out in Georgia. The Soviet Government sent a great many agitators to these regions. Then the Red army advanced in two columns, one of which defeated Denikin and crossed the Kuban to invade Caucasus, and the other spread over Kurdistan, whence, after winning over to its cause the Tatar and pro-Russian elements of the neighbouring regions, it extended its field of action as far as Persia and Mesopotamia.

As early as February the Russian Bolshevists concentrated important forces near the northern frontier of Azerbaïjan under pretence of driving away the remnants of Denikin's army, and after hurriedly getting up a "Soviet Government" at Daghestan, drew near the frontier of Azerbaïjan.

Meanwhile their agents carried on an energetic propaganda at Baku, where the inexperienced Moslem leaders of Azerbaïjan had foolishly left almost all the administration of the country in the hands of functionaries of the old régime or Russian officers who thought that Bolshevism, especially with the national character it had newly assumed, might restore Russia to its former state.

Within the country an economic crisis on the one hand, and on the other hand the Armenians' aggressions, in the course of which they had massacred many Mussulmans, especially at Karabagh, had raised a widespread discontent against the Cabinet.

Emboldened by the success of the Bolshevists, who benefited by these disturbances, their local accomplices, some Russian workmen supported by about a hundred Moslem workmen, helped to organise a series of raids.

During the night of April 26-27 the northern frontier of Azerbaïjan was crossed at the railway station of Jalama by a Bolshevist armoured train, for the main body of the army of Azerbaïjan had been dispatched to Karabagh and Kasakg to repel an Armenian attack, so that only one armoured train and a few hundred soldiers had been left on the northern frontier. This small detachment could not prevent the advance of the Red forces which followed the train, though it did its duty bravely and destroyed the railway track. On April 27 the Bolshevist forces reached the station of Khatchmaz, where they were greeted by a group of local communists.

At Baku, where the population lived in a state of indifference and passivity, the local communists, encouraged by the advance of the Russian Bolshevists, addressed an ultimatum to the Government, which had declared itself in favour of armed resistance, demanding the resignation of the Cabinet and the handing over of the Government to the revolutionary committee which had just been formed. This ultimatum was enforced by the threat of the bombardment of the town by the fleet of the Caspian Sea.

The Government, which had vainly asked Georgia for assistance, and had proposed to Armenia, before the common danger, to put an end to the hostilities at Karabagh in order to withdraw its troops and dispatch them to the northern frontier, was compelled on April 28 to hand over the power to the people's commissioners. The members of the Cabinet, against whom the Bolshevists had issued a writ of arrest, hurried away and the communists immediately resorted to their usual methods of terrorism and plunder.

Instead of the "Moslem Brethren" the Bolshevist emissaries had spoken of, the inhabitants of Baku saw some Russian Bolshevists, accompanied by Armenians who had been expelled by the former Government, take possession of the town. As soon as they arrived, the latter arrested all the foreign missions, except the Persian mission. As the national army was detained on the southern frontier by constant Armenian attacks, the invaders dispatched Russian detachments in all directions, to take possession of the entire country. They addressed an ultimatum to Armenia, demanding the evacuation of Karabagh. At the same time Russian forces were sent via Zakatali towards the Georgian frontier. At Baku the Moslem militia was replaced by Russian workmen, and at the same time orders were given immediately to disarm the population of Ganjha (Elisavetpol), where the governor and some notables were arrested and incarcerated.

It is reported that at Ganjha 15,000 Moslems were slaughtered by the Reds.

A correspondent of *Il Secolo*, on coming back from Caucasus, wrote an article entitled "The East on Fire" on May 25, 1920:

"The information that we have just received from Constantinople, Anatolia, Caucasus, and Persia could not possibly be worse. Bolshevism has won over Caucasus to its policy, and from Baku it is carrying on a more and more energetic propaganda in Persia and Turkistan. The British are already fighting in the latter country with Bolshevism. All this might have been foreseen.

"As it is cut off from Europe and encircled by hostile bayonets, Bolshevism, which originated in Asia, is now spreading over Asia. This does not mean that Caucasus and Asia are ripe for a revolution of the poor against the rich. It would be a foolish thing to say this. In Asia everybody is poor, but nobody starves. In Asia there is no industry, there are no organisations; therefore, there is no socialist movement on the whole. But anybody who has been to Caucasus lately must necessarily have noticed, to his great surprise, evidences of a Moslem Bolshevism headed by Enver Pasha and his brother Noury. The Republic of the mountaineers of Daghestan, the first that joined the Bolshevist movement and made easier the advance of the Reds towards the south, is headed by Enver Pasha. In Azerbaïjan many fanatic admirers of Russia are to be met with.

"And what are the reasons for this? They are many. First, the desperate condition of the new States which came into being immediately after the Brest-Litovsk peace. In Paris the Conference laid down frontiers, but never thought the first thing to do was to put an end to the economic crisis prevailing in those countries. And so an absurd thing happened—wealthy countries living in frightful misery, and issuing paper currency which was of no value on the world's markets. Typical is the case of Azerbaïjan, which had millions of tons of petroleum at Baku, but did not know where or how to export them."

In July it was announced that the situation of the Moslems in Armenia had become critical, as for the last two months the Erivan Government and the "Tashnak" party had been carrying on a policy of violence and massacres against them. What remained of the Moslem populations had been compelled to leave their homes and property and flee to Persia. The Armenian Government had even appointed a Commission especially to draw up a list of the crops left by the Moslems and the Greeks in the district. At the end of June, in the district of Zanguibazar, about twenty Moslem villages had been destroyed by bombardments and their inhabitants put to death. By that time the Moslem population of Transcaucasia was being attacked both by the Armenians and the Bolshevists.

M. Khan-Khoiski, ex-Prime Minister, and Dr. H. Aghaef, former Vice-President of the Parliament of Azerbaïjan, were assassinated at Tiflis, where they had sought refuge, the former on June 19 and the latter on July 19, by

Armenians belonging to the "Tashnak" party, of which the leader of the Armenian Government and most Ministers are members.

This murder of the leaders of Azerbaïjan, who carried on the war against the invaders of their country, served the Bolshevist cause, but aroused much resentment among the Moslems of Azerbaïjan and Georgia, who were exasperated by the Bolshevists' frightful tyranny and now hated Bolshevism as much as they had formerly hated Tsardom.

The delegation of Azerbaïjan handed to the Spa Conference a note in which they drew its attention to the condition of their country. On the other hand, the members of the former Cabinet made energetic efforts to rid their country of the Bolshevist invasion. For this purpose they sent delegates to Daghestan and Northern Caucasus to plan a common resistance, as Daghestan, the tribes of the mountains of Northern Caucasus, and Azerbaïjan were on friendly terms and shared the same views. By this time a small part of the Red armies still occupied the Baku area, whence the Bolshevists sent reinforcements to the detachments fighting in Persia.

About the same time it was announced that Enver Pasha had been appointed commander-in-chief of the Bolshevist forces advancing towards India, and the Bolshevist troops in Caucasus, Persia, Afghanistan, and Turkistan had been put under his command. In this way the Soviets probably sought to compel England to make peace with Russia at once.

At Tabriz a separatist movement was beginning to make itself felt with a view to bringing about the union of Persian Azerbaïjan, of which this town is the centre, with the Republic of Azerbaïjan, the capital of which is Baku.

All this Bolshevist activity naturally caused much anxiety among those who closely watched the development of Eastern events, for Soviet Russia in another way and with different aims merely carried on the work of Russian imperialism both in order to hold Great Britain in check in the East and to give the whole world the benefit of the Soviet paradise. As the Allied policy with regard to Turkey had roused the whole of Islam, the union of the Bolshevist elements and the Turkish Nationalists seemed inevitable when the question of the future fate of Caucasus should be settled. It was only too much to be feared, after what had just taken place in Azerbaïjan, that Soviet Russia, feeling it necessary to get the start of the Turkish Nationalists, would try to take possession of Georgia now she held Azerbaïjan, as a guarantee both against the hostility of England and against the opposition that might sooner or later arise on the Turkish side. It then appeared that the Turkish Nationalists had come to a merely provisional agreement with the Russian Bolshevists to disengage themselves on the Russian side, and secure their help against Europe, which threatened Turkey; and that, on the contrary, the Angora Government, some members of which are Chechens and Ossetes, when brought face to face with the old historical necessities, would be one day compelled to resort to the old policy of defending the Moslem world against the Slavonic world. For notwithstanding the inherent incompatibility between the minds of these two peoples, the Allied policy, through its blunders, had achieved the paradoxical result of making a Russo-Turkish alliance temporarily possible, and to bring together the Moslems—so unresponsive as a rule to the idle verbiage and subversive tendencies of revolutionists—and the Bolshevist Slavs, who were still their political enemies. And so it turned out that the attitude assumed by the various European Powers in regard to the Turkish problem and the solution that was to eventuate were prominent factors in the future relations between each of those Powers and Asia. Now the Turks, who alone are able to bring about an understanding between the Moslems of Caucasus and those of Asia, are also the only people who can bring about a lasting peace in that part of the confines of Europe and Asia, and settle the relations between those Moslem populations and the West.

Footnote:

44 Since the French edition of this book was published, Georgia was recognised, *de jure*, by the Supreme Council in January, 1921.

IX

TURKEY AND THE SLAVS

THROUGH a singular aberration, the dismemberment of Turkey and the Turks' eviction from Europe were being advocated at a time when the idea of the restoration of Russia had not yet been given up, for the various States now detached from the former Russian Empire had not yet been definitely recognised; and among the promoters or supporters of this policy were many defenders of old Russia under a more or less transparent disguise.

Though, from the point of view of European policy, the situation of the two countries widely differed, by dismembering Turkey before the Russian question was settled, at least in its solvable part—viz., with regard to the heterogeneous peoples—the Allies made a mistake of the same kind, or at least of the same magnitude, as the one they had made when they dismembered the Dual Monarchy and yet did not destroy German unity, or rather Prussian hegemony.

Russia had already taken possession of several Turkish territories, and not so long ago she plainly declared she had not given up her ambitious designs on Constantinople.

This open hostility of the Russians toward the Turks is of very long standing.

The first Russian attacks against Turkey, as explained in the early part of this book, date back to 1672. After the victory of Poltava, in 1709, which the next year gave him Livonia, Esthonia, and Carelia, Peter the Great turned against the Turks, the allies of Charles XII, King of Sweden. But Charles XII, who had sought shelter at Bender, in Turkey, after the battle of Poltava, brought over the Grand Vizier Baltaji Mohammed to his views, and induced him to declare war on Turkey. Peter the Great, encircled by the Turks at Hush, between the Pruth and the marshes, was going to capitulate when Catherine I, in order to save him, made peace by bribing the Grand Vizier, who soon after was exiled to Mytilene. The Turks only demanded the restitution of Azov in 1711. In 1732 Peter the Great took from Persia the provinces of Daghestan, Derbend, Shirwan, Mazandaran, and Astrabad. At that time, while Villeneuve was ambassador at Constantinople (1728-41) and Austria and Russia began to turn greedy eyes on Turkey, France declared "the existence of Turkey was necessary to the peace of Christendom," and later on Choiseul-Gouffier, who was the French king's last ambassador from 1784 to 1792, strove to save the Turks from the ambitious designs of Catherine II.

Catherine, taking advantage of the intrigues carried on in the Morea with two Greeks, Papas-Oghlou and Benaki, dispatched a fleet to the Mediterranean to bring about a Greek rising against Turkey; the Ottoman fleet which sought shelter at Tchesmé, on the coast of Asia Minor, was burnt by Russian fireships on July 7, 1770.

After the 1770-74 war, the Porte, which was Poland's ally, lost Bukovina and Lesser Tatary, whose independence was recognised by the treaty of Kuchuk-Kainarji on July 21, 1774, but which became a Russian province in 1783. The treaty of Kuchuk-Kainarji ceded Kinburn and Yenikale to Russia, left to the Christians the principalities lying to the north of the Danube, and guaranteed the Orthodox Greeks' liberty under the patronage of the Russian ambassador at Constantinople. Catherine II also compelled the Turks by the same treaty not to defend the independence of Poland, threatened by Russia with the complicity of the Great Powers, and to give her a right of intervention in their home affairs. The Tatars of the Crimea and Kuban, detached from Turkey, soon after fell under the Russian sway, in 1783. The Sultan even had to sign a treaty granting a right of free navigation in the Black Sea and in the rivers of his empire.

About the same time the European Powers began to interfere in Turkey: that was the beginning of the "Eastern question." In opposition to the Austro-Russian alliance of Catherine and Joseph II, England, dissatisfied with Russia's attitude in the American War of Independence, and wishing to find allies in Germany to counterbalance Russian influence in Europe, concluded an alliance with Prussia, Sweden, Poland, and Turkey. The death of Frederic II soon put an end to this coalition, and Russia's unfriendly attitude, her encroachments in Caucasus, and her territorial claims in Bessarabia, compelled Turkey on August 16, 1787, to declare war on Catherine, and Joseph II entered into the war in 1788. The Austrians took Khotin; the Turkish fleet was destroyed at Otchakov; Belgrade fell on October 8, 1789. Then Leopold, Joseph II's brother, left the Turks and made peace with Turkey at Sistova on August 4, 1791. The Russians, who had defeated the Turks at Machin, were about to invade the Empire when, as a result of the intervention of England and Prussia, a treaty of peace was signed at Jassy, by which the Dniester became the new frontier between the two States. Thus Russia, who owing to the perturbed state of Europe was preparing to dismember Poland, was compelled to give up her dream of restoring the Byzantine Empire.

After the 1809-12 war, Turkey lost the provinces lying between the Dnieper and the Danube which were ceded to Russia by the treaty of Bukharest.

Russia, who, by the convention of Akkerman in October, 1826, had compelled Turkey to recognise the autonomy of Serbia and Moldo-Wallachia and cede her the ports of the coast of Circassia and Abkasia, declared war on her again on April 26, 1828, after the manifesto she had issued to her Moslem subjects on December 28, 1827. The Russians took Braila, advanced as far as Shumla, captured Varna, and laid siege to Silistria, but the plague and food shortage compelled them to make a disastrous retreat. In Asia they took Kars, Akhalzikel, and Bayazid. The next year they entered Erzerum; Diebitch captured Silistria, outflanked the Grand Vizier's army shut up in Shumla, crossed the Balkan mountains, and laid siege to Adrianople. On September 14, 1820, Turkey signed a treaty in the latter town, which put Moldavia, Wallachia, and Serbia under Russian protectorate, and by which she ceded to Russia all the coast of Transcaucasia, granted her the free passage of the Bosphorus and the Dardanelles, and promised to pay a war contribution of 137 million francs.

In 1833 Mehemet Ali, Pasha of Egypt, who, not having been able to obtain the Morea through the Powers' support, wanted to capture Syria, defeated the Turks at Konia and threatened Constantinople. The Tsar, Nicholas I, who hoped he could turn Turkey into a kind of Russian protectorate, then sent Mouraviev to Mahmoud to offer to put at his disposal a fleet and an army to fight with Mehemet Ali. A Russian fleet came and cast anchor before Constantinople, and a Russian detachment landed in the town. But then France, Austria, and Prussia, perhaps foreseeing the danger of a Russian occupation which might pave the way to a definite possession, asked the Sultan to make the necessary concessions to his vassal, and the latter to accept them. The treaty of Kutahia, signed on May 4, 1833, gave the Pasha of Egypt the whole of Syria and the province of Adana. Russia withdrew her troops, but did not lay down arms, and thus Count Orlov compelled the Porte to sign the treaty of Unkiar-i-Skelessi, which stipulated an offensive and defensive alliance between Russia and Turkey, and the closing of the Dardanelles to the other Powers. Turkey was now under Russian tutelage.

After the defection of Ahmed Pasha, who led the Turkish fleet at Alexandria, Great Britain, lest Russia should establish her protectorate over Turkey, offered to France, through Lord Palmerston, to participate in a naval demonstration, but France declined the offer. Metternich then suggested a conference between the representatives of the five Great Powers, in order to substitute their guarantee for a Turkish protectorate. On July 27, 1839, the ambassadors handed the Sublime Porte a note communicating their agreement, and advising that no definite decision should be taken without their co-operation. Then England, having no further fear of Russian intervention, turned against Mehemet Ali, and Baron de Brunov even proposed an Anglo-Russian agreement.

Owing to the intervention of Austria, which was averse to a war with France, the question of Egypt was only settled on July 13, 1841, by a hatti-sherif, which gave Mehemet Ali the hereditary possession of Egypt, and by the treaty of London, which guaranteed the neutrality of the Straits, as Russia wanted to control the Straits and conquer Constantinople to free the Christians in the Balkan Peninsula from the so-called Ottoman tyranny, and "relight the tapers which had been put out by the Turks" in St. Sophia, restored to Orthodoxy. France, following the old traditions of her foreign policy and in agreement with England, confined the Russians within the Black Sea by the convention of the Straits in 1841, and thus secured, not the integrity, but the existence of the Turkish Empire.

But the Tsar, Nicholas I, who was bent on defending the Greek faith within the Ottoman Empire, was anxious to see Turkey pursue the work of the Tanzimat—i.e., the new régime—confirmed by the promulgation by Abdul Mejid of the hatti-sherif of Gulhané on November 3, 1839. In 1844 he made overtures concerning the partition of Turkey, to England, to which the latter country turned a deaf ear. Thanks to the support of Great Britain and France, the Turkish troops, which had been sent to Moldavia and Wallachia after the riots which had broken out after the revolution, compelled the Tsar in 1849-51 to withdraw his army beyond the Pruth.

In 1850 France protested against the encroachments of Russia in the East, who, in order to protect the Greek monks living in Palestine and secure her own religious domination, wanted to deprive the Roman monks of their time-honoured rights over the Christian sanctuaries.

In 1853 the Tsar sent Prince Menshikov to Constantinople in order to demand a formal treaty granting the Greek Church religious independence and temporal privileges. The Sublime Porte, backed by France and England, rejected the ultimatum. The latter Powers then sent a fleet to the Dardanelles, and the next month—on July 4, 1853—Russia occupied Moldavia and Wallachia. At the instigation of Austria, the Powers assembled at Vienna on the 24th of the same month drew up a conciliatory note, which was rejected by Russia. Then the English fleet sailed up the Dardanelles, and on October 4 Turkey declared war on Russia. Austria tried again, at the Vienna Conference which she reopened in December, 1853, to bring about an understanding between Russia and Turkey. But Nicholas I declared that he meant to treat only with England and Prussia to restore peace in the East, which Turkey looked upon as an affront. He also rejected Napoleon III's mediation on January 29, 1854, and the Franco-English summons on February 27, upon which France declared war on him. Notwithstanding the political views which unfortunately are still held by most of the present diplomatists, and in pursuance of which the Powers had already checked Mehemet Ali's success and prevented Turkey resuming her former state,

France and England realised the dangerous consequences of the Russian threat and backed Turkey. In consequence of the manœuvres of Austria and the unwillingness of Prussia, who had declared "she would never fight against Russia," the Allies, who were at Varna, instead of attacking the principalities, decided to launch into the Crimean expedition. Finally, after the ultimatum drawn up by Austria, to which the Emperor Alexander submitted at the instigation of Prussia, a treaty of peace signed in Paris on March 30, 1856, recognised the integrity of Turkey, abolished the Russian protectorate over the principalities, and guaranteed the independence of Serbia, Moldavia, and Wallachia, under the suzerainty of the Ottoman Empire. Our diplomats seem then to have partly realised the extent of the danger constituted by the Slavs, and to have understood that the Turks, by driving back the Slavs and keeping them away from Western and Mediterranean Europe since the fourteenth century, had enabled Western civilisation to develop.

As the influence of France in Turkey was imperilled after her defeat in 1870, Russia took advantage of this to declare she would no longer submit to the most important clauses of the London treaty of March 13, 1871. Russia, whose ambassador in Turkey at that time was General Ignatiev, took in hand the cause of the independence of the Bulgarian Church, for which, in 1870, she had obtained the creation of a national exarchate with its own hierarchy, which had exasperated the Phanar at Constantinople and brought about deadly encounters between Turks and Bulgarians.

In 1875 Russia, alarmed at the reforms instituted by Turkey, and fearing the European organisation she was attempting to introduce into the Empire might strengthen it and thus prove an obstacle to the realisation of her designs, fomented a Christian rising in Bosnia and Herzegovina, which was a pretext for her to declare war on Turkey. Russia, backed by the Bulgarians, obliged Turkey to agree to an armistice and to an International Conference at Constantinople. In consequence of the rejection by Turkey of the protocol of London and the Russian comminatory note which followed it, Russia carried on the hostilities which, after the defeat of Plevna in Europe and the capture of Kars in Asia, led to the negotiations of San Stefano, on March 3, 1878.

Lastly, in the same year, on the occasion of the treaty of Berlin, which gave Kars to Russia and modified the San Stefano preliminaries by cancelling several of the advantages Russia hoped to obtain, France, pursuing her time-honoured policy, showed clearly her sympathy for Turkey, by bringing to bear on her behalf the influence she had regained since 1871.

By so doing, France incurred Germany's anger, for we have already shown the latter country's sympathy for Slavism. As recent events have proved once more, an alliance with Russia could only be brought about by a corresponding understanding with Germany, since Russia, where German influence has been replaced by Slavonic influence, is now being invincibly drawn towards Germany, where Slavonic influence is now prevalent. This twofold understanding could only be brought about by sacrificing the whole of Western Europe and all her old civilisation. The Europe "which ends on the Elbe," as has been said, would become more and more insignificant in such a political concept, and there would only remain in the world, standing face to face for a decisive struggle, the Germano-Russians and the Anglo-Saxons.

Spurred on by the annexation of Eastern Rumelia to Bulgaria, consequent on the rising of September 18, 1885, at Philippopolis, the Macedonian Slavs carried on an agitation the next year, in 1886, in favour of their union with Bulgaria, and resorted to an insurrection in 1895-96.

Lastly, the two Balkan wars of 1912-13, notwithstanding the complexity and intricacy of the interests at stake, may be looked upon to a certain extent as a fresh outcome of the Slavonic pressure and the ambitions of Orthodoxy.

The Russians, who had driven back the Turanian peoples to Turkistan, began the conquest of this country in 1815. From 1825 to 1840 they subdued the Khirgiz. They took Khiva in 1854, and in 1864 conquered the lower valley of the Syr Daria. In 1863 they occupied Tashkent, and in 1867 grouped the territories they had conquered under the authority of the Governor-General of Turkistan. In 1873 they occupied all the country lying between the Caspian Sea and the Aral Sea, and in 1876 took Kokand.

Even before the war, as has already been seen, Russia had turned her attention in the East towards Armenia, who, owing to her situation, could best serve her policy of expansion in Asia Minor. According to the plans of the Imperial Russian Government set forth on June 8, 1813, Armenia was to be converted into an autonomous province under the power of a governor-general, including the vilayets of Erzerum, Van, Bitlis, Diarbekir, Kharput, and Sivas, with the exception of a few territories whose boundaries had not yet been fixed. But in a memorandum presented at the same time, the Imperial Russian Government insisted upon "the close connection between the Armenian question and the problems the Russian administration had to solve in Transcaucasia." These plans lay in abeyance, for they were opposed by the German policy, which was hostile to any Russian encroachment on Turkish territories; and Russia, on the other hand, prevented Germany obtaining the concession of a railway line which was to connect the Turkish ports on the Black Sea, Samsun and Trebizond, with the Baghdad Railway and the Mediterranean Sea at Alexandretta, and settling down on the coast of the Black Sea.

As the Entente had given Russia a free hand, the latter country, as has been seen, resumed the realisation of her plans as soon as war broke out. Russia, who had begun the conquest of Caucasus in 1797 and of the Transcaspian isthmus from 1828 to 1878, occupied Upper Armenia in 1914-15. The Young Turks, who believed in the triumph of Germany, expected that, thanks to the latter, they could hold in check the Russian designs, and for this reason stood by her side.

Meanwhile the Russian policy with regard to Turkey asserted itself more and more energetically, especially in reference to Constantinople, so that the antagonism of the two nations, created by Muscovite ambition, had grown into a deep and lasting hostility.

It was recommended in the testament which is supposed to have been written by Peter the Great—

"Article 9. To draw as close as possible to Constantinople and India, for he who rules over that city will rule over the world. It is advisable, therefore, to bring about continual wars, now in Turkey, now in Persia, to establish shipbuilding yards on the Black Sea, gradually to get the mastery of that sea and of the Baltic Sea—the possession of these two seas being absolutely necessary for the triumph of our plans—to hurry on the decay of Persia, to advance as far as the Persian Gulf, to restore the once thriving Eastern trade, if possible through Syria, and to advance as far as India, the emporium of the world.

"When once we are there, we shall no longer be dependent on English gold.

"Article 11. To show the House of Austria it has an interest in ejecting the Turks from Europe, and to neutralise her jealousy when we shall conquer Constantinople, either by bringing about a war between her and the old European States, or by giving her a share of the conquest—and take it back from her later on."

Russia never gave up this policy; indeed, she did not carry out her plans by force of arms, for the other Powers would have opposed them; but she resorted to all possible means to ensure its triumph. She constantly aimed at the disintegration of the Ottoman Empire by supporting and grouping the Christian elements included in this empire, especially those of Slavonic race and Orthodox faith; and thus she really partitioned the Empire and bound to herself the old Ottoman provinces now raised to the rank of autonomous States. She acted most cautiously, and in order to carry out her plans peacefully she sought to dismember Turkey gradually and weaken her in order to finally rule over her. It has been rightly said that as early as 1770 the

Russians opened the Eastern question exactly as it stands to-day, and already advocated the solution they have always insisted upon.[45]

A century ago Alexander I declared it was time to drive the Turks out of Europe. Talleyrand, in the account he gave of the conversations between that Emperor and the French ambassador, relates that he said one day:

"Now is the time to give the plans laid down by us at Tilsit the liberal aspect that befits the deeds of enlightened sovereigns. Our age, still more than our policy, requires that the Turks be driven into Asia; it will be a noble deed to free these beautiful lands. Humanity wants the eviction of those barbarians; civilisation demands it."

But Napoleon had fully understood the Russian policy, for at the end of his life he said at St. Helena: "I could have shared Turkey with Russia; many a time did I speak about it with the Emperor, Alexander I, but every time Constantinople proved the stumbling-block. The Tsar demanded it, and I could not cede it; for it is too precious a key; it is worth an empire."

At the memorable sitting of the House of Commons of March 29, 1791, some speakers expressed the anxiety felt in Great Britain, just after Catherine II had annexed the Crimea, lest the Russians should capture the whole of the East. But Fox, the leader of the Liberal party, declared he saw no ground for fear in the constant increase of Muscovite power; he did his best to please the Tsarina, who, on her side, continued to flatter him to obtain what she wanted from England; he recalled that the British themselves had opened the Mediterranean to Russian ships twenty years before, and he had told the French Minister Vergennes, who desired him to protest against the annexation of the Crimea, that Great Britain did not wish to raise any difficulty with Catherine II.

Unfortunately, the Marquis de Villeneuve, Louis XV's ambassador, and the Comte de Bonneval, who had been converted to Islam, had been the last Frenchmen who had supported the Sublime Porte against the Russian Tsar's hostility and endeavoured to use Islam as the protector of the liberty of peoples imperilled by the Tsars; and yet this old policy of France had the advantage both of benefiting French trade and counterbalancing the power of the enemies of France.[46] On the other hand, at the Congress of Sistovo in 1791, Sir Robert Murray Keith, who acted as mediator in the conclusion of the Austro-Turkish treaty of peace, recommended his fellow-countrymen "to let the Turks dwindle down in their own dull way." So now French policy and English policy were going the same way.

During the reign of Charles X, the Polignac Cabinet was willing to sacrifice Constantinople to the Russians in return for the left bank of the Rhine, and in 1828 Chateaubriand, French ambassador at Rome, favoured an alliance with the Tsar in order to obtain the revision of the 1815 treaties, at the cost of Constantinople. Moreover, Admiral Sir Edward Codrington, by destroying the Turco-Egyptian fleet at Navarino on October 20, 1827, with the combined fleets of Great Britain, France, and Russia, furthered the Russian Tsar's plans.

As the direct capture of the Straits was bound to raise diplomatic difficulties, Nicholas I, on September 4, 1892, summoned a secret council to discuss what policy Russia was to pursue on this point. The opinion which prevailed was expressed in a memorandum drawn up by a former diplomatist, Dimitri Dashkov, then Minister of Justice, and in a draft partition of the Turkish Empire penned by a Greek, Capodistria. This secret committee, dreading the opposition of the Western States, decided to postpone the partition lest, as Great Britain and France refused their consent, it should not finally benefit the designs of Russia and Greece on Constantinople. These secret debates have been summed up in a book published in 1877;[47] and M. Goriainov, in the book he wrote on this question in 1910,[48] thought it proper to praise the consistent magnanimity of the Tsars towards the Turks—whereas the policy which maintained that no reforms would ever be instituted by Turkey of her own free-will if they were not urged on by diplomatic intrigues or international interference, and that "the sick man" could only be restored to health by the intervention of Christendom and under the Orthodox tutelage, was the real cause of the decay of Turkey and the origin of all the intricacies of the Eastern problem.

In 1830 Lord Holland, Fox's nephew—it will be remembered that on March 29, 1791, Fox had said in the House of Commons he was proud of supporting Russia's advance to the East, in opposition to William Pitt, who wanted to admit Turkey into the European concert—declared he was sorry, as "a citizen of the world," that the Russians had not yet settled down in the Golden Horn.

Besides, whereas the Tories felt some anxiety at the territorial development of Russia—without thinking of making use of Turkey to consolidate the position in the East—the Whigs, on the contrary, to use the words of Sir Robert Adair in 1842, thought they could bring the Muscovite Empire into the wake of the United Kingdom.

In June, 1844, the Tsar himself came to London in order to induce Great Britain to approve his Eastern policy, and Russian diplomacy felt so confident she could rely on the support of the English Liberal Cabinet that in 1853 Nicholas I, in the overtures made to Sir Hamilton Seymour, expressed his conviction that he could settle the Turkish problem in ten minutes' conversation with Lord Aberdeen.

On June 4, 1878, Lord Beaconsfield, who looked upon the part of England in the East as that of a moral protectorate over Islam and a mediator between Europe and Asia, by ensuring the institution of a system of reforms, signed a treaty of alliance with Turkey, by which England pledged herself to protect the Porte against Russian greediness in Asia. Unfortunately, Mr. Gladstone, under the influence of the ideas we have already expounded,[49] soon reversed the Eastern policy of England and unconsciously made his country the Tsar's ally against Turkey.

Russia, to whom it was now impossible, since the Bulgarians and Rumanians were no longer under Ottoman dominion, to reach the shores of the Bosphorus through Thrace and to conquer Constantinople and the Straits, which had been the aim of her policy for centuries, then turned her designs towards Turkish Armenia and Anatolia, as we have just seen, in order to reach Constantinople through Asia.

Tiutshev, in one of his poems entitled *Russian Geography*, said:

"Moscow, Peter's town, and Constantine's town, are theee sacred capitals of the Russian Empire. But how far do its frontiers extend to the north and the east, to the south and the west? Fate will reveal it in the future. Seven inland seas and seven great rivers, from the Nile to the Neva, from the Elbe to China, from the Volga to the Euphrates, from the Ganges to the Danube—this is the Russian Empire, and it will last through untold centuries! So did the Spirit predict. So did Daniel prophesy!"

And in another place:

"Soon will the prophecy be fulfilled and the fateful time come! And in regenerated Byzantium the ancient vaults of St. Sophia will shelter Christ's altar again. Kneel down before that altar, thou Russian Tsar, and rise, thou Tsar of all the Slavs."

The manœuvres in which Great Britain and Russia indulged during the first Balkan crisis in regard to the annexation of Bosnia-Herzegovina are another striking proof of the rivalry between these two nations concerning the Straits, for they plainly show that their possession was still the chief ambition of Russia, and that Great Britain, on the other hand, was still determined to control the Straits directly or indirectly, as she could not possibly seize them openly.

At the time of that annexation, the Western Powers and Russia had proposed that a conference should be summoned to decide the fate of that country. But this proposal did not please Germany, who, though she had a right to be angry with Austria, who had neither consulted nor warned her, yet wanted to reconcile the patronising attitude she had assumed towards Turkey with her obligations as an ally of the Dual Monarchy. So Russia was obliged to submit to the annexation, and the idea of a conference was given up after Prince von Bülow had stated that Germany would back Austria, but that in regard to the indemnity claimed by Turkey as a compensation for the loss of her suzerainty over Bosnia-Herzegovina she would support Turkey. Meanwhile, M. de Tschirschkly, German ambassador at Vienna, did his best both to isolate Austria and to bring her to rely more and more on German friendship by striving to disturb the traditional friendly intercourse between London and Vienna; and he took advantage of the disappointment caused in Austria by the breaking off of the negotiations with Turkey to make England responsible for their failure and embitter the enmity already prevailing between Austria and Russia.

Now at this juncture Russia is reported to have declared her willingness to support Turkey, in return for which she wanted her to open up the Straits to her ships. This secret understanding was revealed to the British Government by Kiamil Pasha, a friend of England, who, at the suggestion of the British embassy, asked Russia whether, in case war should break out, she would take up arms in favour of Turkey. At the same time England hinted to the St. Petersburg Cabinet that she was aware it had opened negotiations, and that, should these negotiations bring about an understanding between Turkey and Russia, the relations between their two countries would be severely strained, and the situation would become critical. And so it turned out that Turkey too submitted to the annexation, and did not insist upon the meeting of the Conference.

Meanwhile Russia had no thought of giving up her designs on Constantinople, as is proved by the revelations made in the Memoirs of Count Witte, the well-known Russian diplomatist and ex-Prime Minister, which were published in the *Daily Telegraph* in January, 1921. In one of his articles, concerning Nicholas II's character, we read that a Russo-Turkish war had been planned at the suggestion of M. de Nelidov, at that time Russian ambassador to Turkey.

"In the latter period of the year 1896, writes Count Witte, there was a massacre of Armenians in Constantinople, preceded by a similar massacre in Asia Minor. In October, His Majesty returned from abroad, and Nelidov, our ambassador to Turkey, came to St. Petersburg. His arrival gave rise to rumours about various measures which were going to be taken against Turkey. These rumours forced me to submit to His Majesty a memorandum, in which I stated my views on Turkey, and advised against the use of force. On November 21 (December 3) I received a secret memoir drafted by Nelidov. The ambassador spoke in vague terms about the alarming situation in Turkey, and suggested that we should foment incidents which would create the legal right and the physical possibility of seizing the Upper Bosphorus. Nelidov's suggestion was discussed by a special conference presided over by His Majesty. The ambassador insisted that a far-reaching upheaval was bound to occur in the near future in the Ottoman Empire, and that to safeguard our interests we must occupy the Upper Bosphorus. He was naturally supported by the War Minister and the Chief of Staff, General Oberouchev, for whom the occupation of the Bosphorus and, if possible, of Constantinople, was a veritable *idée fixe*. The other Ministers refrained from expressing their opinion on the subject, so that it fell to my lot to oppose this disastrous project, which I did with vigour and determination. I pointed out that the plan under consideration would eventually precipitate a general European war, and shatter the brilliant political and financial position in which Emperor Alexander III left Russia.

"The Emperor at first confined himself to questioning the members of the Conference. When the discussion was closed he declared that he shared the ambassador's view. Thus the matter was settled, at least in principle— namely, it was decided to bring about such events in Constantinople as would furnish us with a serious pretext for landing troops and occupying the Upper Bosphorus. The military authorities at Odessa and Sebastopol were instructed immediately to start the necessary preparations for the landing of troops in Turkey. It was also agreed that at the moment which Nelidov considered opportune for the landing he would give the signal by sending a telegram to our financial agent in London, requesting him to purchase a stated amount of grain. The dispatch was to be immediately transmitted to the Director of the Imperial Bank and also to the Minister of the Navy."

M. de Nelidov went back to Constantinople to carry out this plan, and war seemed so imminent that one of the secretaries of the director of the Imperial Bank "kept vigil all night long, ready to receive the fateful telegram," and was instructed to transmit it to the director.

"Fearing the consequences of the act, I could not refrain from sharing my apprehensions with several persons very intimate with the Emperor, notably Grand Duke Vladimir Alexandrovich and Pobiedonostzev.... I do not know whether it was the influence of these men or the influence of that Power which rules the whole world and which we call God, but His Majesty changed his mind and instructed Nelidov, soon after the latter's departure for Constantinople, to give up his designs."

After the attack by the Turkish ships on October 29 and 30, the Emperor Nicholas, on November, 1914, issued a manifesto to his people, which, though sibylline in tone, plainly asserted Russia's designs on Constantinople and showed that she meant to avail herself of circumstances to carry them out.

"The Turkish fleet, led by Germans, has dared treacherously to attack our Black Sea coast. We, with all the peoples of Russia, feel quite confident that Turkey's rash intervention will only hurry on her doom, and open to Russia the way to the solution of the historical problem bequeathed to us by our forefathers on the shores of the Black Sea."[50]

In the course of an audience which Nicholas II granted to M. Maurice Paléologue, French ambassador, at Tsarkoie-Selo on November 21, 1914, and in the course of which he laid down the main lines of the peace which he thought should be dictated to the Central Powers, he considered how the settlement of the war would affect the other nations, and declared:

"In Asia Minor I shall have naturally to take care of the Armenians; I could not possibly replace them under the Turkish yoke. Shall I have to annex Armenia? I will annex it only if the Armenians expressly ask me to do so. Otherwise, I will grant them an autonomous régime. Lastly, I shall have to ensure for my Empire the free passage of the Straits....

"I have not quite made up my mind on many points; these are such fateful times! Yet I have arrived at two definite conclusions: first, that the Turks must be driven out of Europe; secondly, that Constantinople should henceforth be a neutral town, under an international régime. Of course, the Mussulmans would have every guarantee for the protection of their sanctuaries and shrines. Northern Thrace, up to the Enos-Midia line, would fall to Bulgaria. The rest of the country, between this line and the coast, with the exception of the Constantinople area, would be assigned to Russia."[51]

About the end of 1914, according to M. Maurice Paléologue, public opinion in Russia was unanimous on this point, that—

"The possession of the Straits is of vital interest to the Empire and far exceeds in importance all the territorial advantages Russia might obtain at the expense of Germany and Austria.... The neutralisation of the Bosphorus and the Dardanelles would be an unsatisfactory, mongrel compromise, pregnant with dangers for the future.... Constantinople must be a Russian town.... The Black Sea must become a Russian lake."[52]

In the formal statement of the Government policy read on February 9, 1915, at the opening of the Duma, after mention had been made of the victories gained by the Russian armies over Turkey, the following sentence occurred: "Brighter and brighter does the radiant future of Russia shine before us in yonder place, on the shores of the sea which washes the battlements of Constantinople."

Sazonov only hinted at the question of the Straits in the speech which followed, but he declared: "The day is drawing near when the economic and political problems arising from the necessity for Russia to have free access to the open sea will be solved."

Evgraf Kovalevsky, deputy of Moscow, stated in his turn: "The Straits are the key of our house, so they must be handed over to us, together with the Straits area."

Then, M. Miliukov, after thanking M. Sazonov for his declaration, concluded his speech in these terms:

"We are happy to hear that our national task will soon be completed. We now feel confident that the possession of Constantinople and the Straits will be ensured in due time, through diplomatic and military channels."

The question of Constantinople captivated public opinion at that time, and in February, 1915, it engrossed the minds of all prominent men in Russia. Public feeling agreed with the declarations we have just read, that a victorious peace must give Constantinople to Russia.

At the beginning of March, M. Sazonov could not refrain from raising this question with the ambassadors of France and Great Britain, and asked them to give him an assurance that the Governments of London and Paris would consent after the war to the annexation of Constantinople by Russia.[53]

On March 3, at the dinner given in honour of General Pau, Nicholas II talked on the same subject to M. Paléologue. The Emperor, after recalling the conversation he had had with him in November of the previous year, in the course of which he had said France could rely upon Russia, and telling him he had not altered his mind, said:

"There is a point, however, about which recent events compel me to say a few words; I mean Constantinople. The question of the Straits engrosses the Russian mind more and more every day. I consider I have no right to impose on my people the dreadful sacrifices of the present war without granting as a reward the fulfilment of their age-long aspirations. So I have made up my mind, sir. I do not want half-measures to solve the problem of Constantinople and the Straits. The solution I pointed out to you in November last is the only possible one, the only practical one. The city of Constantinople and Southern Thrace must be incorporated into my Empire; yet I have no objection, as far as the administration of the city is concerned, to a special régime making allowance for foreign interests. You know that

England has already sent me her approval. If any minor difficulties should arise, I rely on your Government to help me to smooth them."[54]

On March 8, M. Paléologue told M. Sazonov that he had just received a telegram from M. Delcassé, and was in a position to give him the assurance that he could rely on the French Government's friendly offices in settling the questions of Constantinople and the Straits according to the wishes of Russia. M. Sazonov thanked him very warmly, and added these significant words: "Your Government has done the Alliance a priceless service ... a service the extent of which perhaps you do not realise."[55] On the 15th the French Government, having examined the conditions of peace which the Allies meant to impose on Turkey, informed the Russian Government of the compensations France required in Syria.

On March 16, after being received by the Emperor at the General Headquarters at Baranovitchi, the Grand Duke Nicholas, speaking as commander-in-chief of the Russian armies, had a formal conversation with M. Paléologue, speaking as French ambassador, and requested him to inform his Government that he considered the immediate military co-operation of Rumania and Italy as an imperative necessity. The French ambassador suggested that the Russian claims on Constantinople and the Straits would, perhaps, prevent Rumania and Italy joining the Allies. Upon which the Grand Duke answered: "That's the business of diplomacy. I won't have anything to do with it."[56]

Finally, the following letter of M. Koudashev to M. Sazonov, Minister of Foreign Affairs, printed in the collection of secret documents of the Russian Foreign Office published in December, 1917,[57] shows how deeply the leaders of Russia and the Russian people had this question at heart, that it commanded all their foreign policy, and that they were determined to use any means, to resort to any artifice, in order to solve it in conformity with their wishes. No wonder, then, as we pointed out at the beginning of this book, that Turkey, being fully aware of the Russian enmity, should have consented to stand by the side of Germany in a war in which her very existence was at stake.

IMPERIAL HEADQUARTERS,
February 5, 1916 (o.s.).

"Most honoured Serguey Dmitrievich,—At the request of General Alexiev, I waited on him to discuss how the capture of Erzerum could be best exploited.

"Such an event obviously points to a certain state of mind in Turkey which we should turn to account. If a separate peace with Turkey was to be contemplated, it should be borne in mind that such favourable circumstances are not likely to occur again within a long time. It would undoubtedly be our advantage to start the negotiations after a victory which the enemy rightly or wrongly fears will be attended with a new catastrophe.

"Considering that our forces on the secondary front of Caucasus are insignificant and it is impossible to take away one soldier from the chief centre of operations, it would be most difficult, in General Alexiev's opinion, to derive full profit from the glorious success of our Caucasian army in a strictly military sense.

"Though he does not wish to advocate an immediate peace with Turkey, the general desires me to bring to your knowledge some of his views concerning this eventuality that the situation created by our recent success may be carefully considered and fully utilised.

"According to him, it would be most important to specify the war aims of Russia. Though the brigadier-general is fully aware this is a question to be settled by the Government, yet he thinks his opinion might be of some weight.

"In the course of our conversation, we have come to the following conclusions:

"Whatever may have been our prospects at the time when Turkey entered into the war, of securing compensations at the cost of the latter country when peace is concluded, we must own that our expectations will not be fulfilled during the present war. The longer the war lasts, the more difficult it will be for us to secure the possession of the Straits. General Alexiev and General Danilov agree on this point. I refer you to my letters of December, 1914, and January, 1915, as to Danilov's opinion.

"The defeat of the chief enemy and the restoration of the parts of the Empire we have lost should be our chief war aim. Our most important enemy is Germany, for there cannot be any question that at the present time it is more important for us to recover the Baltic Provinces than take possession of the Straits. We must by all means defeat Germany. It is a difficult task, which will require great efforts and sacrifices. The temporary abandonment of some of our hopes should be one of these sacrifices.

"Considering the advantages a separate peace with Turkey would bring us, we might offer it to her without injuring our real 'interests'—the occupation of the Straits being merely postponed—on the basis of the *status quo ante bellum*, including the restoration of the Capitulations and the other rights acquired by the treaties. We should also demand the dismissal of the

Germans, with a promise on our side to defend Turkey in case of German reprisals. If a separate peace could be concluded with Turkey on such a basis, all our Caucasian army would be available. We could send it to Bessarabia and thus—who knows?—bring Rumania to our side, or, if Turkey asks for it, send it to defend Constantinople. England would heave a sigh of relief when the dangers of the Egyptian campaign and of the Muslim movement thus vanished. She would then be able to send her Egyptian army—nine divisions—to Salonika and Kavala, bar the way definitely to the Bulgarians and liberate Serbia with the help of the French, the Italians, and the reconstituted Serbian Army. If Turkey were no longer our enemy, the situation in the Balkans would be quite altered, and we should be able to keep in touch with our Allies by clearing the southern route of Europe. In short, the advantages of a separate peace with Turkey are innumerable. The chief result would be the defeat of Germany, the only common war aim of all the Allies. No doubt, we all—they as well as we—will have to waive some of our cherished schemes. But we are not bound to give them up for ever. If we carry on the war with Turkey, we delude ourselves with the hope our ideal can be fulfilled. If we interrupt the war with that country, we postpone for a time the fulfilment of our wishes. But in return for this, we shall defeat Germany, the only thing which can secure a lasting peace for all the Allies and a political, military, and moral superiority for Russia. If a victory over Germany gives us back the paramount situation we enjoyed after the Napoleonic wars, why could not the glorious period of the treaties of Adrianople and Hunkiar-i-Skelessi occur again? In concluding that treaty we should have only to take care not to offend the Western Powers, and yet meet the requirements of Russia.

"Perhaps I have stated General Alexiev's opinions too unreservedly, as I wished to give this report a definite form. Though the brigadier-general does not wish to be the advocate or promoter of the idea of a separate peace with Turkey, I am sure he looks upon this as a highly profitable scheme.

"Of course, many difficulties will have to be overcome in the conclusion of such a peace; but is not every matter of importance attended with difficulties? Public opinion should be warned that we cannot possibly secure the fulfilment of all our wishes at once, that it is impossible for us to shake off German hegemony, reconquer the shores of the Baltic, and the other provinces now in the hands of the enemy, and at the same time take Constantinople. The conquest of Tsarigrad in the present circumstances must necessarily raise many a political and moral question. The Turks, too, will have to be convinced. But they may be influenced both by logical and pecuniary arguments. If once the question of the loss of their capital is waived, it will be pretty easy for us to convince them that the Germans merely want their help for selfish purposes without any risk to themselves. If some of them turned a deaf ear to logical arguments, we might resort to more substantial arguments, as has always been the way with Turkey.

"But the discussion of such details is still premature. For the present, the important points are:

"1. Plainly to define our real war aim.

"2. To decide, in connection with this aim, whether a separate peace with Turkey should not be contemplated at once.

"3. To prepare public opinion—the Duma is to meet tomorrow—and our Allies for such a turn of events.

"I want to conclude this long letter by stating that General Alexiev and I share the feelings of all Russians in regard to Constantinople, that we do not disregard the 'historical call of Russia,' in the solution of the Eastern question, but that we are actuated by the sincere wish to clarify the situation by distinguishing what is possible at the present time from those aspirations whose fulfilment is momentarily—only momentarily—impossible."

It is obvious that if, at the beginning of the war, General Kuropatkine maintained that it was a military necessity to occupy part of Turkey, it was because the only aim of Russia in entering into the conflict was the conquest of Constantinople.

In an article entitled "*La Neutralisation des Dardanelles et du Bosphore*," which was written at the beginning of the war, M. Miliukov confirmed the Russian designs on the Black Sea and consequently on all the part of Europe and Asia Minor contiguous to it. He recalled that, by the former treaties concluded with Russia before the European nations had interfered in the Eastern question—those of 1798, 1805, and 1833—the Porte had granted Russian warships the free passage of the Straits, though the Black Sea was still closed to the warships of any other Power, and that when the treaties of 1841, 1856, and 1871 had laid down the principle of the closure of the Straits, Russia had always preferred this state of things to the opening of the Black Sea to the warships of all nations. This article throws a light on the policy pursued by Russia and the propaganda she is still carrying on in the hope of bringing about the annihilation of the Ottoman Empire. So the writer recognised that it was the duty of Russia to oppose the dispossession of Turkey and that, if the Straits passed under Russian sovereignty, they ought not to be neutralised.

Taking up this question again in an interview with a correspondent of *Le Temps* in April, 1917, M. Miliukov stated that the map of Eastern Europe, as it ought to be drawn up by the Allies, involved "the liquidation of the Turkish possessions in Europe, the liberation of the peoples living in Asia Minor, the independence of Arabia, Armenia, and Syria, and finally, the necessity of recognising Turkey's right to the possession of the Straits." Nobody knows what was to become of the Turks in such a solution, or rather it is only too plain that "the liquidation of the Turkish possessions in Europe" meant that Russia would take possession of the Straits and rule over the Turkish territories in Asia Minor.

Though both the Conservatives and the Bolshevists in Russia were plainly drawing nearer to Germany, M. Miliukov, who seemed to forget the pro-German leaning of Tsardom and the tendency he himself openly displayed, came to this conclusion:

"The Straits to Russia—that, in my opinion, is the only way out of the difficulty. The neutralisation of the Straits would always involve many serious dangers to peace, and Russia would be compelled to keep up a powerful war fleet in the Black Sea to defend our coasts. It would give the warships of all countries a free access to our inland sea, the Black Sea, which might entail untold disasters. Germany wants the Straits in order to realise her dreams of hegemony, for her motto is 'Berlin-Baghdad,' and we, Russians, want the Straits that our importation and exportation may be secure from any trammels or threats whatever. Nobody can entertain any doubt, therefore, as to which Power is to own the Straits; it must be either Germany or Russia."

Prince Lvov, M. Sazonov, M. Chaikovsky, and M. Maklakov, in a memorandum addressed to the President of the Peace Conference on July 5, 1919, on behalf of the Provisional Government of Russia, stated the Russian claims with regard to Turkey, and the solution they proposed to the question of the Straits and Constantinople was inspired by the agreements of 1915 and showed they had not given up anything of their ambition. For, though they had no real mandate to speak of the rights of New Russia they declared:

"New Russia has, undoubtedly, a right to be associated in the task of regeneration which the Allied and Associated Powers intend to assume in the former Turkish territories.

"Thus, the question of the Straits would be most equitably settled by Russia receiving a mandate for the administration of the Straits in the name of the League of Nations. Such a solution would benefit both the interests of Russia and those of the whole world, for the most suitable régime for an international road of transit is to hand over its control to the Power which is most vitally interested in the freedom of this transit.

"This solution is also the only one which would not raise any of the apprehensions which the Russian people would certainly feel if the aforesaid mandate were given to any other Power or if a foreign military Power controlled the Straits.

"For the moment, Russia, in her present condition, would be satisfied if the control of the Straits were assigned to a provisional international administration which might hand over its powers to her in due time, and in which Russia in the meantime should hold a place proportionate to the part she is called upon to play in the Black Sea.

"As to Constantinople, Russia cannot think for one moment of ceding this city to the exclusive administration of any other Power. And if an international administration were established, Russia should hold in it the place that befits her, and have a share in all that may be undertaken for the equipment, exploitation, and control of the port of Constantinople."

Some documents, which were found by the Bolshevists in the Imperial Record Office, concerning the conferences of the Russian Staff in November, 1913, and which have just been made public, testify to the continuity of the aforesaid policy and the new schemes Russia was contemplating. It clearly appears from these documents that M. Sazonov, Minister of Foreign Affairs, had represented to the Tsar the necessity of preparing not only plans of campaign, but a whole organisation for the conveyance by rail and sea of the huge forces which were necessary to capture Constantinople, and that the Crown Council was of opinion this plan should be carried out in order to bring the Russians to Constantinople and secure the mastery of the Straits.

At the present time, forty or fifty thousand[58] Russian emigrants, fleeing before the Bolshevists, have reached Pera and have settled down in it; others are arriving there every day, who belong to the revolutionary socialist party—an exiled party temporarily—or who are more or less disguised Bolshevist agents. It is obvious that all these Russians will not soon leave Constantinople, which they have always coveted, especially as the Bolshevists have by no means renounced the designs of the Tsars on this city or their ambitions in the East.

Not long ago, according to the *Lokal Anzeiger*,[59] a prominent member of the Soviet Government declared that, to safeguard the Russian interests in the East and on the Black Sea, Constantinople must fall to Russia.

Being thus invaded by Russian elements of all kinds, Constantinople seems doomed to be swallowed up by Russia as soon as her troubles are over, whether she remains Bolshevist or falls under a Tsar's rule again; then she will turn her ambition towards the East, which we have not been able to defend against the Slavs, and England will find her again in her way in Asia and even on the shores of the Mediterranean Sea.

On the other hand, as Germany is endeavouring to come to an understanding with Russia and as the military Pan-Germanist party has not given up hope of restoring the Kaiser to the throne, if the Allies dismembered Turkey—whose policy is not historically linked with that of Germany, and who has no more reason for being her ally now, provided the Allies alter their own policy—they would pave the way to a union of the whole of Eastern Europe under a Germano-Russian hegemony.

Again, the Turks, who originally came from Asia, are now a Mediterranean people owing to their great conquests and their wide extension in the fifteenth century, and though in some respects these conquests may be regretted, they have on the whole proved beneficial to European civilisation, by maintaining the influence of the culture of antiquity. Though they have driven back the Greeks to European territories, they have not, on the whole, attempted to destroy the traditions bequeathed to us by antiquity, and the Turk has let the quick, clever Greek settle down everywhere. His indolence and fatalism have made him leave things as they were. What would have happened if the Slavs had come down to the shores of the Mediterranean Sea? The Bulgars and Southern Slavs, though they were subjected to Greco-Latin influences, displayed much more activity and were proof against most of these influences. But the Turks checked the Slavs' advance to the south; and, were it only in this respect, they have played and still play a salutary part of which they should not be deprived.

The new policy pursued by France towards Turkey becomes the more surprising—coming after her time-honoured Turkish policy and after the recent mistakes of her Russian policy—as we see history repeat itself, or at least, similar circumstances recur. Even in the time of the Romans the events of Syria and Mesopotamia were connected with those of Central Europe; as Virgil said: "Here war is let loose by Euphrates, there by Germany." Long after, Francis I, in order to check the ambitious designs of Charles V, Emperor of Germany, who, about 1525, dreamt of subduing the whole of Europe, sought the alliance of Soliman. The French king, who understood the Latin spirit so well and the great part it was about to play in the Renaissance, had foreseen the danger with which this spirit was threatened by Germany.

Moreover, a recent fact throws into light the connection between the German and Russian interests in the Eastern question, and their similar tendencies. For Marshal von der Goltz was one of the first to urge that the Turkish capital should be transferred to a town in the centre of Asia Minor.[60] Of course, he professed to be actuated only by strategic or administrative motives, for he chiefly laid stress on the peculiar geographical situation of the capital of the Empire, which, lying close to the frontier, is directly exposed to a foreign attack. But did he not put forward this argument merely to conceal other arguments which concerned Germany more closely? Though the Germans professed to be the protectors of Islam, did not the vast Austro-German schemes include the ejection of the Turks from Europe to the benefit of the Slavs, notwithstanding the declarations made during the war by some German publicists—M. Axel Schmidt, M. Hermann, M. Paul Rohrbach—which now seem to have been chiefly dictated by temporary necessities?

Thus the Turkish policy of the Allies is the outcome of their Russian policy—which accounts for the whole series of mistakes they are still making, after their disillusionment with regard to Russia.

For centuries, Moscow and Islam have counterpoised each other: the Golden Horde having checked the expansion of Russia, the latter did her best to bring about the downfall of the Ottoman Empire. It had formerly been admitted by the Great Powers that the territorial integrity of the Ottoman Empire should not be infringed upon, for it was the best barrier to Russia's claims on the Straits and her advance towards India. But after the events of the last war, England, reversing her traditional policy, and the Allies, urged on by Pan-Russian circles, have been gradually driven to recognise the Russian claims to Constantinople in return for her co-operation at the beginning of the war.

The outcome of this policy of the Allies has been to drive both the new States, whose independence they persistently refused to recognise, and the old ones, whose national aspirations they did not countenance, towards Bolshevism, the enemy of the Allies; it has induced them, in spite of themselves, to come to understandings with the Soviet Government, in order to defend their independence. England in this way runs the risk of finding herself again face to face with Russia—a new Russia; and thus the old Anglo-Russian antagonism would reappear in another shape, and a more critical one. Sir H. Rawlinson[61] denounced this danger nearly half a century ago, and now once more, though in a different way, "India is imperilled by the progress of Russia."

However, there is no similarity between Pan-Turanianism and Bolshevism, though an attempt has been made in press polemics or political controversies to confound the one with the other. They have no common origin, and the utter incompatibility between Bolshevism and the spirit of Western Europe exists likewise to another extent and for different reasons between Bolshevism and the spirit of the Turks, who, indeed, are not Europeans but Moslems, yet have played a part in the history of Europe and thus have felt its influence. The Turks—like the Hungarians, who are monarchists and have even sought to come to an understanding with Poland—have refused to make an alliance with the Czecho-Slovaks, who have Pan-Slavic tendencies; and so they cannot become Bolshevists or friendly to the Bolshevists. But, if the Allies neither modify their attitude nor give up the policy they have pursued of late years, the Turks, as well as all the heterogeneous peoples that have broken loose from old Russia, will be driven for their own protection to adopt the same policy as new Russia—the latter being considered as outside Europe; and thus the power of the Soviet Government will be reinforced.

We have been among the first to show both the danger and the inanity of Bolshevism; and now we feel bound to deplore that policy which merely tends to strengthen the Bolshevists we want to crush. Our only hope is that the influence of the States sprung from old Russia or situated round it on Soviet Russia—with which they have been obliged to come to terms for the sake of self-defence—will complete the downfall of Bolshevism, which can only live within Russia and the Russian mind, but has already undergone an evolution, owing to the mistakes of the Allies, in order to spread and maintain itself.

As to the dismemberment of the Ottoman Empire, it seems that far from solving the Eastern question, it is likely to bring about many fresh difficulties, for it is a political mistake as well as an injustice.

This dismemberment, impudently effected by England, is not likely to turn to her advantage. Of course, owing to the treaty, British hegemony for the present extends over Mesopotamia, Palestine, and Kurdistan, and is likely to prevail over the international régime foreshadowed by the same treaty; but the organisation which Great Britain wants thus to enforce on the East, if ever it is effective, seems most precarious. For, even without mentioning Turkey, which does not seem likely to submit to this scheme, and where the Nationalist movement is in open rebellion, or Armenia, whose frontiers have not been fixed yet, the condition of Kurdistan, which England coveted and had even at one moment openly laid claim to, is still uncertain; the Emir Feisal, who is indebted to her for his power, is attempting to get out of her hand; finally, by putting Persia under her tutelage, she has roused the national feeling there too, and broken of her own accord the chain she intended to forge all round India, after driving Germany out of Asia Minor and capturing all the routes to her Asiatic possessions.

Now it is questionable whether Great Britain—in spite of the skill with which her administration has bent itself to the ways of the very various peoples and the liberal spirit she has certainly evinced in the organisation of the Dominions belonging to the British Empire, the largest empire that has ever existed—will be powerful enough to maintain her sovereignty over so many peoples, each of which is proud of its own race and history, and to organise all these countries according to her wish.

As to France, she is gradually losing the moral prestige she once enjoyed in the East, for the advantages she has just gained can only injure her, and also injure the prestige she still enjoys in other Moslem countries; whereas, by pursuing another policy, she might have expected that the German defeat would restore and heighten her prestige.

It follows from all this that the Turkish problem, as we have endeavoured to describe it—considering that for centuries an intercourse has been maintained between the Moslem world and Mediterranean Europe, and that a Moslem influence once made itself felt on Western civilisation through Arabic culture—cannot be looked upon as a merely Asiatic problem. It is a matter of surprise that Islam, five centuries after Christ, should have developed in the birthplace of Christianity, and converted very numerous populations, whose ways and spirit it seems to suit. One cannot forget either that Islam acted as a counterpoise to Christianity, or that it played an important part in our civilisation by securing the continuance and penetration of Eastern and pagan influences. So it is obvious that nowadays the Turkish problem is still of paramount importance for the security of Western civilisation, since it concerns all the nations round the Mediterranean Sea, and, moreover, all the Asiatic and African territories inhabited by Moslems, who have always been interested in European matters and are even doubly concerned in them now.[62]

Footnotes:

[45] Albert Sorel, *La Question d'Orient au XVIIIe siècle*, pp. 81, 85, 277.

[46] Albert Vandal, *Une ambassade française en Orient sous Louis XV*, pp. 4, 8, 331, 447.

[47] Martens, *Étude historique sur la politique russe dans la question d'Orient*, 1877.

[48] Goriainov, *Le Bosphore et les Dardanelles*, 1910, pp. 25-27.

[49] See *supra*, p. 114.

[50] *Daily Telegraph*, January 5, 1921.

[51] *Revue des Deux Mondes*, March 15, 1921, pp. 261, 262: Maurice Paléologue. "La Russie des Tsars pendant la guerre."

[52] *Ibid.*, pp. 274, 275.

[53] *Revue des Deux Mondes*, April 1, 1921, p. 573.

[54] *Revue des Deux Mondes*, April 1, 1921, pp. 574, 575.

55 *Ibid.*

56 *Ibid.*, pp. 578, 579.

57 The editor was M. Markine.

58 Now there are about 200,000.

59 August 10, 1920.

60 Von der Goltz, "Stärke und Schwäche des turkischen Reiches," in the *Deutsche Rundschau*, 1897.

61 H. Rawlinson, *England and Russia in the East* (1875).

62 The French edition of this book bears the date August, 1920.

Milton Keynes UK
Ingram Content Group UK Ltd.
UKHW042143281024
450365UK00010B/571